BUILDING BRIDGES

Can We Love & Relate in a Polarized World?

Michael Sullivan

Copyright © 2024 by Michael Sullivan

All rights reserved.

No part of this publication may be reproduced, distributed, or transmitted in any form or by any means, including photocopying, recording, or other electronic or mechanical methods, without the prior written permission of the publisher, except as permitted by U.S. copyright law. For permission requests, contact SullyWorks Media LLC at 1205 Williamson St., Easton, PA, USA, or visit our website, https://sullyworks.com.

For privacy reasons, some names, locations, and dates may have been changed. Additionally, a few facts have been altered for artistic purposes and to streamline the narrative.

Design, Production, Editing, and Illustration Credits

Book Cover by Sabrina Awdi
Typesetting by Jacob Smith

Publisher

SullyWorks Media LLC
1205 Williamson St., Easton, PA
Website: https://sullyworks.com

ISBN:978-969-569-270-7

DEDICATIONS

First and foremost, to my Mother—
I'm finished! I hope you enjoy it!

To my wife, the Queen of 'Liki,' Jen Sullivan—
I love you. We will grow old together.

To my daughter, Khenyz—
May you grow powerful, confident, and with the courage to say 'no.'

To my sister—
Thank you for protecting me and for having a faith greater than mine.

To my granddaughter, Mace; my future daughters-in-law; my adopted daughters, Anak Marie and Anak Nichole; my nieces, and my endless adopted sisters all over the planet.

To Fatma Dodurka—
May your legacy live on in our hearts and in the lives of the girls from Be the Voice of Girls.

To Jen and Nikki—
I wish you fair winds and following seas. Thank you for putting up with me, Shipmates!

Table Of Contents

Dedications — 4
Part 1: Me... Mike Sullivan — 6
   Chapter 1: Beauty School Dropout — 8
   Chapter 2: Mamma Mia! — 20
   Chapter 3: The Gambler — 44
Part 2: What Divides Us? — 58
   Chapter 4: America the Beautiful? — 60
   Chapter 5: 음양 'Eum-Yang' — 76
   Chapter 6: A Stained Glass Masquerade — 88
   Chapter 7: In Between — 114
   Chapter 8: Crossing the Colored Chasm — 128
Part 3: A World Away — 152
   Chapter 9: Crime and Punishment — 154
   Chapter 10: My Ride to Work — 174
   Chapter 11: Chaperones — 190
Part 4: A Broken Road — 204
   Chapter 12: A Rescue — 206
   Chapter 13: Can We Love & Relate in a Polarized World? — 222
Endnotes — 253

Part One:
Me... Mike Sullivan

I should not be left to my own devices
They come with prices and vices
I end up in crisis (tale as old as time) ..

.. It's me, hi ..

- Taylor Swift (performing "Anti-Hero")[1]

Chapter One

Beauty School Dropout

Beauty school dropout
No graduation day for you
Beauty school dropout
Missed your midterms and flunked shampoo

Frankie Avalon (performing "Beauty School Dropout" in *Grease*)[2]

Uncle Dusty and the CIA

In 1996, we were the largest graduating class in the history of our tiny missionary school in Chiang Mai, Thailand. We had added two fresh recruits to the famous donut crew of eighth grade. Back then, two of our teachers left five 13-year-olds alone with instructions and a few hours to our own devices before lunch. One of those teachers, 'Uncle' Dusty—we were convinced—worked for the CIA and used his role as a Christian missionary as a cover. He was always running secret errands for God and the US government. Our donut run scheme came to fruition in a plan that he and Jack Ryan would be proud of. We wrote all over the whiteboard, promising we'd save a donut for our teachers, and off we went, leaving one of our risk-averse classmates behind. When 'Uncle' Dusty found us at lunchtime, he congratulated us with fire in his eyes and offered instant letters of recommendation to join his next mission.

The other teacher was my dad. I was grounded for three weeks.

Fast forward to my senior year. I was the only student to serve an in-school suspension, and graduating on time was perilously in jeopardy. I had to report on *Hard Times* by Charles Dickens, which is about 800 pages, or else I couldn't walk the aisle with my graduating classmates. I had two days to do it. I remember someone falling into a well in the book. It was hard to get them out.

My weight fell to 115 lbs. I was having uncontrollable diarrhea in my bed, in my sleep, every night and every hour. After a humiliating colonoscopy, where they pumped water up my anus and told me to hold it, I couldn't—since I hadn't held it for over a month already—so I helplessly squirted on the Thai nurses, who were shouting, "Wait five minute, wait five minute!" They discovered nothing.

Then, my parents had me sit down with a therapist, Mr. Green, with a candlestick in the library. I learned that I didn't have to please everyone, and if someone was angry with me, it wasn't entirely my fault. It was found that this 'Atlas' syndrome I imposed on myself was causing an extreme case of IBS.

I got into no fewer than three motorcycle accidents, with no permanent trophies to show for any of them. In one of them, my friend and I had snuck out of the house at three in the morning to crash a girl's slumber party, armed with smoke bombs and a sparkling fountain. 'Uncle' Dusty wasn't in on this one. Instead, we crashed into another motorcyclist. My parents woke up to the ringing telephone, hearing my voice on the other end.

"It's me, Mikey."

"Where are you!?"

My mother, in disbelief, cracked open the door to my bedroom and peered in at the empty bed.

"We're at the hospital. We've been in an accident."

Born to Be Wild

After graduation, we left Thailand and returned to the US. I decided to enter a community college in Warren County, NJ, on a Pell Grant. Due to my mother's battle with cancer, I had been in the US my junior year prior, put in the hard yards at Ponderosa Steakhouse, and saved enough money to buy my first car, an '87 Pontiac Grand Am. It was ten years old, but it felt new in my mind until I noticed the engine overheating anytime I turned the air conditioning on.

I'd sit in Brian Bradford's office and talk for hours. He was my writing professor. We'd exchange stories. He would always tell stories about his Japanese wife, and when mimicking his wife's voice, his voice would suddenly change to high-pitched 'broken' English. He would rattle on about the good ol' days in the '80s when someone could live on being a valet at a nice restaurant or hotel. I took a film appreciation course and a writing course with him. I remember scraping along the bottom of the grade pool and passing barely with an essay based on the song "Born to Be Wild" by Steppenwolf.[1] It's funny because this has been my go-to song at every karaoke event for as long as I can remember. I couldn't tell if Brian's nostalgia for the '80s made me feel better about drifting, or worse—at least in his time, drifting could pay the bills.

My sister and I have a thing with storms. We like watching them drift in and materialize from thunder and lightning to an eventual downpour. One day, I got into my 'new' car, skipped my college classes, and headed out to watch the remains of a hurricane that pummeled Florida or North Carolina. I headed to the shore to listen to the wind and waves, hoping they might jar my mediocre existence and kick my future into gear. Coming over an arched bridge, I failed to see the red light and brake lights of the cars in front of me. I slammed on my brakes, but my car hydroplaned and skidded into the car in front of me, setting a chain reaction between three vehicles beyond us. It was enough force to wreck my car to an unrepairable state. I called my parents.

"Where are you?!"

"I'm in Perth Amboy, at the hospital."

Washed Up Liberals

After my wreck in Perth Amboy and Warren County Community College, I joined two of my high school classmates one spring semester at Pensacola Christian College, down near the white sandy beaches of the Gulf of Mexico. PCC was for fundamentalist evangelicals who couldn't hack it at Bob Jones University in Greenville, South Carolina. We were 'washed-out liberals' by their standards, but PCC was still pretty strict. For instance, they had a 'pink' and 'blue' beach designated for us to go to. Unaware of the school's seriousness about their guidelines, a few buddies and I ended up on the 'pink' beach wondering why girls were running around with skirts past their knees rather than status quo beach attire. Some form of the PCC Gestapo reported the college parking sticker on my car, and the dean called me into the office to ask why I was at the 'wrong' beach.

It was at PCC where I met Suzanne, a sugar coma in a long skirt. The only woman to come close is my third-grade teacher, Laura Hoppkeppel. Suzanne's sweet southern tenor, dripping with honey, would break into a smile and laugh, lifting her dark eyebrows in delight as we talked. Her father and mother didn't allow her to wear jeans or go to the movies in the back hills of Alabama. On the other hand, my parents took me to see *Scream* and *Tommy Boy*. I didn't meet her at the 'wrong' beach. She was a freshman nursing student from Ohatchee, Alabama. During the summer, I visited her at her family's home on a road called Six Foot Lane, which turned out to be one of those never-ending dirt roads in an alternate version of the movie *Wrong Turn*. Their spacious manor, hidden behind a long driveway, was not 30 seconds down the road, but it was too hard to spot. Twenty minutes later, I ended up in one of those scenes with seven dogs barking at me around a dilapidated trailer home. This is the part in the movie where someone with missing teeth and a shotgun suddenly arrives and shoots out my back window. Suzanne and I stayed up until the sun rose the following day talking in her kitchen.

On campus, I made friends with another young lady, a half-Arabian girl whose family had been estranged from her wealthy father. He refused to pay for a Christian school, so I scrounged up some funds to help her pay. I had Suzanne leave the money on her bed, so she had no idea it was me. When the semester ended, she talked me into piling all her things with mine into my dad's '86 Dodge Aries, and I told her I'd drop her off at her home in Philadelphia. On the way, we got into a tussle at a truck stop after a cast iron breakfast. She insisted that because her brother was a former cop and taught her to drive, she should take over the driving duties. I told her I was fine and that we could continue with me at the helm. Not happy with my sentiments, she threatened to tell the truck drivers that I had violated her in some way. Shaken, I gave her the keys and got into the passenger seat, fuming and staring out the window. I was trapped in my own car, with thoughts of regret spinning around in my mind like clothes in a dryer. Countless mileage signs passed, and after 50 years, we were on the outskirts of Philly.

I decided not to go back to PCC the following semester, and I could hear a catch in Suzanne's throat as we talked about it over the phone. Eventually, she met someone else and let me know he was interested in her. She asked if it was ok if she entertained the idea, possibly hoping I would put up with a blue beach for a while longer and come back into her life.

A Candle in the Wind

Instead, with six hundred dollars to my name, I headed off to Joplin, MO, in my dad's '86 Dodge Aries. I moved in with one of my best friends, Zavian, and his family, who had recently returned from Thailand for a furlough from their mission work. On my way, I was visiting an old friend in South Carolina, and the CV boot on one of my wheels started malfunctioning. Guess what the cost of the repairs was? Six hundred dollars. My dad decided he'd use his credit card over the phone to, hopefully without any other incidents, get me to Missouri.

It was at this time that Zavian's younger sister, Kaelira, became a close friend. She and I would go on to be in each other's lives whether we were on opposite sides of the planet or not. Kaelira would have been my best man at my wedding if… she were a man. We had this famous trip to Columbia, Missouri, to visit fellow missionary kids we grew up with in Thailand. It was the day the 'candle in the wind' blew out. Princess Diana was killed in a high-speed car accident trying to shake off the 'papa' paparazzi chasing her down. They promised to be kind. Now she's dead. I rattled on without pause the whole weekend journey, obsessed with how ironic it was that the world's fixation on Diana's celebrityhood was partly to blame for her death.

My driving record became a concern for my manager at Pizza Hut. Drivers needed a clean record, and it looked like I would lose my job. I was a waiter for an evening and dumped a piece of pizza on the lap of my very first customer. My managers were both Jehovah's Witnesses and loved talking about religion and why my mainstream religion was wrong. We'd talk until the sun would come up some nights as we made pizzas to take home for ourselves.

Unfortunately, Zavian also found new friends. We shared the basement of his grandparents' home, but friction between his parents, his new friends, and me clogged our relationship down to spurts. When he ran up my long-distance phone bill while talking to his girlfriend in California, it was time to go. With the impending phone bill to be paid and the potential loss of my delivery job,

I called my dad.

"Dad, I want to come home. I'm sinking here."

He agreed to bail me out of my phone bill dilemma and provided me with the means to drive back home. I packed all my things in Joplin, MO, and returned to New Jersey.

Dr. Zang

I had a weird complex where visions of grandeur took me to heights unfathomable, allowing me to escape the reality I was in. I had landed a decent-paying temp job at Hoffman-La Roche, a vitamin manufacturing monopoly in Warren County. I worked in the mixing department, providing pre-mix packages of vitamins for food processing companies such as General Mills (Cheerios!).

In the quiet solitude of taping together hundreds of boxes we'd use later to package the mixes, I imagined myself as the President of the United States, crafting political campaign speeches or debate answers. I also saw myself as a successful entrepreneur who would change the world with a product everyone wanted to get their hands on.

I would eventually be told not to come back. They never told me why. It could have been for turning 15-minute break naps into 35 minutes or for spearing expensive bags of chemicals with the forklift forks. At least I wasn't the other guy who wrote "free blow jobs" on a woman's hard hat. He wasn't invited back either.

Within two years of leaving high school, I had about eight or nine tries at jobs. I worked at a video game store called Electronics Boutique. That's where I met the 'Beanie Baby' people who sold collectibles at a kiosk outside my store. Furbies were selling for more than $250 that Christmas. I aspired to help them with their technology needs. As the Internet bubble grew before bursting, so did the need for business owners to better understand how to connect in these fledgling new digital ways. Their adopted son was an aspiring rapper with the 'crazy' idea of providing downloadable versions of his songs on the Internet. He was asking me for help. My buddy Todd, who was still in high school then, helped me make a website for these Electrolux vacuum salesmen trying to steal sales from other regions. I'm pretty sure we broke many copyright laws, and they were operating outside their company's policies. We demoed it for them and disappeared.

One night, I was headed out and fingering around my seat for bridge tokens because I was headed across the river to Easton in Pennsylvania. While doing so, I failed to see the car in front of me stop to turn left. The damage from the encounter pushed in my door, and the bent vehicle frame made my dad's '86 Dodge Aries uninspectable without a ton of work necessary to get the passenger door to open again. I drove it until the last possible day, until the registration expired. We found a beautiful plot for it to lay to rest at my grandparents' estate, and we could visit her every now and then and rub the dust off her blue paint and reminisce about the times we had together, delivering pizza and going to the pink beach. My dad let me borrow the 'Beast,' an '85 Chevy station wagon that could probably win the war for Ukraine against Russia as the tanks did for the British in WWI.

I landed a job pumping gas on Route 78 in New Jersey at an Exxon station, Exit 12. I'd fall asleep constantly and wake up to people pumping and running. I woke up one night to a man digging for the cash box in our cabinets. He calmly put it back and told me he was getting change. In another incident, I was the last to see a wanted drug dealer getting gas with his mother's stolen credit card before he disappeared out of state.

For the longest time, I never knew one had to suck cigarette smoke into their lungs to get the full effect of the nicotine in your bloodstream. Perhaps that's why people cough a lot? I was sitting at the gas station one night, contemplating suicide, smoking menthol-laced cigarettes like cigars.

I landed in therapy with 'Dr. Zang'. He was performing the 'dark arts' of figuring out what led to a developing self-destructive pattern in my life that could have landed me in serious trouble.

I would tell him about a five-hour marathon phone conversation with a former crush, a girl from Missouri. Her name was Charity. She was a waitress at Pizza Hut, where I was a delivery driver. I scared her off one night by neatly folding the wrapping paper of her gift to me. I was her Secret Santa recipient during our work Christmas party. We stayed friends and talked over the phone, long distance.

"A woman likes you enough to talk to you for five hours?" I shrugged. "I'm not sure." My thoughts wandered back to the wrapping paper.

Early on, 'Dr. Zang' said with a somber tone, "Mike, if you are here thinking I can give you a magic pill to solve all your problems, you have come to the wrong place. You may face these struggles for the rest of your life."

My thoughts tumbled along in silent despair. "Oh God. I don't want to end up in jail or, worse, some rehab facility somewhere."

My parents went out of town for a few days, leaving me at home alone. They were never quite sure what would befall their son while they were gone. For instance, one time, I made it all the way to Chicago to start a new life and suddenly acknowledged that I had no money to do so. It was far less than six hundred dollars. I had to turn around, drive back, and plead with the supermarket I worked for to let me keep my job. This time, in their absence, I went out to a Navy recruiting office, took the ASVAB, and was told by the recruiters that if I signed my life away, I could do whatever I wanted in the Navy.

Chapter Two

Mamma Mia!

Look at me now, will I ever learn
I don't know how, but I suddenly lose control
There's a fire within my soul
and I can hear a bell ring
(One more look) and I forget everything, whoa
Mamma mia, here I go again

ABBA (performing "Mamma Mia")[3]

Geography Skills

I put on twenty pounds of self-esteem. There was a moment in boot camp when I thought my Navy career would end after a few weeks. At around 5:55 a.m., my bunkmate caught me marching next to the bed in my sleep, just before Reveille. We were told sleepwalking could end it all. I was half hoping it would. Sleepwalking is dangerous in the Navy. Need I explain?

I was muttering our cadence call, "1, 2 .. 1, 2, 3, uh 4 .. 1, 2 .. 1, 2, uh, 3, uh 4 ahhh .."

My most famous sleepwalking incident came when I was twelve. We were home from Thailand for a year, living at my grandmother's ancient fieldstone house sandwiched between a busy two-lane road and a huge cornfield. I had a dream that I heard something outside and went to investigate out the back entrance facing the cornfield. I woke up running around the house. We aren't sure, but it's possible aliens had beamed me up to their spaceship, saw a brain scan of my future, and dropped me back outside. At least they didn't drop me off in the cornfield or, worse, the busy highway. I had to have walked out three doors, traveled down two hallways, and a narrow set of stairs while unlocking the front door facing the highway. The witnesses were my mother and grandmother, terrified of someone knocking on the door. My mother grabbed an iron skillet.

"Mommy, it's me, Mikey," I cried.

In my boot camp unit, I was also in charge of laundry because, for some reason, they looked at our ASVAB score, and since I had the right to do whatever I wanted in the Navy, they gave me the job. The highlight came when our division had just come back from the 'confidence' chamber. It was a gas chamber designed to help us figure out quickly why we needed to secure our gas masks properly. We were asked to take off our masks in the gas and yell out our name, rank, and identification number. Many couldn't complete it without coughing violently. There was vomit and loads of mucus drenching the clothes, and as my new shipmates shed their clothing, they failed to put it in the laundry bags properly. I was there to make sure it all made it in, and the bags were tied and ready for pickup.

My parents came to my boot camp graduation. To this day, my mother finds Navy or military-related content on TV or the Internet, cries, and sends me the link or tells me about it during our weekly calls. She and my wife prominently display my mug in my Navy blues all over our houses.

After boot camp, when I went home that winter, I met Deanna. She was a prom princess without a date. Unfortunately, I had to attend my technical training school and could not take her the following week, but my first romantic relationship was kindled. We would talk on the phone until doubts about it lasting clouded me due to her poor American geography skills and disinterest in intellectual pursuits.

Bill Clinton

There were a lot of firsts for me in London: first official duty station in the Navy, first kiss, first sexual encounter, first real girlfriend, first time drunk, first time in Europe, first sighting of white powdery substances being snorted on a bus stop bench, first time being in a cult, and the first time meeting the President of the United States.

I had a colleague working with me in London, UK. Her name was Janine. Her dark cascading curls framed her face perfectly and were only let loose out of uniform. They accentuated the elegant contours of her New York nose and gymnast frame. We were assigned as electronics technicians to maintain communication equipment for a small detachment, existing just in case the Russians nuked the main facility in Italy.

We raced out to Hyde Park one day to see if we could catch a glimpse of President Bill Clinton a few days before the inauguration of George W. Bush. He was visiting Queen Elizabeth and decided to stroll the length of the park with Hillary and Chelsea. We wore our dark blues to be easily recognizable, and lo and behold, President Clinton walked over to shake our hands. He towered above us. His phallic nose was bigger than my fist. He shook my hand, and then he shook Janine's. He continued to shake Janine's hand. And while shaking her hand for what felt like eight years, he started talking about how the last time he was in London was when he was our age (or possibly just Janine's age at that point), in his southern drawl.

36 Holes

I was hanging with a British buddy of mine, Adam, from church. He had moved to London from the quaint village of Orford. His mother had an obsession with owls, which awkwardly prompted me to ask, on a weekend visit, why such an ugly bird. It sent him running out of the room, leaving me alone with his mother. I became pregnant each night with mince pies and other delightful countryside cuisine.

He was a deckhand on a sailing vessel out of St. Katharine Docks. He'd often take up jobs handling the rigging and other duties on ships owned by people wanting to go back in time and sail as far as the Caribbean. I'd visit him onboard often, especially if his best friend, Laura, was there. She didn't have curly locks or a New York nose, but her form was poetry inside and out. Her British vernacular was a Beatles song.

Adam and I were having shots of whiskey with his boss in St. Katharine's Docks over the weekend. 9/11 had come, and the 'War on Terror' had started. There were reports that on the anniversary, another landmark in Europe might become a target.

I piped up, "If anything, they should aim for the Eiffel Tower; it's the ugliest building in Paris."

My buddy's boss returned after a pause, "My mother's French."

My first drunken episode was when two colleagues fed me fruity cocktail drinks called Bacardi Ice at the Barley Mow down the street from our workplace. By three of them, I was shouting obscenities

I had practiced in high school. We were on the way home on the Underground. My shipmate, escorting me, politely pointed out later the rules of drinking.

"The goal, Mike, is to see how much you can drink without appearing too drunk—no spitting on yourself and/or others, and still be able to get yourself home."

A Navy reservist named Luis, Janine, and I decided to take a weekend trip to Paris. We took the high-speed Eurostar through the 'chunnel' (the link between Europe and the UK underneath the English Channel). There was complimentary wine for the whole journey. I don't remember much of Paris on the first night. I don't even remember where I slept that night.

In the morning, as we were going out to see Paris, we managed to get stuck in the elevator at our hotel. We laughed and talked for three hours, waiting for the repairman. We saw Paris and the Eiffel Tower. It looks much better at night.

They had complimentary wine on the way back. On the way back, we had so much wine that Janine and I had to carry each other home when we got off. Where was Luis? I'm honestly not sure. I had the urge to pee on the way home, but I had never peed in public before. I peed at a bus stop. As I was carrying out my business, some strangers approached my pit stop.

"Janine, JANIIINE .. Oh my God, they can see me."

We made it back to our barracks in Kennington. Janine bit my neck, and we went our separate ways to bed.

On a random Friday night in 2002, I attended a going-away party in the basement of our office building in downtown London. Janine's curly locks were on full display. I remember her floating across the floor while I sang the Backstreet Boys' "I Want it That Way." I had started celebrating long before the party with shipmates and civilian support staff again at the Barley Mow, where I lost my sobriety for the first time. I went and saw *Mamma Mia!* in West End with one of my supervisors, Jodie, because she had two tickets, and her husband didn't want to go. I sobered up in the middle of it, returning later to the party that ensued in our office building.

In my drunken enthusiasm that night, I told the crowd of astonished listeners that I was a virgin. Our command master chief was there. She played the role of Eva Gabor in *Green Acres*. She was in her late 30s and playfully suggested she'd steal it from me one night. Mamma Mia!

I slid off my bar stool at something o'clock and staggered out of the establishment. The security detail told me afterward that, in a failing effort to go home, I tried to slide my credit card instead of my security badge to exit the revolving doors. I gave up and left.

The next thing I remember was being woken up by that same security detail outside the elevator on the 10th floor (the top) and outside our workspace. They could have just rung the buzzer so my shipmate on duty could let me in to sober up, but they didn't. They reported it, which became an official incident requiring accountability, lots of paperwork, and yelling superiors.

I stood before the Chief's mess at a DRB (disciplinary review board), trying to explain why I didn't make it home and became an embarrassment to the unit. As I stuttered out my excuses, all I could think about at that moment was Master Chief and her gleeful prod the night before that she might take my virginity. As long as she had role-played Eva Gabor, I'd have been okay with that. Instead, I was cajoled and pounded down to about three feet tall by the folks in khakis.

I faced the officer in charge of our unit. I was slapped on the wrist for my foolishness and had to, of course, take a screening test for alcoholism at the local medical center to see if I had any underlying alcohol issues. I arrived at the unit, completed the survey, and left. I figured this would be the end of this misadventure.

I was wrong. I failed two line items. I had had an incident with alcohol, official and insufficiently documented. Check one. I also admitted to one more informal incident within my unit that impacted my workplace. Check two.

A few months prior, I was at a going-away party in the same basement, again, singing boy band karaoke tunes. My roommate had snuck out early as usual because he was handsome and liked to avoid trouble with a lonely shipmate, or he was sneaking around with a lonely shipmate, but I wasn't ever sure. I had too many fruity cocktails, and when I slithered off my seat, I could barely stand up. They recommended I go up to our work space and sober up. Unfortunately, I kept my supervisor, Jodie—the *Mamma Mia!* one—awake, who was eight months pregnant, entertaining her for hours with confessions of my deepest and darkest secrets. The following day came around, and I was reprimanded by my chief for annoying Jodie with my confessions all night. I was forced to work through the hangover as well.

So, I failed the alcohol screening process. The local DAPA (Drugs and Alcohol Program Advisor) was a recovering alcoholic himself and was concerned with the frequency and increasing tolerance I had for alcohol. He recommended I go to a treatment facility for rehab.

I called my father and mother and angrily blamed the drinking culture and everyone around me for my demise. I told them I would legally fight back because the security detail didn't handle the incident correctly, as a lawyer suggested I could do. My dad had other thoughts to share.

"Maybe this is God being faithful to you and preventing something worse. Sometimes, we need to be stopped in our tracks to evaluate the direction of our life."

Because the inpatient facility at the local US Air Force base at Lakenheath in the UK had no vacancies, they sent me to sunny and beautiful Rota, Spain. There, there is a huge naval hospital facility with a full alcohol treatment center for military personnel stationed in Europe and the Middle East.

I was assigned there for 28 days. The only way out of rehab was to write my own recovery plan. I needed to convince the facility that I had identified the underlying causes for drinking too much and knew the steps to avoid getting into trouble again.

We watched the movie *28 Days* with Sandra Bullock. We had group sessions. I met a man who had one too many driving incidents after a few too many beers. He worked out of Cornwall in the UK, took me under his wing, and showed me how to play golf. I forgot to put sunscreen on my arms one day while I played 36 holes without a golf cart. I played twice and walked 10 miles of golf course and another 10, chasing the ball in the woods. I had horrible sweat rashes in tender locations, and my arms hurt, but I still went out later to enjoy the endless night culture in Spain. Siesta in the hot afternoons, but things come alive at night!

I was done in 10 days, but tickets were non-refundable, so my unit in London, possibly enjoying some time without me, said I needed to stay there for 18 more days. I would get my breathalyzer test each morning and make a call in the afternoon to ensure them I was still alive and staying sober. Other than that, I was free. I would spend my evenings watching the sunset at a beachside villa up on a cliff, drinking lemonade. I was befriended by a family living in the villa. They were running a Christian ministry alongside the military installation.

The villa's name was Victory Villa. Was this name an ironic gesture in a story of failure, or was there a victory to be claimed here? My problem wasn't with alcohol. I discovered, with the help of the DAPA team at the facility, that I had a serious problem with boundaries. Hanging around other drinkers, I couldn't say 'no' to drinks or go home on my own accord. Eager to please, I drank beyond an appropriate limit. Along with Mr. Green with the candlestick in the library, untangling my battle with IBS in high school, my friends at Victory Villa and counselors in the treatment facility were there to stop me in my tracks and help me evaluate the direction of my life.

The Mess Decks

Because the Navy was concerned with my alcoholic tendencies, they were unwilling to send me abroad again for my next duty station. In the winter of 2002, I was sent to the USS *Bulkeley*, DDG-

84, a Flight 2A guided missile destroyer out of Norfolk, Virginia, the largest US military facility in the world. It was the homeport of no fewer than five nuclear-powered aircraft carriers, the symbols of America's global military reach. The surrounding Tidewater area included the carrier's shipyard facility in Newport News, the Portsmouth maintenance repair facility, and dozens of other ancillary military bases supporting the greater effort of national security for the world's most powerful nation.

I stayed onboard until I was permitted to move off the ship. I had found a church community and a welcoming family in Chesapeake who let me stay in their converted attic. This family would go on to provide me with love and support during some very tough moments in my life.

I struggled, especially with my anger. I survived mainly because I was smart. My low EQ might have been a ticking time bomb, but my technical skills often kept defusing it just in time, keeping both the ship and me in working order. In one incident, however, I wasn't so lucky.

I had been assigned double kitchen duty, and I was frustrated with not making the next rank and getting stuck with the duties for an indefinite period of time. I was working in the wardroom, serving the officers their meals. They'd often come by and comment about my perusing *The Economist* magazine. It was rare to meet an enlisted kitchen staff member who could wax on about the monetary policy of the Federal Reserve and the relationship between Iran and the US.

There weren't enough junior enlisted members to rotate into the kitchen, and because of the pecking order or outright favoritism in the Chief's mess, one of the units failed to provide a body to the main mess kitchen for the enlisted crew. I pointed this out to the command master chief. She was NOT interested in taking my virginity. She directed me to the Mess Chief, who proceeded to get in my face and explain to me that we ETs (electronics technicians) were lazy and talked back like 16-year-olds. The 16-year-old part applied to me. I got in his face, yelling that he was the 'biggest fucking disgrace in Navy history'—screaming it, in fact. The Mess Decks Master-at-Arms rushed over, grabbed me, and pulled me out of harm's way.

I refused to apologize at first. I wanted it to be sincere. I wasn't sorry. I was angry. Angry at Master Chief for pawning me off and dismissing my complaint. Eventually, I apologized convincingly at Captain's Mast, a ceremonious version of receiving non-judicial punishments such as restriction to the ship or docking of our paycheck, depending on the severity of our failures. My supervisor, ET2 Nikki Foster, was there to remind my chain of command about my technical prowess and the hard work I had done for the unit. Again, as in London, I was slapped on the wrist. I was given a stiff sentence, but it was all suspended, and I was on probation for six months. They also decided to take me out of kitchen duty.

Here I was, a week later, sitting with a man who had chased someone into their own home with a gun, a woman who was beating her children, and another man whose road rage led him to rip another driver out of their car. What could I have possibly earned to get here? This incident landed me in anger management therapy.

600 Dollars

Did you ever hear the joke of an Irishman, a Russian, and an American lawyer sitting on the train together? No? Okay. I'll tell you. The Russian was eating his caviar and suddenly chucks half of it out the window to the other two men's amazement. The American exclaims,

"Why did you do that?"
"We have lots of caviar where I'm from .."

A moment later, as they are all sharing a bottle of Guinness, the Irishman suddenly picks up the bottle and tosses it out the window, to the astonishment of the other two. The Russian gets in his face, grabs his shirt, and shouts,

"Comrade! Why did you do that?"
"We have lots of Guinness where I'm from .."

A few moments later, the lawyer gets up and starts climbing out the window to the disbelief of the Russian and Irishman. The Irishman stands up to restrain the American.

"Wha the hell are ya doin', lad?!"
"It's ok; in America, there are too many of us."

He jumps.

Possibly, the forklift misfortune got me fired at the vitamin plant. I never really inspired confidence behind the wheel. While driving, I noticed my passengers always fidgeting a bit. One time in London, three of us sailors went to get our 15-passenger van license, and we had to sit in the back while each of us demonstrated our driving. I looked in the mirror to see two grown men huddled in the back, almost hugging each other and white-knuckling the seat handles. My Asian children now talk about how great a driver their mother is (polite and indirect). I tried ramping and catching air with my dad's '86 Dodge Aries with five people in it down in Florida, costing me x amount of dollars at different stages of my penny-pinching years (that CV boot!). I did it again unintentionally on my way to my friend Caleb's wedding. I had the whole groomsmen party with me, and it knocked off the muffler to my '88 Mercedes SEL. In high school, I had been in no fewer than seven motorcycle accidents. In my early 20s, I almost died waking up in another lane of traffic due to playing *World of Warcraft* until three in the morning before work. I tell that story to gaming addicts all the time. And like all good Americans, you have to hit a deer at least once. I hit one on my way to Hoffman-La Roche for a night shift with my dad's '85 Chevy station wagon, a.k.a 'The Beast'. The deer didn't have a chance, and it merely moved the bumper a few centimeters and tattooed the grill with fur.

I have been pulled over and ticketed around the world from Thailand to the UK (parking Nazis). But the most remarkable feat was my driving record in the US.

Thankfully, I could never get my license revoked because I moved around the country a lot. No, I didn't move around the country simply because of my driving record. I just had a hard time staying in one place. I blame my parents, who had me travel around the world three times before I hit puberty.

NJ, PA, MO, KS, NE, OH, IL, DE, AL, MD, and VA .. yes. I had driving altercations in all of those states. I passed a cop in the passing lane going about 100 in a 75 in Nebraska because I was sleepy. Another cop pulled me over in Illinois and expressed his utter dissatisfaction with my inability to see him out in the open on a narrow median between lanes.

When I moved to Missouri to live with Zavian and Kaelira, I got no fewer than four tickets. That's why my boss at Pizza Hut was contemplating giving me a promotion from driver to manager to get me off the road. One night, I gave my customers a nice show, getting pulled over in front of their hotel room at Motel 6. I even got pulled over on my way to get my New Jersey driver's license converted to a Missouri license. On another night, on the back country roads of Joplin, on my way home, I was pulled over for drunk driving. The only problem was ... I wasn't drinking. I had a habit of looking over my shoulder at cars behind me riding my bumper. I thought the driver of the car was flashing their headlights at me, but it was just his car hitting bumps on the road. Every time I'd look over my shoulder, I'd jerk the wheel a bit, causing the car to swerve. The car behind me was a cop. He let me go, not because he was convinced I wasn't drinking. It was because he pulled me over in front of my driveway. I was already home.

I was the only white man in my 20s to own a 2003 black Impala Super Sport in all of America. While stationed on the USS *Bulkeley*, on a brisk Christmas Eve morning, a Saturday in 2006, I was headed to work. In the Navy, we rotated shifts for standing duty to keep things operating and the ship protected in port. It was my turn. We had just come off a deployment called a 'Med cruise.' We'd traveled through the Mediterranean Sea to the Middle East through the Suez

Canal. We were mainly responsible for anti-piracy operations similar to those highlighted by the movie *Captain Phillips*, starring Tom Hanks.[4]

I hadn't driven my car much. Our unit cautioned the sailors that they shouldn't drive during their first few weeks at home. Our sea legs were no longer reliable on land, and we needed time to adjust. I ignored them and hit a parked car in the Best Buy parking lot on the first day.

I had already been 'on land' a month or so, but I hadn't blown the cobwebs out of my Impala's engine since being home. I approached the onramp for I-64 in Chesapeake and mashed the accelerator .. again. With a full sport suspension guiding my turn up the ramp, I could feel the G-forces pushing me up against the door as my car approached 95 miles an hour before having to merge onto the highway. There were no cars on the road at the time. It was 5:30 a.m. The road was four lanes wide on my side. My car quickly reached 110 mph, and the governor kicked in to keep the car from traveling faster. On the median (like in Illinois), there was a cop in plain sight.

I immediately knew he'd come to get me, so I just pulled over and waited for him to arrive. He was angry and had me get out of my car and sit with him in the front passenger seat while he chewed me out for being so stupid. He said his family and others were traveling this time of year because of the Christmas holidays. There were construction signs along the route as well, lowering the speed limit to 50, so he clocked me doing well over twice the speed limit. He gave me a summons to come to court, and I got back in my Impala and continued my journey to work that day.

One of my shipmates at work told me to get a lawyer to reduce the penalty. My violation was in Chesapeake, but his lawyer was in Newport News. I traveled out there, was given a $600 bill, and we were on our way to possibly getting another slap on the wrist.

My court date arrived, and I waited for my lawyer to come. I sat and watched five hours of cases go by. One man was driving drunk and well over the limit, and because he showed them calibration paperwork for the car's speedometer, they knocked off the reckless driving charges and gave him six days in jail over three weekends so he didn't miss work. This was good news for me! I wasn't driving drunk; surely, I would get slapped on the wrist for just driving fast early in the morning with little or no traffic. My lawyer never arrived. He said he got stuck in traffic driving from Newport News to Chesapeake, so they rescheduled it for three months later.

Three months arrived, and he delayed my case again because he was a very fat man and was getting surgery for a gastrointestinal life-saving operation.

Another three months passed, and the final day came. My supervisor and I dressed up in our finest Navy outfits, as we are inclined to do for formal events such as weddings, award ceremonies, and Captain's Mast.

My lawyer was late again but eventually arrived and ushered me into one of the side rooms to discuss my case before the judge summoned us. He asked me,

"Do you have your calibration paperwork?"

I stared at him. He'd never told me to get calibration paperwork. In fact, he didn't communicate anything for six months other than to tell me he wasn't coming ... twice.

"No ... I was doing over twice the speed limit in a construction zone. Why would that help?"

We went back into the courtroom and waited our turn. When my name was called, I stood up. When the judge asked us to support my case, my lawyer said this:

"Your honor, my client chose a good time to drive at this speed because it was 5:30 in the morning, and there was no traffic."

Six hundred dollars .. six months.

The judge asked me if I had anything to say. I said, "No, your honor." That's why we hire lawyers, right?

The judge took a moment to deliberate and then read my sentence.

"I find the defendant guilty. I sentence him to 180 days jail time. One hundred forty days suspended with three years probation, a suspended license for six months, and a 480-dollar fine."

Out of the corner of my eye, I saw my supervisor swaying in the breeze. There was no wind, we hadn't been drinking, and his face was whiter than the whites he was wearing.

I didn't fully understand my sentence. It whistled in, but I couldn't understand the lyrics. Nothing was sinking in. Jail time? What about the drunk driver from six months ago?

Soon after, it was explained that I'd have to take a leave of absence from my Navy duties to serve my sentence. I was given 40 days jail time, but it's cut in half if you behave in jail and don't cause any trouble. So, I was looking at a 20-day vacation in Chesapeake City Jail.

My Chicken Leg

I wasn't arrested immediately. I was given a date that I had to turn myself in to start my sentence. I was brought before the commanding officer of my ship. My chief defended my conduct as a sailor, and I was reassured that the Navy would not punish me when I returned.

I turned myself in. They emptied me of my possessions (my wallet, my phone, etc.). It felt like Navy boot camp again for a moment, minus the haircut. Another gentleman then directed me to a place to shed our clothes and get our new uniforms on.

I sat in a holding cell for four hours with another man. We had nothing to do but talk to each other. He told me his story. He had just gotten out of prison a few months back. His younger brother was berated by his neighbor for walking on her grass. She was drunk. It started out with abusive language and escalated to punches. Her partner came out to see what the commotion was.

This young man was on his way out the door to break up the fight with his brother when his cousin suggested bringing a gun. In his mind, in a split second, he thought, "No .. not a good idea" .. but did what his cousin suggested. He walked out. Things further escalated to some shoves, and this man pulled the gun out and shot the lady's partner in the leg. And now here he was. He was already on probation and looking at getting locked up for years.

"What are you in for?"
"Speeding."
"Get out .. You're lying .."
"Nope."

I was eventually ushered into the non-violent ward that had 100 open cells (no bars like in the movies). The cells were all in a honeycomb-like fashion in a semi-circle facing the warden's desk, where he had visibility and could monitor all activities.

There were toilets for each, just like the movies, and when we wanted some privacy, we'd drape a sheet up and tie it in a way to separate us for a moment. The showers were in the middle. They were private stalls. I remember dropping the soap one time, and it slid across eight stalls. I didn't ask for it back. The soap was always stacked up in a big soap castle at the end of the row of stalls. I remember humorously getting angry at someone cutting in line for the shower. We had to figure out how to get the soap and not lose our opportunity to get a stall or get sent back to the end of the line.

Meals. They weren't enough. The economy ran on the money people would send to our 'canteen' fund. Once a week, we would fill out a form telling them what we wanted. The most popular items became currency that would be exchanged for extra plates of food, especially the Sunday meal, which included a colossal chicken leg. I had two young guys who were serving time on good behavior from prison sentences challenge me to see if I'd bail and give them my chicken leg. I implored that I, too, valued my chicken leg and wasn't willing to give it up. Some idle threats and smirks, and they moved on.

I would do pull-ups, pushups, and sit-ups underneath a grated staircase in an area outside that also had a half-court basketball setup for our ward. At night, many of us would go out there, hold hands, and say the Lord's Prayer.

Nobody believed my story. Not even the warden. He laughed at me.

"No one goes to jail for just speeding unless you were running from the cops."

"No .. I pulled over immediately."

"No drugs?"

"No .. I wasn't drinking either."

"Not possible."

I read quite a few books. *Men Are from Mars, Women Are from Venus*, Walter Cronkite's autobiography, a story about a fair-skinned Black woman in a poor neighborhood, and another 800-pager about how we destroyed Native Americans. I wrote a journal.

I had a few visitors. It was like the movies. They had to talk to me through a glass window. My parents came on my birthday to hang out with me three days before I would be released. The running joke was that I went to jail at the same time as Paris Hilton, 2,725 miles away in Lynwood, California. She got out on good behavior as well, three days after I did.[5]

My parents stayed around for three more days to pick me up. That day, another gentleman from another ward and I were released. In the blink of an eye, we were standing next to the warden, a bit disconcerted in our regular clothes and phones in hand. The warden sauntered along in a nonchalant gait, escorting us to the exit. The moment before sliding open a thick steel door with frosted glass, coaxing us back into our other reality, he said,

"Thank you, gentlemen .. if it weren't for you guys, I wouldn't have a job .."

I was standing next to a man who had been in jail for over a year and had a daughter who hadn't seen her father yet. My parents were on the other side of this chasm, talking with his wife before we were released.

I hugged my parents. I had just seen them on my birthday and only spent 20 days in jail, but when I got to the parking lot, I broke down and started to sob.

Newport News

Despite my short vacation in Chesapeake City Jail, I was still on target to transfer to Camp David in Maryland for special duty. I would be working for POTUS (the President of the United States) on their elaborate security system. It was a career booster, and considering my current relationship with a beautiful girl from back home in Pennsylvania, I was excited about my prospects.

Days away from transferring from the USS *Bulkeley* to Camp David, my Master Chief called me. He told me the orders were canceled, and I was no longer transferring. When I pressed for details, I found out the Secretary of the Navy's Office at the Pentagon was squeamish when they discovered I failed to report a reckless driving incident in Newport News.

Months before, I had been pulled over for speeding in Newport News, and the cop eventually handed me the citation. When I went to pay it, there was no record of the citation at the courthouse. Several months passed, and when I was pulled over for passing a cop (again) in Yorktown, he put me in handcuffs and informed me that my driver's license had been suspended and my personal details matched those of someone wanted by the Federal government. He let me go when I promised not to drive home.

While filling out the paperwork for my special assignment, I completely forgot about it. The Secretary of the Navy's office found the discrepancy and didn't feel good about allowing me near the President.

It felt right. An unbelievable assignment remained unrealized. I probably didn't deserve it anyway. As I pondered my next move for the following six months, a critical role in Singapore became available for someone with my qualifications. I broke up with my girlfriend, packed my bags, and headed back to Asia for the first time since graduating high school.

The Filipino Mafia

I'm sorry to sound like a kid in the show *Wonder Years*, but when I saw the Japanese flight attendants, something really clicked .. in my brain! It was as if I was moving closer to a place where I belonged. When I arrived in Singapore, it wasn't my new job that really had me excited about being there. The Navy unit there was small, and my responsibilities weren't challenging at first. I found an Asian community quickly, and the world became much smaller when a middle-aged movie producer I met there knew my high school classmate and his family from Thailand.

My ambition was to find a well-educated Chinese woman from church, but I was destined in a different direction. Six out of eight of us sailors arrived single and left married; one was with a Singaporean, but the other five were from Myanmar, Thailand, and the Philippines. My boss had met his wife in the Philippines as well when the US Navy was present there. She was a splendid lady! But I was skeptical. Filipinas were infamous in 7th Fleet sailor sea-story lore for their trickery and were often labeled gold diggers. I didn't want to have anything to do with them. Local bars were full of them, and my Navy buddies introduced me to one of those places on my first weekend in Singapore.

My buddy Todd has been an immovable force my whole life. He was 16, and I was a 21-year-old adult when we first met. I was helping out with the youth group at my dad's church, and I would drive him home after events. He knew the reasons I had to see 'Dr. Zang.' He witnessed me use Lysol spray on my armpits on my way to interact with Cristen, a beautiful neighbor of ours. He and Cristen came to see me at my technical 'A' school training. He visited me in London as well with our mutual friend Stephen. He has this habit of bringing up embarrassing stories, such as never letting me forget that I lost my camera in London at the airport or when we both went to Osaka, Japan, for a few days, informing me and a number of strangers that I snore. He deletes messages constantly from his phone but never deletes the recording of me snoring, just in case he needs to share it one more time. He was supposed to be my best man at my wedding but decided to attend at the last minute. So, I technically had three best men: Kaelira (if she had been a man), Todd, and Leon, my Singaporean friend, who was the official best man in the entourage.

He decided to visit me in Singapore as well. He brought my adopted Russian niece, Sasha, with him. We were out at a beachside park in Pasir Ris and decided to stop for dinner at a restaurant and bar.

Todd had fallen in love with a girl he had met online from Australia. She sang "Only Hope" from the Mandy Moore film *A Walk to Remember* to him, so it became his go-to song request even after the embers had chilled. The bar and restaurant had a live band, and they sang it for him. As always, when we're together, Todd helped me come out of my shell, and we connected with the band and our waitress—all from the Philippines. Todd likes to regularly frequent Apple stores throughout the world, and of course, we perused through one of them in downtown Singapore. One of the attendants, Vanessa, invited Todd, Sasha, and me to a Christmas party with her friends—all from Cebu, Philippines.

Todd had his eye on a girl behind the bar that night in Pasir Ris. Her name was Marisol. She, too, was from Cebu. Marisol eventually caught my eye as well. I would go on to repeatedly visit the place to see her and hang with the band and my growing number of friends in the Filipino community. We'd have a Monday crash night at my 1,900 sq. ft. place in the Navy quarters provided for us in a beautiful part of Sembawang. Our quarters were renovated army barracks from the British military back in the '50s. We were surrounded by pristine rolling hills of crabgrass and rain trees with umbrella-shaped spreads. I never saw my electricity bill, and I had four AC units for two master bedrooms, an enormous living room, kitchen, dining room, and a maid's quarters.

My romantic interest in Marisol came to a head as I realized I was constantly running out of money. After yet another anger management incident with my chief at work, I realized I had deeper issues to address. I had let four folks working at the Pasir Ris place move in with me, and I was buying all the groceries. Marisol was one of them.

I have to give her credit—she never took advantage of my situation outside of the groceries, no rent, and no utilities. Despite the pressure from others who said I could provide financial security, she stayed true to herself. Even with financial problems at home, she never gave in to the pragmatic choices many in her position might have. Not even a limo ride, roses, and a fancy dinner on her birthday could sway her. Eventually, she moved out after I asked her to clean up after brushing her teeth—a small issue, but it felt like the last straw. In reality, it was clear she wasn't interested, and it was time for me to move on. It was almost a relief to see her go.

One night, one of my Filipino friends decided to lick his wounds from a breakup by going out for the band leader's birthday at a bar downtown. I went with them, and that's where I met Jen, my lover, best friend, and mother of my kids. I have never tired of her voice, her laugh, definitely her singing, and her face first thing in the morning.

Heart Palpitations

My lack of boundaries with the mafia inadvertently brought me the joy of my life (my super lady and my kids). Work didn't pan out quite the same.

My Senior Chief would nag me to clean up my desk before leaving for the day. One night, while she was standing duty, she passed by my desk and saw I had not cleaned it. She decided to swipe it all off my desk onto the floor.

My supervisor came in before I did and had to pick it up. In his high nasal tone, he said something to the tune of not paying the piper and covering my ass by just following orders.

I felt violated, having my personal work and things scattered carelessly on the floor by a superior. I refused to sign the disciplinary form, and thus the discussion moved to Senior Chief's office. It was there that I repeated the incident on the mess decks a few years before, blacking out, screaming in her face, and telling her that she was the last person on earth who should tell me to be more professional. I walked out shaking and staggered into our locker room.

Master Chief down the hall suddenly had flashbacks of her abusive husband and instantly dialed security. She, too, had no desire to take my virginity.

One more DRB and an Academy Award-winning performance to explain my lack of boundaries and empty bank account, and it was a slap on the wrist once again. Of course, I apologized immediately to Senior Chief for screaming in her face and Master Chief for giving her flashbacks of her worthless ex-husband.

They sent me to counseling at the prestigious Singapore American Club downtown.

I had heart palpitations that scared me one night. I had only shit my bed or had a scratchy anus when life got too tough before. I also had an annoying habit of sweating, and only my right armpit would stink if things got too stressful or the girl was too pretty—hence, Todd witnessed me spray the Lysol in desperation one night. These new anatomical reactions startled me. I thought something was seriously wrong.

The counseling was once a week during the day, and it allowed me to unload all my troubles and concerns. It gave me time to think about my past and its impact on me and my career. It was great timing because I would soon meet my wife. They flew me all the way to Okinawa to figure out if I was crazy or not. When the psychologist asked me if I needed anything, I told him to please send the positive report (that I'm not crazy), but that I would like the counseling to be extended for six more months because of the life changes going on behind the scenes.

I was doing comparatively well in my rating (electronics) and rank. I was up for chief, and I was handling some very challenging assignments. I coordinated the Defense Information Systems Agency node from our tiny facility, where we all had to wear more than one hat. We would go on missions setting up and training other militaries on communications equipment designed to allow them to collaborate tactically with the US securely using real-time displays of pertinent information and everyday tools like email. We would bounce the links off of commercial satellites, and voila—there it was. I worked with the Filipino, Thai, and Singaporean Navies.

When it came time to get our evaluations, I was hugely disappointed. They had given early promotion recommendations to someone who had been there less than six months, which is completely against protocol. Since only a few of them could be given, I missed my chance and attained a 'Must Promote,' which was ok but not what I expected.

I had been sitting in church wondering how I would continue a Navy career and be a husband and father. My wife and kids were in the Philippines. I knew the divorce rate in the Navy was higher than in the civilian world because of the unique challenges of regular deployments.[6] At one point on the USS *Bulkeley*, my whole division chain of command had divorced at least once. I sat quietly one Sunday and prayed, asking God to find the answer.

A month later, the Navy mysteriously denied my request to re-enlist.

Chapter Three

The Gambler

You've got to know when to hold 'em
Know when to fold 'em
Know when to walk away
And know when to run
You never count your money
When you're sittin' at the table
There'll be time enough for countin'
When the dealin's done

Kenny Rogers (performing "The Gambler")[7]

Sorry!

I had talked to a Filipino shipmate in Singapore whose family lived in the Philippines. Upon retirement, he was going to move back as well. He owned a laundry business in Dumaguete, on the island of Negros, but he told me one steamy night over drinks:

"It's easy to make money in the Philippines, Sullivan, but keeping the money is the problem."

I got married in December of 2010, and had my son in February. I processed out of the Navy in San Diego, California, in July of 2011 and then rejoined my family in Cebu, Philippines, to start our new life together.

I had left the Navy with 35,000 dollars to my name. Like my Pinoy shipmate, I invested in a laundry and water filtration business. Having spread the money too thin, our revenue didn't come close to matching our lifestyle. I borrowed money with my good credit rating and racked up credit card debt, and soon, the ship began to sink, torpedoed by a lack of planning, knowledge, effort, support, and the list goes on. Not only was I new to the Philippines and entrepreneurship, but I was newly married. My wife knew we didn't have enough money, but we hadn't learned to communicate yet. Her calculated assumption was,

"Surely, my white husband from the rich world knows what he is doing, maybe, but it doesn't look like it."

She kept her mouth shut, trusted me, and showed immense loyalty until the money melted away, and we could only afford two packets of ramen noodles and rice one night. I went out to negotiate with my old landlord for a bit of my deposit money back. I scored and proudly displayed the thousand-peso bills to her, but she was already fuming about me not telling her where I went. I told her I was going to step out in front of a big truck on the highway and end it all. I didn't. She was stuck with her husband with rich skin and an empty wallet.

If you see my smile, you will see a trophy of mine—a chipped tooth. Each time I look in the mirror, I am reminded of my time wrestling with my water filtration system that kept breaking. Thus, it broke us financially and caused us to throw in the towel and sell off its parts to a middleman. He didn't give us a good deal and later failed to pay up on a $4,000 business loan. It was a sad day for me. But thankfully, I have my chipped tooth and a 50-foot water tower on our property to remember this time by.

In our journey through the financial valley, my wife and I, both with our two youngest children, ended up in Thailand while I was teaching English. It was there that our marriage went through the fire and barely avoided divorce. People often tilt their heads to the side privately as they see our public posts. I call her "My Friend," and she calls me "Friendship." The gossip, I'm sure, is juicy, but we merely learned to treat each other kindly rather than succumbing to a tyranny of expectations that often plague marriages. Our terms of endearment are a reflection that kindness comes first.

She went back to finish her college education at the university she had dreamed of as a child. With notches in my belt as a maturing husband, I was more than happy to help her in this regard. However, I felt that our new start in our marriage wouldn't survive if I stayed in Thailand. I found a job in Manila working as a consultant for the BPO (business process outsourcing) industry.

I got fired. Yes. Add that to the list. My managers weren't comfortable with some of the jokes I made about my assignments. The project management software I was expected to manage and train six staff members on sounded like a drug used to combat heart disease, and it was used by medium to large-sized enterprises in the automotive manufacturing and space industry. Of course, I made fun of it. It represented the inflated ego of all involved who chose it. So, I went about making the management feel as ridiculous as it sounds. Of course, I was ushered in by my manager and the HR head and told to pack my things.

After the firing, my poor assistant manager had to get in the elevator with me all the way to the ground floor. It was like a *Seinfeld* episode. He was on his way to a lovely tropical beach vacation with a lover or two, and I jovially wished him a great holiday. He probably wondered whether or not he should lock his doors or leave town early that night. My friend Sarah, who had quit a few months before, took me out for pizza and beer a few hours later.

Anger crept in, over the next few days, and I was too ashamed to tell my wife. I stayed in my apartment for two more weeks before letting on.

Before leaving Manila, Sarah invited me to a conference for entrepreneurs. It was my introduction to the startup world. The keynote address was about small business incubators worldwide and the Web 2.0 revolution. I listened to pitch contest after pitch contest. Blue ocean, as some refer to it—ideas and innovation that transform lives by becoming future businesses.

We all know of the likes of Steve Jobs, Bill Gates, and Jeff Bezos, whose startups are now the most valuable companies in the world. I met founders of fledgling companies trying to get started, and I realized we had so much in common. Each time I shook hands with a founder and heard their pitch, a heavily chained door was opened to a cavern, illuminating a piece of me.

They were about solving problems—difficult problems—not 9-to-5 drudgery that feels like most people are pretending to work. They definitely did in my workplaces in the past. They put their heads down, and people seemed okay with that. Patrimony was the fuel that kept the lights on. I hated it. My boss even called our driver a cockroach, his statement dripping with racist and classist sentiment that he carried with him effortlessly around Southeast Asia for years.

Manila had chewed me up and spit me out. With little left to lose, I found myself looking for something else. I eventually had to tell my wife that I had been fired and needed to move back to Cebu. I was studying at the time, and my college loan money buffered the transition.

One night, sitting in my office, toying with energy sector ideas, my thoughts wandered into a different problem to solve. I envisioned a new platform here in the Philippines that would help create financial rapport in a siloed and disparate third-world economy. It would help those who had cash-based businesses, like my mother-in-law, establish more financial leverage with the businesses and institutions they depended on. In an environment that stigmatized the poor and kept them there, this would democratize their information privately and seek winners and losers, encourage losers to .. not be losers, and create higher business standards in an otherwise predatory and inefficient market.

I fell behind in my studies and was put on academic probation, but something fueled my desire to solve a societal need I saw so dire in the world around me. I had a bright young lady as my cofounder and protégé. I did focus groups and interviewed customers with the help of my wife and her college friends. I solicited many to invest in my ideas and pitched to Silicon Valley investors, angel investors, and USAID. I came up empty. My school kicked me out. College loans weren't an option anymore, and I was so broke. Again. My wife had to quit school as well because of her husband's poor pockets.

To my horror, my mother and father had long planned to visit for Christmas in 2016. The timing was humiliating because my parents arrived to a son who was at the end of his resources and wit's end. I had to ask them to pay for the groceries and more. They stayed in our home. They had a great time with my kids playing *Sorry!* and listening to them sing in the bathroom.

I sat down with my dad on the couch one night and asked him for advice.

"Why do I have so much trouble providing for my family?"

He put his hands up like a duck quacking and said,

"You tend to run your mouth."
"True."
"I'm sure if you apply for work tomorrow, you will find a job within the week. God will be faithful."

He handed me the equivalent of 80 dollars in Filipino pesos, and they flew back to the US. Within ten days, I had two interviews and a job.

My new Korean manager was lamenting his English academy without a token white man to complement it. I was his guy. He did find another one a few months later and paid him twice my salary because he was a Canadian rockstar from China who had developed his own IELTS curriculum. He was 58 years old and a former professional hockey player who landed in Asia running from the law. He had stories. I'm not sure how many of them were true. I'd give him relationship advice as he lamented the roller coaster he was on with a Filipina Amazon half his age.

When I found this job teaching for 800 dollars a month, and my wife was working at the call center, I would drive to work on my 10-year-old motorcycle for 45 minutes both ways, sometimes in almost unbearable traffic. I would see the sunrise out on the water on one side and the beautiful mountains on the other side and suddenly become aware of how small I was. Being devoutly religious, I believe God had a message for me at this time.

I had no insurance and meager pay, but I started to control that sarcastic tongue of mine. I started to relax a bit and cherish the relationships with my students and fellow teachers—especially when I saw how much less those teachers made than I, yet with laughs and smiles and life.

jjimjilbang

One of my colleagues from New Zealand got married. At his wedding reception, I was getting a second glass of wine when a beautiful woman approached me.

"How are you? How is the wedding going?"
"Um, uhh, fine I guess. I'm sorry, do we know each other?"
"I'm the bride, Mike … …"

It was the fourth wedding in Korea I had attended. When I attended the first wedding, my boss ushered me in to find a seat. I looked and saw a procession going on and thought we were late. We weren't.

It was someone else's wedding that was finishing up. Most of the patrons had already gone down to eat at the buffet. In Korea, their public wedding ceremonies were like their manufacturing lines, efficient and without time to spare. Guests were there to get selfies with the bride and provide financial honor to the family as a whole, but it wasn't that necessary to stick around and chitchat. How did I end up in Korea, you might ask.

While in the Philippines on the margins of financial existence, my buddy Todd told me he could get me a job at the kindergarten where he worked. Thankfully, Jen could give those self-entitled first-worlders on eBay the middle finger and quit the call center. She went on to become the number one events host in Cebu. Often, her customers are other young Filipinas stealing love and money from more foreigners. At least they had money.

And so I went, leaving my family behind in Cebu. Korea was a lovely place—chic cafes and conveniences that left European and American cities in their dust. I was especially proud of myself for getting over my fears of walking around naked at their *jjimjilbang* (찜질방) to sit in the hot tub and get a few hours of sleep before work the next morning.

I'll never forget the little faces of my 5-year-olds (Korean 7-year-olds)—Elsa (English name) and her architectural dreams, accidentally throwing Anthony and Princess Bella, and the beautiful scarf her parents bought me for Christmas. I bring it everywhere with me, even if it's a tropical country. It holds the special memory of surviving kindergarten and the little smiles and moments we had together.

At the beginning of 2019, I found a follow-up job teaching corporate English to Hyundai Motor Group, the world's fifth-largest auto manufacturer. This job gave my family the boost necessary to regain some financial territory.

When COVID-19 struck, we had to move our operations online. I had had a terrible back injury involving lifting at the gym the night before 'patient 31' caused a super-spreader event attending the birthday party of her cult leader.[8] The night after my injury, while lying in bed, wondering if I'd ever walk again, a vision came to me of the rows and rows of Chinese people dying alone of a disease no one really knew what to do with yet. I had trouble putting on socks and pants the next morning, but eventually, I made it to work on time.

We had to bring all of our things home, and I wasn't sure if I'd be employed in a few weeks, let alone run and walk normally again. On the bus ride, because of my back, I could not lift my suitcases onto the bus and required assistance.

My salary had been cut in half, but on a better note, through research, I found that I had slipped a disk, and it wasn't severe enough to get surgery. I couldn't lift myself on the balls of my left foot for weeks. I reinjured it twice more, and each time, I rehabbed feeling back into my left foot as the swelling stopped pinching the nerves that caused the numbness.

My mother and brother-in-law were hospitalized soon afterward with COVID-19 and weren't given great prospects to survive. It was discovered that my brother-in-law had diabetes, which had complicated his recovery and the safety of his liver. My mother was older and immune-compromised, having fought off breast cancer twice. There came a point where she was lying in a hospital bed alone, wondering if God had abandoned her.

I knew I had to go home either to funerals or recoveries. My sister had nine children. It scared me to hear my mother scared, and the breathing device wasn't just background noise—it hissed death and uncertainty for the woman who gave birth to me.

My boss, Dianne, went to bat for me and allowed me to be home in the US for a month and a half.

It seemed the night my mother and I talked was the low point for her. She was congratulated by the staff in the intensive care unit for being in the best condition out of all there. Considering her oxygen level sat at a stubborn 30%, that didn't bode well for the rest of them.

My brother-in-law made a turn as well and was released long before my mother. My dad and I waited at home. Finally, when my mother fought with the doctor to leave, we knew she was ready to come home.

I slept on the couch in my parents' living room, playing *Civilization 6* and seeing a lifetime's worth of senior citizen ads on TV. We'd watch game shows from the '60s and a Canadian series called *Heartland* about a family and their ranch. The main character was a horse whisperer.[9] I sat through maybe two episodes of my dad's emergency service drama and told him my heart couldn't take it. I would stick with the horse whisperer and other choices my mom preferred.

I shared breakfast, TV, and hours of conversations with the two people who brought me into this world and put up with my antics. From that point on, I try to call once a week to talk to them without fail.

I returned to Korea and went back to work. Our program had moved completely online. As COVID-19 had mutated into more benign strains and vaccines were perpetuated throughout the world, Korea slowly started to open up. Eventually, we had in-person classes, with only a few mishaps with COVID-19 cases that would send us all scurrying back online again.

In the midst of the COVID-19 mayhem and drug wars in our neighborhood back in Cebu, a typhoon made a beeline for our house in Talisay. I always complained over the years that they would cancel events for typhoons that had already passed or ones whose trajectories were clearly not going to hit us. Strangely, no one seemed to care about the one heading straight for them. It was quite rare because there are lots of islands and mountains between Cebu, and the typical routes these typhoons take normally downgrade them to mere storms before they arrive. Not this time. Before the Internet and electricity disappeared, I was barking orders from Korea for the kids to move downstairs. I stared helplessly at the computer monitor as 200 kph winds destroyed the second level of my home, ripping all the windows out, destroying beds and electronics, and knocking out electricity for two months. Our roof was a sieve. Drinking water was pedaled for the desperate willing to pay. Lines for everything were extremely long. Jen's back troubles started around this time.

It was time to leave Korea. The English Language Program, sponsored by the US Department of State, picked me up for a prestigious fellowship in Türkiye teaching in Isparta at Suleyman Demirel University.

I hadn't seen my wife and kids in the Philippines for two and a half years. Because of COVID-19 restrictions in both Korea and the Philippines, it became virtually impossible to go home. In July of 2022, I was reunited with them, and we found the 10-month fellowship I'd have in Türkiye to be a short vacation compared to what we had just gone through.

Earthquakes

"Our future is darker than your shirt, *Hocam*," one of my students remarked with a smirk on his face. I sat having a *tavuk dürüm* with them during my last week in Türkiye.

As soon as I met these young guns in Isparta at Suleyman Demirel University, I fell in love. I loved their lives and their potential. I knew that if I was given a 40-day vacation period between semesters, I needed to come see them in their hometowns. And so I did.

I set out on my journey on the first day of 2023. My first visit was in Kayseri. When I arrived, it was -8 degrees Celsius, but I was so excited, I just walked around completely lost for a moment, looking for a bus. I made Instagram friends with a random stranger in the process who also couldn't find his bus. I finally met the warm and wonderful Yaren and her friends, and we would go on to have an amazing day that ended at her home with *mantı* and a long list of other delicious Turkish cuisine on the table.

I would go on to visit 26 cities in 35 days. I met scores more of my students, their friends, and family members. None of my students were wealthy. I wasn't involved in a glossy affair. I was teaching prep school at a mid-tier public university. These kids were all from middle-class Türkiye. Many of their parents had never been to college. One of my student's parents had recently lost his job but still rented a car to take me around town and then drove me to my next stop—an unexpected road trip, listening and singing to Adele.

I know people come from all over the world to see Hagia Sophia in Istanbul (not Constantinople). Great. It was amazing for me too, but much better with my student and her sister. We lay on the plush carpets there as if it were a park lawn and talked about life, and infamous Turkish dissidents that are hiding in my home state of Pennsylvania—all while staring up at the famous dome art.

I had students who braved the elements to be hospitable. I was in this beautiful coastal town on the Aegean coast in the wrong season. The weather was icicles coming down as rain. It was windy and terrible. My student and her brother, with no money, still insisted on walking me around town. We ended the night at a coffee house and talked about the obstacles in the way of young people and the insurmountable challenges they face in dismal economic times with a real inflation rate close to 60%.[10]

I had the chance to stick my feet into the steaming hot springs of Pamukkale with the ancient city ruins of Hieropolis in the background—Awesome, but not nearly as awesome as listening to my student translate her dad's story about his open-heart surgery and tasting her mom's homemade Turkish pasta. Greek, Roman, and Ottoman history were no match for the bonds that were made over meals and Turkish tea.

On February 5, I came home. It was Sunday, the day before our Spring semester was about to start. I got off my bus too early in my excitement. I had to trudge through snow that was several inches deep. I didn't feel it. I didn't care. I was on top of the world, and the 35-minute journey through the snow was a celebration dance of all that transpired thus far in 2023. I felt like Alexander the Great having reached the Indus River. I had endless memories in the bank with my students and their immediate communities that we would cherish forever. More than one student said it was the best time they've ever had. I had mothers and brothers cry when I left.

The next morning, at around 4 a.m., I was woken up by my bed shaking. It shook for a while, and it was frightening. I thought it was the wind for some reason or my apartment's heater exploding. But I soon realized it wasn't. It was an earthquake. I was on the top floor of a 7-story apartment building, that shook anytime someone slammed a door, so I thought possibly I should get dressed and get out of there, but then it stopped. I went back to sleep.

What I didn't know in the early dawn was that a 7.8 magnitude earthquake with the epicenter in Kahramanmaraş had ripped through Eastern Türkiye and Syria and took tens of thousands of lives, leaving millions homeless and almost a quarter of the country paralyzed.[11] It was 750 km away from me. One of the aftershocks was almost as severe.

When I heard the news, I contacted my students closest to the epicenter. Thankfully, they all answered. I contacted my new friend Fatma in Hatay. She had taken me to her brother's house at 11 p.m. to learn how to cook Hatay's finest dessert, *künefe*, a sweet, cheesy dessert soaked in syrup and topped with crushed pistachios. No answer. I reached out to Fatma's student Deniz, who, only a week before, was telling me about her dreams of traveling to space and writing poetry. No answer.

Not only a month before, I was in Gaziantep, Iskenderun, and Antakya, now scenes of utter chaos and destruction. I saw the world's largest mosaic museum in Antep. I was in the foodie capital of Türkiye, having more Baklava than I thought healthily possible. My students were humorously repulsed by any Baklava made without pistachios. I had UNESCO-protected food in Antakya with three awesome ladies from my classes who had now lost their homes and best friends. I spent a magical afternoon in Iskenderun with Fatma Dordurka and her amazing program, Be the Voice of Girls, working with marginalized girls through art and English. She, her daughter Alara, and students Deniz and Cemre. Gone forever.

Many young Turks asked me why I was in their terrible country, and I replied, "I was chosen to be here. Türkiye chose me. I allowed the doors to open, and I walked through." And I'm glad I did, despite the anguishing pain of falling freshly in love with everyone around me, having lost some of them, and watching others suffer.

Earthquakes. They are no one's fault. No one owns the fault lines far beneath us. We can't even blame climate change. They are unstoppable forces of nature. They have proven time and time again how fragile and precarious life can be, no matter what heights of innovation we have available. Earthquakes tell us that no matter how mobile or elevated in society you may be, choices are not always yours. I didn't choose to be abused as a child by school teachers. I didn't choose the religion I was brought up in. I didn't choose my skin color, my class, my citizenship, my genes, or my heritage.

I didn't choose to come to "terrible" Türkiye and enjoy the best breakfast culture on the planet. But I did choose to love and relate to people there, and the hundreds of places around the world that I've been. I, at each turn, have stopped to appreciate, hug, encourage, and embrace those in my path, regardless of their social status, religion, armpit smell, or lifestyle.

Part Two:
What Divides Us?

*So I could ask myself really what is goin' wrong
In this world that we livin' in people keep on
givin' in
Makin' wrong decisions, only visions of them
dividends
Not respectin' each other, deny thy brother
A war is goin' on but the reason's undercover
The truth is kept secret, it's swept under the rug
If you never know truth then you never know
love
Where's the love, y'all, come on? (I don't know)*

Black Eyed Peas (performing "Where Is the Love?")[12]

Chapter Four

America the Beautiful?

And he raised his hand and smiled at me
As if he seemed to say
Here's hoping we both live
To see us find a better way
Then the devil's clock struck midnight
And the skies lit up again
And the battlefield where heaven stood
Was blown to hell again
But for just one fleeting moment
The answer seemed so clear
Heaven's not beyond the clouds
It's just beyond the fear
No, heaven's not beyond the clouds
It's for us to find it here

Garth Brooks (performing "Belleau Wood")[13]

Airports

When something goes wrong, we often reimagine the events over and over again, trying out different ways of saying or doing whatever we think will make it okay. I do this when thinking about my endless mishaps at the airport, with luggage weight, missing luggage, customs officials wanting bribes, and detainments.

For a time, I was stopped almost every time I entered the United States. I can only remember once when I was not from September 11th, 2001, to 2022. I will never forget the first time. It was the November after 9/11. I was standing in Newark Airport looking at all the other detainees with me. I was the only one with a US passport. I was in the US Navy at the time with a top-secret clearance. The woman asked for my military ID, and I showed it to her but refused to give it to her.

"You can take it out of my cold dead hands. I work for the government too, and they conveniently lose things."

I have discovered slowly, through each murky detainment and my mystery encounters with the police in Virginia, that my personal identification matches that of someone wanted by the country. That person of interest traveled with a woman named Samantha at some point. That's all I know. To make myself feel better, I often try to imagine Samantha looking like one of the femme fatale characters in a James Bond film, wearing a short skirt and looking strangely close to Barbara Eden in the show *I Dream of Jeannie*. Of course, the Barbara Eden from 1965.

While I was traveling to the US to be home with my mom, fighting for her life with COVID-19, I was detained again at Detroit Metropolitan Wayne County Airport. I walked up to show my passport to the DHS (Department of Homeland Security) officer. While he was checking, one of his colleagues with 'POLICE' written on his flak jacket walked up. The DHS official checking my passport points to me with my passport and says with a laugh, "Hey, I thought you were here to get this guy."

I flinched. I had just watched these folks berate a woman and ask her how much money she had and then proceeded to make her take everything out of her bags. How do I know this? Because they didn't have it walled off for privacy. Passengers from up to 140 different places around the world could stand there and watch people get humiliated as they entered the United States of America—showing off their branded underwear, store-brand shaving cream, or worse.

After clenching my teeth, I was soon directed over to the same tables as the young Asian woman who had her money and undies counted in front of her. The same two DHS ladies took their turn counting my undies as if they would suddenly reveal the secret identity behind Samantha's mysterious travel mate. There was no cash to count, of course. I was broke, as usual. And there was very little time between flights. How long were they going to keep me there? When one of them came upon my doctor's notice that I needed to leave Korea, telling whoever needed to know that my mom was not in good condition, she suddenly looked up and said in a hushed voice,

"Oh, this is why you are coming home."

"Yes. And my next flight leaves in an hour."

The Star-Spangled Banner

It happened while I was in the US Navy, stationed in London, UK. It was about 3 p.m. or so when we saw the news of the plane that hit the WT towers and then witnessed in horror as the second plane pummeled into the second tower. I called my parents. With a wavering voice, I left a message saying I was safe. The building went into lockdown. Every US military installation around the world went into lockdown, especially as news crept in that the Pentagon had been hit as well. A fourth plane went missing.

I had grown up overseas. I rolled my eyes at outward displays of unabashed patriotism that failed to take into account the side effects of America's place in the world. My patriotism was fledgling. I would get teary-eyed when *The Star-Spangled Banner* was played at sporting events. My Aunt Deena, my dad's sister (may she rest in peace), was born on the 4th of July, so it was common for us, when we weren't overseas, to celebrate eating huge hoagies in her home on the large deck overlooking their inground pool with Philadelphia in the distance. Being shuttled back and forth from Thailand as a kid fractured my sense of continuity with my passport country, despite wearing her uniform proudly in the United States Navy.

However, this time, I felt a twinge of anger caked over my horror as we watched everything unfold. A terrorist group was mocking the freedom and relative safety we espoused that allowed us to walk all the way to domestic gates to send our loved ones off on flights around our big, beautiful country. This senseless bloodshed would usher in two wars that America would fight halfway around the world in Afghanistan and then Iraq.

I suppose at this point, I don't need to tell you how topsy-turvy my career in the Navy was. I was often at odds with my supervisors, and I landed in therapy, jail, and rehab. But I was depended on to do some very difficult tasks that were far beyond my pay grade. Cruise missile qualifications were on schedule due to pulling off miracle repairs on the USS *Bulkeley*. President Obama's pivot to Asia required me to have our tiny facility in Singapore upgraded and ready to expand and support forward-deployed naval and specops units to the AOR. The relationships we developed with the Singapore Navy were intangible signs of gifts I had no idea I possessed at the time.

But in 2010 or so, despite having made rank earlier than most of my peers, despite having put on a Superman cape to solve some very difficult problems for the Department of Defense—despite many things, I was told to leave. I served in the United States Navy for 12 tumultuous years. I'm super proud of my service. The bonds and experiences I had there are irreplaceable, but in the end, they said they didn't want me.

No explanation was given. The Navy was weeding out underperformers in my electronics rating. I was in the best shape of my life, kicking ass and taking names. Yeah. I had a bit of an attitude problem, but there wasn't an iota that spoke of this in my service record. The slaps on my wrists and DRBs are not permanent marks reflected in the paperwork. It gets thrown out if there are no further problems from one unit to the next, giving me a fresh start.

One of my lingering thoughts was that I was a squeaky wheel at times that possibly poked at the wrong power structure that had the ability to whisper my name into the database of people to be removed. It sounds conspiratorial because, without an explanation, I'm still left guessing.

Americans all know about the 100-dollar toilet seats and the 50-dollar screws. The military would try to limit waste, fraud, and abuse, but it was just too big. The Navy alone is huge. Our military budget is bigger than the next nine countries' military budgets combined.[14] When I was on the ship, I replaced a PC unit in a communications device that should have cost about 400 bucks. It cost 8,000 dollars. This space-age technology didn't work under heavy rain conditions, but it could withstand an electromagnetic pulse caused by a nuclear explosion. I watched the construction of minor things cost enormous funds at the behest of local contracts through larger defense suppliers like Lockheed Martin and General Dynamics. I saw the money being tossed around when it shouldn't have been. Maybe I made one too many comments. I have doubts this could be true because I was low-ranking and had no authority to act on these things.

When I would go on missions in Thailand, as mentioned, and the Philippines, our transportation arrangements were made by a local contract company based out of Singapore called Glen Defense Marine Asia (GDMA). The locals would show me how much it cost. It blew my mind. I would repeatedly tell my bosses that a lot of this was unreasonable. What we were paying for a van could have gotten me a police escort around town in the day and several escorts at night. I would get slight nods in agreement, but little was done to stop it. And it happens every day. We spend enormous amounts of money for "national security," but in reality, it is a bunch of opportunists capitalizing on the sluggish oversight and rules associated with Contract America.

A year after I left, I was vindicated when the biggest scam in Navy history landed. GDMA was owned by a man named 'Fat' Leonard. They had a virtual monopoly over the port services for our ships operating in the Pacific. He was always the largest donor to our Singapore Navy Ball each year. He'd ask for several front-row tables and, one year, gave us a 15-meter replica of the *USS Eisenhower* to display out front while everyone was prestaging the drunkfest it would become by the end of the night. He'd pull up to the 5-star hotel in a stretch Humvee. It turns out he was bribing US Navy personnel for information to gouge them of money for port services such as sewage waste removal and transportation. Often, classified information was coughed up. Supply personnel would give him a blank check with no accountability. Even someone I knew from NCIS in Singapore was implicated in the whole thing. They were paid through tickets to concerts, prostitution, and parties at ports crawling with paid escorts.[15]

While in the Navy, along with noticing the waste, I had very negative opinions after the second war in Iraq. I felt duped. There were no weapons of mass destruction .. there was just mass destruction caused by American bombs. And I was a part of it. Contract America, again, received billions of dollars to rebuild Baghdad and other places while Americans were losing jobs to Asia.[16]

In high school, my friends in Chiang Mai, Thailand, as missionary kids used to hang out at Burger King in the Night Bazaar. We'd watch in humor as tourists would regularly get ripped off heavily by the vendors selling silk shirts that would never be worn more than once and teak wood carvings that would most likely end up in an attic or basement somewhere. We were talking to a US Vietnam vet named Tony, who had stayed in Thailand for years. He was full of venom toward the United States, and when we asked him about ever going back, he told us, "I'd rather die."

I started to understand Tony. Coupled with my removal from the military and anger issues that caused me to flame out every now and then, I began to consume media that presented America as evil.

Indiscriminate drone strikes, Benghazi, Edward Snowden. I started to believe it.

When I was teaching English in northeast Thailand, making tiny amounts of money, I delved into this amazing new information that the US was spying on its own people.[17] I thought Edward Snowden was a hero. When I inferred as such one night on Facebook, suddenly I was locked out of my account.

With the wounds of being kicked out of the Navy freshly bleeding again and my economic status plummeting, I hated America. I even flirted with the idea of becoming an Irish citizen. I was convinced 'they' (whoever they were) were reaching out and punching me in the face. I imagined some nameless warrior at the NSA toying with my life.

The Imperial Language

A few years after the Facebook incident, my disillusionment with America was still there but lay dormant, dulled under the strain of survival. I was teaching English in Cebu. It was a boutique academy on Mactan Island next to Cebu City, and a 45-minute drive on my 10-year-old motorcycle through sun-melting traffic and shin-deep monsoon rain deposits on roads crumbling under the weight of unchecked corruption. I had a two-dollar budget for lunch. All of this while making 800 bucks a month, with my super wife working graveyard at a call center arguing with self-entitled first-worlders over five-dollar discounts.

I had students from all walks of life: Vietnamese bitcoin millionaires, Taiwanese doctors, lawyers, and movie producers; an AI engineer from China who wanted to escape to Canada with his 16-year-old daughter. She is still, to this day, my most brilliant student in memory. I remember another student, a Korean Calvin Klein exec, who quit his job to learn English and travel around the globe with his family instead of running the rat race presented to him back home. I taught engineers from the Japanese Ministry of Energy. They taught me everything a layperson could understand about the hydrogen economy.

I liked interesting statistics, so I'd show graphs of the average size of an American home. I'd talk about my time in the Navy. With each new convening class, I'd show immigrants to America from their countries. I shared the history of my ancestors' Irish immigration path as well.

One day, I had a picture of the Statue of Liberty up on the screen. I shared Ms. Liberty's poem:

> *Not like the brazen giant of Greek fame,*
> *With conquering limbs astride from land to land;*
> *Here at our sea-washed, sunset gates shall stand*
> *A mighty woman with a torch, whose flame*
> *Is the imprisoned lightning, and her name*
> *Mother of Exiles. From her beacon-hand*
> *Glows world-wide welcome; her mild eyes command*
> *The air-bridged harbor that twin cities frame.*
> *"Keep, ancient lands, your storied pomp!" cries she*
> *With silent lips. "Give me your tired, your poor,*
> *Your huddled masses yearning to breathe free,*
> *The wretched refuse of your teeming shore.*
> *Send these, the homeless, tempest-tost to me,*
> *I lift my lamp beside the golden door!"*

Emma Lazarus wrote the poem to contrast the Colossus of Rhodes as a symbol of old-world conquest with our Statue of Liberty, which embodies refuge and hospitality.[18] "Give me your tired, your poor, your huddled masses yearning to breathe free, the wretched refuse ..."

At this moment, standing in front of a whiteboard and projector with the Statue of Liberty displayed, it dawned on me that all countries suffer. For my Irish ancestors, the United States was a beacon of light in a very, very dark time. For an endless number of people I've met, America presented a very different future for their families, often breaking the shackles of an economic destiny based on their disposition or class. In America, there was potential for all of that to change.

As I showed up each week as an American, presenting the culture of America to others, a strange old lump in my throat started to form when I'd see her flag or an icon of American success displayed for the primary purpose of teaching English, but suddenly and therapeutically, breathing life back into my sense of belonging to Her.

One day, I was showing how much Americans loved experiences over comfort. Comfort food, couch potatoes, driving to mailboxes ... those are all very American. Yes, but so is going to a football game in negative freezing temperatures, camping, hiking the Appalachian Trail, going to the moon, and, frankly speaking, being the best at something. Being at the top is the only comfortable place for many Americans. Michael Jordan, Tom Brady, Simone Biles, and Steve Jobs were not interested in comfort. They were interested in being the best. Intriguing facts and accomplishments of Americans that have inspired billions of people started to spill out of me each week.

Many students coming to our academy needed a qualification for work or education somewhere in the rich world. Many looked for more pragmatic leaps to Singapore, Australia, or the UK—not America, the Wild West, the land of dreamers. America really represented something different.

When I moved on to Korea, and I was a boot camp instructor at our intensive English program for Hyundai execs and senior engineers, part of our curriculum involved teaching them public speaking. We had two sample speeches we used from President Barack Obama's political career. The first one was his 2004 speech at the Democratic National Convention. The nominee that year will be a trivia game answer in the difficult category forever. Everyone remembers his speech. He would go on to be the 44th president of the United States of America.

In the speech, he says:

"Through hard work and perseverance, my father got a scholarship to study in a magical place: America, which stood as a beacon of freedom and opportunity to so many who had come before. While studying here, my father met my mother ..."[19]

My Korean students helped me better understand how free America is, from their point of view. The undertones of their society were like shackles and whips. Of course, I was "free" in Korea. I wasn't Korean. I was a guest enjoying the chic cafes, crazy bus drivers, and one of the most well-paid English teaching jobs in the country.

We would have two 8-week boot camp sessions with the expatriating Koreans headed to branch offices of Hyundai and KIA all over the world. Many of them were headed to the auto manufacturing plant in Montgomery, Alabama, or to their testing facility and design centers in Ann Arbor, Michigan, and Orange County, California. They were excited at the prospect of having a yard, not having an apartment and noisy neighbors, or angry nosy ones. They wondered aloud, though, how Americans could possibly be so efficient and prosper in the ways that they do with so much freedom.

I ignored a lot of the curriculum I was supposed to teach. Instead, I put them on a path of researching their destinations in detail and sharing their findings with each other. I would show them house listings in the locations they would be serving, call private schools on their behalf, and bridge the gap between their homogeneous Korean identity and a country that brought me so much pain before. We'd meet at night on the soccer field, and I still have a dozen requests to visit them all over the world if I ever get the chance. Ann Arbor, Los Angeles, Washington, D.C., ...

Making America Great

In Obama's second speech, we'd show our Hyundai students what an impromptu speech is. We used his speech at the Betty Ong Convention Center in San Francisco in 2013, focusing on the urgent need for immigration reform. His well-prepared teleprompter speech was shouted down by a group of young people chanting, "Stop deportation, stop deportation." President Obama stopped and turned away from the camera because those shouting were behind him and said, "That's what I'm trying to do." As things got out of hand, and a security detail off-screen headed to escort the hecklers out, President Obama started shouting into the microphone to let them stay. The crowd burst into applause, and he continued on to give an otherwise unremarkable impromptu answer ... but the "he can stay there" part made its mark in history and brings tears to my eyes every time I watch it.[20]

Here was the most powerful man on the planet saying, "He can stay there, I respect the passion of these young people because they feel deeply for concerns for their families."

We had some immigration challenges ourselves. When my wife, daughter, and son came over to Thailand with me, I was able to sponsor my wife and my biological son with Thai immigration, but Khenyz, my daughter, since my wife didn't have a work visa, could not be sponsored. We couldn't leave her home in the Philippines. She was too young. She had to be there illegally with us. So, after that experience, it was better for Jen to stay with the kids in the Philippines while I continued to figure out work options abroad that would move the needle for us economically. Many people asked us why I hadn't moved my family to the US yet, and I tried to explain to them that in the Philippines, you need connections to get paperwork done. My kids had issues with their birth certificates, thus making it impossible, like Khenyz in Thailand, to legally process them.

Thankfully, my best buddy, Todd, provided me with the opportunity to work in Korea at the kindergarten and the follow-on job at Hyundai. I wanted to go home to my family, and I missed them. While in Korea, I bumped into loads of people from the US and other English-speaking countries teaching English like myself. I met most of them through the church I was attending. Many of them were young college graduates venturing to Korea to experience a different culture and a fresh start. It was these young guns that gave me purpose far from home. They were inspired by my family's story and cheered us on as we moved along this murky path. In turn, I was a listening ear for their relationships and struggles. Let me tell you about three of them.

Lue and I met at the kindergarten and would regularly park ourselves at our favorite coffee places called Gravity or Melbourne on the edge of Ssangyongdong (쌍용동) and Bongmyeongdong (봉명동). Melbourne had this amazing vanilla ice cream concoction with thickly brewed coffee poured on top that would send both of us running home to use the toilet, but it was so good! We'd talk until closing about our students, relationships or lack thereof, and politics would seep in at times.

Lue was Hmong. The Hmong people are a nationless group of people spread over the national boundaries of China, Vietnam, Laos, Thailand, and Myanmar. During the Vietnam conflict, his family sought asylum in the US and successfully made the enormous journey and settled in the state of Colorado. Lue and his siblings were born there and helped their parents navigate American life, by doing such things as answering calls or figuring out how to pay the bills.

Abigail, or 'Abi,' is Mexican-American. When we first met, she was aghast at this old, balding white guy who was leading the young people's group at church. Now, she's my younger sister—*mi hermanita*. I would cut my arm off and sell it to make sure she was okay. When I finally left Korea, I gave her my ugly orange lucky jacket.

Abi is the daughter of immigrants who crossed the border, not legally, but eventually, they were naturalized and became American citizens. Wealthy American citizens. Not murderers and not a burden to our social system.

Finally, Basirat, or 'Bee Sunny' as we know her, was a rugby goddess. She had left on a hiatus to another country and then returned to us a few years later. She is the only one of the three who wasn't born in America. She arrived from Nigeria as a 16-year-old. Her father won his American citizenship by getting his green card in the lottery system, which is available to a tiny percentage of the world, with chances extremely small of winning. He then sponsored his family, including his eldest daughter, Basirat, to come to California.

Their stories resonated with me because we were all caught between worlds ... the world of our parents and the world we grew up in. It was fascinating to hear Bee tell her story because it sounded very Korean. She admitted that the power distance and cultural norms of Korea and Nigeria were much more similar than those of the US and Korea. Her consternation was with her dad's expectations of her when it came to her education and career. Despite English being spoken in Nigeria, she was dropped into special classes for her to learn English. I often accuse her of having a much better vernacular than any of us born there. Write a book, Beee!

Abi had struggled because she was the only sibling to be born in the US and was constantly told by her older siblings how lucky she was and how her life was not a struggle like theirs, and she should have more than they did. For Lue, it was his desire to separate himself from Hmong culture and experience something else. I guess, in a way, they were all doing that in Korea. Korea was a wonderful place for single American young people to experience a homogeneous culture, benefit from Korea's safe streets, and be compensated well with pay and housing. If possible, I will be at their weddings, and I know they will be at my funeral, given the chance.

We were all in Korea, far from home, but it's not unusual to find Koreans far from home as well. The English academy that I was at in the Philippines is one of hundreds of tiny schools run by Korean or Japanese folks who have found a new life all over the Philippines. There are at least ten little Koreatowns in Cebu alone.

On a passport renewal trip from Thailand to Laos, I stayed at a Korean hostel. I couldn't get much sleep due to a guest on the other side of the wall vomiting all night, and because the walls didn't reach the ceiling, the resulting odor wafted over. The next morning, while waiting at the Thai embassy, I got my best reaction to my joke about why the American dictionary is shorter than the British one. I was talking to an elderly British man named Tony, who lived in Thailand with his Thai girlfriend, and he guffawed out loud for a good minute or two. The punchline involves the Pilgrims getting into a storm across the Atlantic and needing to lighten their load so they didn't sink, so they tossed their dictionaries overboard.

Around five million Americans are living abroad. Although we are often accused of myopic lives and bad geography, many Americans have settled elsewhere, like Tony, our angry friend in Chiang Mai. While I still had my '87 Grand Am, I would try to get my cousins to venture into the outskirts of Philadelphia, only an hour away. They were pretty happy staying put.

Eventually, though, two of them got involved with an Australian Football League in the US and eventually made it further than me Down Under for training and tournaments. The youngest of the brothers would find love there, settle in Melbourne, and have four kids. We were reunited in an unexpected way in London for an 'Aussie footy' tournament while I was serving in the Navy in 2001.

Let's go back to Lady Liberty.

"Give me your tired, your poor, Your huddled masses yearning to breathe free, The wretched refuse of your teeming shore. Send these, the homeless, tempest-tost to me, I lift my lamp beside the golden door!"

As Americans, "the refuse" designed our nuclear and missile programs, built our homes, and lead our Fortune 500 companies these days. "The refuse" of others' teeming shores has made my country, the United States, the greatest country by a multitude of measures. Hollywood, nuclear-powered aircraft carriers, and the Nasdaq are signs of being at the top. We gave a tiny percentage of our military arsenal to Ukraine, and they have held back the 2nd most powerful military in the world.[21] We are immensely rich as a country because of our people who come from everywhere. Abi, Lue, Bee, their parents, and millions of others are making America great by taking the risk of starting anew in a whole new world, a dazzling place called the United States of America.

Chapter Five

음양 'Eum-Yang'

우리는 오렌지 태양 아래
그림자 없이 함께 춤을 춰
정해진 이별 따위는 없어
아름다웠던 그 기억에서 만나

IU (performing "에잇")[22]

10 Minutes

In October 2022, I got a boutique hotel room with the loudest jacuzzi in Old Town, Antalya, where my Korean friend, Dong Hyuk (동혁, a.k.a. William), and his newly minted bride were staying during their whirlwind honeymoon tour of Türkiye. We had a fantastic night together, having dinner, and it was great to finally meet the mystery woman he'd been dating for quite some time. The jacuzzi was not fun at all. It was like hanging out in a bathtub at a club with a genre you loathe playing all night.

My friend was my long-time neighbor in Cheonan, South Korea. I had moved to Korea to do what my wife declares as 'finding money.'

My best buddy Todd got me a job at a kindergarten in Korea to help me recover from the financial mayhem of going bankrupt for the second time. Dong Hyuk, a mutual friend, was a local firefighter who regularly hung out with another friend, Dong Ho (동호, a.k.a. Won, not Juan). Dong Ho had provided me with companionship and translations that sometimes led to arguments with customer service reps. He also gave me a desk and office chair from his father's treasure trove.

My time in the kindergarten was my first exposure to Korean society outside the Philippines. My little kindergarteners had better table manners than I did. At a picnic, I was watching 3-year-olds keep all their rice on their plate while I had it spread around as if I was throwing it at a fictitious bride and groom no one else knew about. I had a 5-year-old, 'Lily,' who reminded me of those military academy videos of the West Point dining hall.

Ten months in, our ownership decided to shut down the English immersion kindergarten due to laws closing a loophole they could exploit for more money. I frantically looked for another job teaching English, and I stumbled on a business English job in Gangnam and applied.

On my first day on the job, I saw a Hyundai Motor Group calendar in front of me and thought, "Hmm, maybe they are our client." It turns out that SPEP, my employer, was indeed the sole provider of English coaching and training for the world's fifth-largest auto manufacturer.

I would become a commando at intensive English boot camps for executives and senior engineers. They were either preparing to be expats at their various facilities around the globe or just being rewarded with a 4-week break from work to improve their English.

We mainly worked at a 4-star accommodation in Yongin (용인) near Seoul. Everything was provided for us at their global campus: ridiculously amazing food, sports facilities, and private accommodations. I wouldn't say I like this cliché, but I remember pinching myself to make sure it wasn't a dream. I was actually pinching myself as I rode up the elevator to my classroom at first. Everything was perfect. The lawns, the facility—there wasn't a broken light or spill on the carpets. Eventually, though, I discovered that they built it in a valley, and if I played basketball too early, it echoed into the rooms of students who weren't early birds. We would watch the perfect universe where deer would frolic unabated along the hillsides until one day, we were reminded the world was real by a wild dog chasing down a fawn. The sounds ruined our vibe at our soccer match that evening.

My trainer and boss, Dianne, became the linchpin of my success. She had no clue about my fears of powerful women in charge and the amount of sweat that would pour from my armpits each time I stood in front of her to give a training demo or be observed in the classroom. One time, my students humorously commented on my drenched shirt after a session. "Mike, does she make you nervous?" Absolutely.

Both Dianne and our administrator, Hyunjee, would chastise me regularly. Hyunjee was especially horrified that I would run to class if I was running late.

She and Dianne were quintessential parts of Korean cultural norms as they drove the machinery of our program without much applause and would go on to be the backdrop of my soaring confidence for the first time in my life. They were secretly endeared to my less 'professional' acumen, and they knew these were essential to me building rapport with a demanding client.

During the pandemic, while we were still studying online, three of my students met me in Seoul and took me to my favorite jazz bar for my birthday. My student with the English name 'Jake' was primarily responsible for negotiations and policy with the European Union and was headed to Belgium. He got up in the crowded jazz bar, announced my birthday, and gave me a warm speech.

It became clear to Dianne and Hyunjee that I was taking the best and brightest in the country, and creating a safe space for them to do something they'd never done before. They would come in thinking they'd be putting their hard hats on and drilling in on more English. They had no idea they'd make new friends from other parts of the company. They didn't predict the laughs and emotional heights they could attain in the corporate veneer of HMG. I was sincerely interested in their work and the struggles of balancing it with their demands at home. I would know about secret corporate expansion plans or divorces before anyone else would.

The gift was equally reciprocated. What they gave me was the drive and determination to fulfill my duties each day and complete two master's degrees in the process online. I finished up my Master of Education in the early going. During COVID-19, 'Korean' survival panic kicked in, resulting in completing my MBA as well.

Koreans work too hard. But I'm eternally grateful to them for showing me how to do it. I've struggled my whole life with focus and consistency.

Before I arrived in Korea, my Korean manager, 'Mr. Kim' at Philinter, the boutique academy in Mactan was often mystified by my complaints that my Filipino coworkers worked too many hours.

The academy was run by a Korean couple who used to be the cooks for the school and then bought it from the previous owner. 'Mr. Kim,' would say to me,

"Mike, if you give someone 45 minutes to do something, it will take them 45 minutes. If you give them 10 minutes to do something, they will take 10 minutes."

Bali Bali (빨리 빨리) culture, they call it. *Bali* means "hurry" or "hurry up."

Working with Hyundai, we had to be on our feet almost 50 hours a week, facilitating our training. We would start early in the morning and sometimes wouldn't leave work until 8 or 9 at night. We had little time besides those 10-minute breaks to plan or catch up on something.

It's crazy that I walked away from Philinter in Mactan, Cebu, telling myself I'd never work for Koreans again. I had a lot wrong. I had so much wrong. And in Korea, it was turned upside down.

Itaewon

Starlings are known to fly in patterns called murmurations, moving in concert with each other, creating stunning, sometimes ghostly, forms in the sky. They don't require a leader but gauge their movement based on up to seven other starlings around them.[23] On December 11, 2019, about 200 starlings were found dead on the road in Anglesey, North Wales, in the UK. Upon further investigation, it was determined they died of severe trauma, having flown into the pavement while taking emergency 'avoiding action' to evade a bird of prey, leading to their deaths. This phenomenon has been discovered in a few other places as well, such as Spain, Canada, and the Netherlands.[24]

The morning after Halloween, at the place with the grunge rock jacuzzi in Antalya, Dong Hyuk (동혁), his wife, and I were enjoying breakfast. Upon glancing at our phones, we briefly became aware of the nightmare in Itaewon the night before. 158 young people lost their lives in a crowd crush during the yearly Halloween celebration.[25]

Itaewon has been a go-to spot for shedding Eastern inhibitions for many. Minutes away are all the world's embassies in Seoul, Korea, and a range of international cuisine, stretching as far as the east is to the west. It is also the go-to spot for US Army personnel blowing off steam. Almost 30,000 US personnel are serving in South Korea as a deterrent in an unresolved conflict with North Korea, dampened by years of a cease-fire behind the DMZ. On a Friday night search for Mexican food, I saw uniformed patrols of American military police keeping their fellow soldiers out of trouble. It reminded me of the days we had 'shore patrol' as sailors, keeping people like me out of trouble. The only known gay clubs are in this part of town as well. During COVID-19, a spreader event took place in one of them, and suddenly, young men were outed by the medical system, and their demographics (22 years old, male, etc.) could be seen on real-time information displayed on apps for everyone avoiding exposure.[27]

In Itaewon, Irish pubs played the US Superbowl or the Rugby World Cup. A South African joint there had the largest ribs I've ever seen. Most Koreans prefer more traditional Korean foodie places with scenic views or in close proximity to work or other, more insidious places. As women gained a bigger foothold in the economy, cafes that match their luxury purses have become more pronounced. There is no need to advertise loudly. Word of mouth spreads almost as fast as tiger mom chat groups looking for the next best place to take social media stills of their best life at a new cafe or glamping spot. But Itaewon has grown on a younger generation. There was a popular Korean drama called *Itaewon Class* that featured more diversity than is typically shown, largely based on its context in the most multicultural corner of Seoul.[28]

Korean COVID-19 restrictions heavily impacted crowds throughout the pandemic, and a seemingly innocuous announcement lifted most of those restrictions in time for the regular Halloween celebration in Itaewon. There were no organizers for the event. Young folks thronged the tiny streets in the thousands. The packed crowds, with an unhealthy fervor, pushed unsuspecting people down one of the steep alleys and couldn't be stopped, looking like an I-95 pile-up, but with people. People trapped below were instantly crushed, and others were mangled and suffocated. Paraphernalia brought as part of costumes led to some clumsiness and bodily peril for those trapped. A frustrated crowd, unable to see in front of them, continued to push. Abi, as mentioned before, horrifyingly witnessed a long line of lifeless forms on gurneys while stuck in traffic on a bus. If she had been on time, she might have been one of them.

As Koreans do, they move in large chunks. When it came to COVID-19, as an American, it was breathtaking to watch society move in concert to counter the spread of the deadly disease. It was equally breathtaking to see them provide their society with the tools to combat the spread. Without question, Korea came out with far fewer casualties than any Western country. Their ability to mobilize and utilize available technology was remarkable.

Similar to other Eastern cultures, Koreans have what is called *nunchi* in their language, which is their 'awareness factor' in society. To those of other cultures, it looks like politeness, and Koreans would agree to a certain extent, but it is more than that. *Nunchi* is a sixth sense that allows them to move horizontally.

I was at a language exchange one night in Cheonan, and a young British lady complained to me that no one helps people with their luggage when disembarking a bus. I told her that the bus driver and staff were getting out of the way because people wanted to handle their own luggage. The silent movements of their society are often bizarre to an outsider but understood by all of them. If you've ever seen an accident in parts of Asia, you will notice a fascinating pause from everyone, scanning the scene. It's a much longer pause than any Westerner is comfortable with. In our brains, we are screaming, "What is going on? Why isn't anyone jumping in to help? Don't these people care about the victim?" What do we fail to see in the silent and sometimes deadly hesitation to help a stranger? If they get involved, then they have to go all the way. I would constantly have

Koreans willing to go to great lengths to provide honor that requires resources. Any step toward a victim puts you at risk of losing that honor if something goes wrong.

I was serving in the Navy in Singapore when a 9-magnitude earthquake took place off the eastern coast of Japan, creating a tsunami that easily subdued the protective seawall, flooding the Fukushima nuclear facility.[29] The news will never say how much the US Navy played a role in investigating the aftermath or leading support to the Japanese government. But I know! I had to sit in on high-level meetings the sitting flag officer had via virtual video conferencing. They wanted a standby technician to ensure the calls were not interrupted. US military personnel had been evacuated, and I met some of them who had temporarily moved to Singapore.

The wife of one of the personnel and I were talking about the Japanese reactions. She told me it was surreal. There was no panic, no pushing, no looting, nothing. People patiently waited in lines for water and food. She couldn't imagine anything like this happening in the US. Judging from what we saw during Katrina, with people firing at law enforcement trying to save them, and looting being commonplace anytime there is chaos.

In many Asian societies, from Türkiye to Japan, there is *nunchi*. We joke that if we leave something in a restaurant or a park, if we come back three weeks later in Japan or Korea, it will still be there. The constant silent assessment has to do with relationships. If you don't know someone, you don't say hi or ask them questions. In America, we will ask, "How ya doin'?" but we don't give a rat's ass about how they are doing most of the time. It depends on the relationship with the person we are asking.

The power distance also makes a huge difference in what kind of language you use or how quickly you respond to someone. The famous incident I always teach when discussing polite forms of expressions in English is when the Vietnamese doctor was dragged off a US flight because he was unwilling to give up his seat.[30] In his society, he had never been asked to give up his seat. He's a doctor!

Asians often move like starlings in concert without the need for leadership to tell them what to do to protect themselves. We constantly berate our kids to be more like the Japanese, who clean up their own messes at school and in public spaces. The country is so ridiculously clean. In Korea, I was watching a Psy concert on YouTube and laughed as the crowds, in almost complete synchronous form, started jumping. It would have taken years of practice to get crowds from the West to do so.

Comfort Women

But what if the crowds move in the wrong direction?

The Korean War left most of the country deforested due to massive artillery and bombing by both sides.[31] Impoverished by war, today's South Korea stands as a remarkable economic miracle in contrast to the country it once was. When asked to comment (or not) on Korea, I tell people that you could walk from one end of the country to the other through trails over a very mountainous and beautifully green countryside. Their manicured trails to the tops of each peak are admirable, to say the least.

Despite Korea being one long, immaculate garden trail from one end to the other, I rarely took vacations or went anywhere. I had a wife and four kids at home in the Philippines and would feel guilty spending money on myself. But one summer, I decided to climb one of the most beautiful mountain ranges in Korea, Mudeungsan (무등산), with its exposed and squared-like patterns of dacite rock. It wasn't the tallest, but the scenes on the Internet looked breathtaking.

Mudeungsan was the guardian peak of the city of Gwangju (광주) in Korea's southwest region. One of my students, who worked in HR at KIA's automotive plant in Gwangju, had also invited me down for a meal.

I decided to stay at an Airbnb that was converted from an old missionary home of historical significance from the time of the Japanese colonial period. There was an adjoining art museum. It was shaded by planted trees from the West, such as cherry and holly, that provided a spectacular view canvased in front of a shared kitchen window that stretched from floor to ceiling.

My first morning there, I woke up early to climb. I met two other fellow travelers at the kitchen table. One of them was Japanese.

We started talking. He was a Japanese historian. He had recently returned to Korea for work. He had lived in Germany for eight years prior and was down with a friend from Europe to visit an art exhibit in the local area. As the conversation deepened, it became apparent he wasn't just any historian. He was also a curator of a museum called the House of Sharing in Gwangju (Gyeonggi-do) in the north.[32] Not only was he a historian and curator of a museum, but he was also the caretaker of the 'Comfort Women,' the remaining living Korean victims of sex slavery by the Japanese soldiers in World War II.[33] He was Japanese. In Korea.

Korea and Japan have had a fraught relationship when it comes to territorial disputes and resolving the wounds of a brutal period of Japanese colonial rule over Korea. Thanks to the Japanese losing World War II, Korea was then set free. August 15th is celebrated each year as Gwangbokjeol (광복절) or Liberation Day. One of the disputes has been the desired reparations for people who suffered under the hands of Japanese rule and the Japanese industrial complex at work in the country. The Japanese government wisely moved early in the 1980s when Korea was a fledgling economy compared to Japan. Now that Koreans were on par or wealthier than the Japanese, of course, they felt the repayment was too small. It was politically salient for both countries' politicians to stir up old feelings of disgust with each other to generate votes.[34] When Shinzo Abe's party in Japan was facing political pressure, his government suddenly struck Korea from preferred trading status, expediting customs controls for necessary materials in the chipmaking process. They alleged that South Korea was allowing dual-use materials into North Korea that could be used to make ballistic missiles.[35] At that time, Korea made 60% of the world's memory chips and 18% of the world's semiconductors. Koreans started boycotting Japanese brands immediately.[36]

The term 'Comfort Women' is a Japanese term. The first time I heard it in class with my students, I was offended. I asked them why they were all stuck referring to these poor women under a Japanese language term that mocks them. As Westerners, we see the single quotes around the word and know it is denoting a special meaning, but surely it was a disgrace to continually refer to them as comfort women in Japanese. The Koreanized term *wianbu* (위안부) comes from the Japanese term *ianfu* (慰安婦). Surely, this reference was a constant wound in society's side.

Because I was required to follow the news with my students regularly as part of our course, I was familiar with a huge scandal that had broken out regarding the 'Comfort Women'. This man's organization, which cared for these women and the history of *wianbu*, was receiving money from a large nonprofit advocating for the rights of the 'Comfort Women'. After further discussion with this Japanese historian, I found he was one of seven whistleblowers exposing his organization's lack of care for the victims and theft of money.[37]

I was supposed to hike up and down Mudeungsan before dinner with my student and some of his friends, but I couldn't back out of this moment under the shade of the holly trees outside our kitchen window. We talked about the history of Japan, the Philippines, Black slavery, human trafficking, and current affairs in Afghanistan.

We then walked around with the caretaker of the Airbnb, and he talked about the history of its former missionary owners and their role in starting the hospital nearby. We also were a stone's throw from the monument in honor of the Student's Rebellion that contributed to fighting back against the brutal Japanese regime in 1929.[38] I saw all this with a Japanese historian. In Korea. Caring for the women whose lives were plundered by his own people.

Chapter Six

A Stained Glass Masquerade

Is there anyone that fails?
Is there anyone that falls?
Am I the only one in church today
Feeling so small?
'Cause when I take a look around
Everybody seems so strong
I know they'll soon discover
That I don't belong.

Casting Crowns (performing "Stained Glass Masquerade")[39]

Blah, Blah, Blah .. Thailand!

ET2 Nikki Foster, my supervisor who always tried her best to keep me out of trouble on the USS *Bulkely*, would go on to have a brilliant career as an officer. We had lots of inside jokes to keep us humored on boring cruises over the world's largest bodies of water. She would mimic me all the time when I told them that I "hate TV" and then catch me watching *Love Actually*, elbows resting on the electrical test bench, watching it for the 4th time. Another one was when I'd wax on about my time living in Thailand.

She'd roll her eyes, laugh, and say, "Blah, Blah, Blah … Thailand!" Yes indeed. I grew up there.

When I was 7, I was brought halfway around the world. My parents were called to be missionaries in Thailand. From bearded, rock' n' roll-loving people to more austere fundamentalists with Mennonite roots, the missionaries joined together under one common mission: to tell people who had not heard about God sending his son Jesus to die on a cross for their sins. If they didn't believe, they would spend an eternity in Hell. How could they believe if they had never heard?

Before we arrived in Thailand, my parents had been in and out of missionary boot camps and language training centers in Canada and the Ozarks in Missouri. While in Missouri, I was five or six years old when I had my first crush. Because I didn't choose one of my sister's friends, they all told me they weren't coming to our wedding. I saw a prayer card (missionary marketing that goes on people's refrigerators) of her family after she blossomed several years later. She was gorgeous.

In my early childhood, I had an unearthly imagination. With Lego sets and my friend Matt, we built our own sagas. He was great at Legos. I was subpar at first, but as his apprentice, I improved over the years. My spaceships stopped looking like dead dinosaurs, and my navy ships eventually became impressive-looking war machines. I spent hours with atlases in the library, imagining my own country, inventing its economy and history, and bringing my stuffed toys,

Construx, and Lego sets along for military conquests. When hanging with my Canadian friend, Kenton, I'd tell him these long tales of commanding armies out of caves when we lived in Missouri. He was polite.

At nine years of age, my sister told me one night that if I didn't believe in Jesus I would not go to heaven with her and my parents. I sat on my top bunk that night, looking into the dark abyss below, and told God or Jesus or both that I didn't want to be left behind. Wherever my sister was going, I wanted to go too. Like many second-generation Christians growing up in a bubble, I don't have a dramatic conversion story where I was in rehab or jail and found Jesus. I did that after I found Him.

I wrote my own commentary on the Psalms in 3rd grade. I read many of my parent's books about the Christian faith, and without their knowledge, the ones about Christian sex. I had an insatiable consciousness of God. There would be these missions conferences, where all the missionaries around Thailand would meet for a week at a resort on the beach near Pattaya City. A friend and I stood on the beach one night feeling the warm breeze and, thanks to a couple who taught us, felt the warmth of knowing for the first time about God's grace. We discovered that, as Christians, we were free from shame for the bad things we had done. There wasn't any stored-up impending doom hanging over us as we'd assumed.

I had some very difficult years during my 4th and 5th grades. I had a teacher; she was a Dutch immigrant to Canada who became a full-time missionary. She was practically married to her cat. She didn't appreciate how forgetful I was or my inability to pay attention. I was in constant trouble. When I'd get distracted and fail to finish my lunch, she'd add eggplant to my plate and force me to eat it despite not liking it. I was constantly getting pulled into the kitchen to get spanked by a little green spoon. When I failed to produce a spelling assignment, I would have to write the spelling words hundreds of times. If I didn't do it on time, I would have to start again. We had this little book that I would take home. No other students had it. If an assignment was written in blue, it was ok. If it was written in red, I would have to go to bed 30 minutes earlier.

It hurts to write about it. Mainly because I don't want my parents to have to think about it one more time. They collaborated thinking at the time it was the right thing to do, and they have asked me for forgiveness so many times. I want them to know one more time, as they read this, about the warm breeze my friend and I felt on the beach in Pattaya. God was not angry with me. Everyone deserves forgiveness and grace, including them and even my 4th and 5th grade teacher. Having kids of my own later would provide me with the challenge of not operating under a similarly austere and unimaginative punishing regime when my kids failed to meet expectations.

We took two furloughs back home to the US. The first one was during my 7th grade year. I went to the local Lopatcong Elementary School in Phillipsburg, New Jersey. I worked my way up the social ladder. At first, I was friends with the rejects, the kid who drew elaborate and detailed recollections of running over rabbits with the lawn mower, and another kid with fish bowl glasses that would later in the year shove me out of the lunch line to remind me I was no longer welcome in their group. Another guy I'd sit with at first for lunch would tell me crazy stories about his father owning airports—almost as crazy as my tales to Kenton. When I ditched him, he decided to jump up over the bathroom stall wall and spit in my face.

I joined the basketball team and the baseball team. I was horrid but regular. My parents were faithful in bringing me to all the practices and games. During the baseball season, I think I may have walked a few times to first base, and I remember throwing someone out at first from right field. That was my place ... Right field. We didn't face a lot of left-handers. The coach's son befriended me and ushered me into the world of cool kids and pretty girls. It all culminated in me being allowed in their group on the class field trip to Philadelphia towards the end of the year.

Speaking of baseball, when I returned in 8th grade, the famous year of the 'Donut Run,' I made friends with Darren. He knew a lot about sex. When we'd have sleepovers, instead of looking at porn, we'd listen to him tell us a tale about the 'housekeeping' at a hotel room that got saucy. Pamela Anderson on *Baywatch* made her first appearance in our lives. More innocently, we were obsessed with *Baseball Digest* and baseball statistics and tossing the baseballs over each other's heads into the rickety tin fences of the third world. Darren was a great athlete, and I was a good sport.

Our second furlough was unexpected. My mother found a lump in her breast and caught on to potentially having cancer early. It saved her life. It was my sophomore year of high school. I was funny, loved, and was having an incredible year. It was suddenly cut short. I remember people praying with me to overcome my sadness for my mother. I didn't have feelings regarding my mother's state. I was sad about leaving high school and my friends. I would have to start over in another year. I'd have to make new friends and possibly get spit on in the toilet again.

I went home my junior year and started out at a technical high school, but didn't fit in well. I was well outside my bubble of Christianity. I felt lonely and my academic acumen was far above my classmates. Ominously, I had chosen electronics to study there, having no inkling that I would become a journeyman electronics technician for the world's most powerful navy.

So my parents decided to put me in the Christian high school my dad was teaching at. I won over quite a few folks. I wouldn't say I had tremendously close friends, but girls would pay attention to me. I ran in the halls. Sorry, Hyunjee (현지)! I had an English teacher who absolutely loved to hear my stories and opinions about the world we lived in. I wish I remembered her name. I had a thing for a young lady named Chrissy White. When she comes to mind, I always think about one of her favorite songs ...

Daaamn ... I wish I was your loooover ... I'll rock you 'til the daylight comes[40] ... Nah, nah, nah, nah, na, nahhh. I was terrible with lyrics.

My dad and I spent a lot of time together in the car. He'd drive me to school and back. We'd listen to 100.7 FM, the light rock station. Delilah would be on. I went on to find out she had three divorces and four husbands. She was on each night to help people through their difficulties and loneliness.[41] I guess failure can teach others.

He'd also bring me to work and pick me up at Ponderosa Steakhouse. Many thought I was a pothead at work because I often gave the deer in the headlight look on the job, but I still worked my way up from dishwashing to the cold and hot buffet food. They trusted me with the chicken wings and powdered mashed potatoes.

I returned my senior year and, in addition to managing to graduate by finishing *Hard Times* by Charles Dickens, shared one more story in front of all the missionaries in Thailand at our ceremony. My parents decided it was time to retire after ten years and come home as well.

PCC

It's funny because after joining the Navy, people would ask me which was more difficult or strict: Pensacola Christian College or the Navy. Easy answer: PCC. Along with the 'pink' and 'blue' beaches, it was against the school rules to listen to secular music (anything remotely distant from the narrow confines of allowable music sung in fundamentalist churches). Even contemporary Christian artists were frowned upon. The Gestapo that found me on the 'wrong' beach would check parking lots at other churches hosting gospel singers or Christian rock bands alike. I had a radio that I would listen to. I could put it under my pillow so that only I could hear it. I'd listen to the sinful tunes of the Top 40. My roommate, in his third year, discovered this and challenged my backsliding habits. I suggested to him that Jesus partied with sinners and probably would listen to Top 40 music if given the chance. Gasp! He might even dance.

He slapped my face.

My other roommate chastised his girlfriend about her tight skirts. Many girls wore very tight skirts because the length requirement prevented them from showing off their legs, so they pushed the rulebook by fitting into a size too small to create eye-popping, head-turning effects on our 18-year-old eyes. Tight, showing their panty lines, etc.

I was a working student on campus, helping pay my bills. I washed the dishes. Oh yes. The tales of what went on wafted through the steamy double doors of the enormous kitchen behind the cafeteria. The girls were waitresses and patrons for school events or food handlers. We heard about the ones who would sneak out and party with local Navy guys at the aviation training facility nearby. They had a covered garage that could easily conceal their exit from the roving Gestapo and cameras, and the guy's parking lot was like crossing a minefield in Ukraine.

My dad and I were big *Star Wars* fans. While at PCC, Lucas Films released digitally enhanced versions of all three original films to the theater. There was only one problem. Along with secular music, watching movies was also forbidden. We had signed our lives away and agreed to follow these policies to receive a Godly education. It was a great education, I must say. The teachers were competent and had academic standards per penny that exceeded the best schools in the country. This came at a tiny fraction of the cost. But at the expense of *Star Wars*?

I planned my escape on Saturday. To elude the Gestapo, I signed out to an adjoining mall, parked there, and walked to the movie theater. I sat in the theater and watched all three movies at once, and only left for popcorn. I don't even remember taking a bathroom break. I felt guilty. I remember arguing with God or Jesus or the Holy Spirit—or all of them, or maybe just my conscience—on the way there and then on the way back.

I liken my time at PCC to being like the girl I took home to Philadelphia: beautiful on the outside, but with some serious problems when you stick around long enough to find out. Could following God be as simple as wearing the right kind of clothing and avoiding certain entertainment choices? I sincerely wanted to discover who God was. I felt I was on the right path, but much of this felt wrong.

Then there was Suzanne. Every once in a while, I search social media for her. At the time, I wasn't mature enough to think her wearing skirts and leaving movies behind for love was possible. I want her to know now that her affection and her family's trust are near and present in my mind today. She and other childhood missionary friends had a part in helping me love and appreciate my time at PCC. They remain tangible signs that the icy and cold legacies of superficial religious practices can melt away in the bright, hot sun of sincerity and love.

Mother Teresa

We were all crowded in the living room of one of our discipleship leaders in Camden Town, London, listening to a conversation about Mother Teresa. Someone was a bit offended by the thought that she didn't make the cut for the team to be with Jesus. The discipleship leader said her works appeared to be good, but she was doing 'good' with the wrong motivation. Her spiritual 'fruit' had to be fake because she wasn't baptized and part of the church and its movement that started in 1984 by a group of apostles called the 'remnant.' I know. It sounds like a horror movie. Mother Teresa, then, in their view, was going to hell.

When I was in London serving in the US Navy in 2000, I was invited by one of my colleagues to join his church. When I arrived on a Wednesday night for the first time, I was greeted with hugs and lots of smiling faces. I was swept up quickly by the small Bible study group of my colleagues, and they excitedly invited me back on Sunday. Before long, I'd even join them on Saturdays to greet random people in the street and invite them to church. I couldn't think of a place that was more welcoming in my whole Christian life than here. I concluded that this was tangible evidence of what it meant to be devout.

As the new guy, I arrived at a Valentine's Day party as the only man without a jacket and tie. No matter—my date was the party coordinator. We had met at a gathering at her house in Oxford with other 'disciples' from their local congregation. We hung out until the a.m. hours, talking and laughing. I had arrived in London not three months before, and now, an hour outside of London, by train, making new friends. She invited me to their Valentine's Day celebration and hinted at not having a date. I was fresh meat on a platter as the FNG (Navy term). And there was dancing! Dancing wasn't a sin! They assured me, of course not... as long as you danced with fellow Christians, and there were many forthcoming, beautiful Christians to dance with!

About a month into discovering nirvana with more than 72 *houris* milling around to dance with, I was headed to a Wednesday night gathering when I was stopped by a homeless man trying to sell me a bum Underground ticket for money. He and all his worldly possessions were pooled together in a tiny circle in an underpass walkway, enabling people to avoid crossing the street above. It was in my part of town, Kennington, in South London—not the most affluent neighborhood. We had lots of opportunities to get the good stuff, whatever it might be, on various corners of the block.

I sat next to him as he spilled out his whole life story and why he ended up homeless. He hated God for his circumstances. Eventually, I told him to keep the ticket and gave him 20 pounds. I never made it to church.

That Sunday, I went back to church. My discipleship leader and another in my group had a look of concern on their face.

"Where were you on Wednesday?"

I told them about the homeless man near my home in Kennington. They grew quiet, and then one suggested I should have let him be and come anyway. Another asked why I didn't bring him along. I was a bit perplexed. I had expected some high-fives for connecting with someone in need, but maybe there was something to what they were saying, and I needed to keep an open mind.

Another night, we were out at a pub, sitting around a large circular table and having a conversation with some folks who claimed to be Christians from a Pentecostal denomination. They politely pushed back on my new brothers when it was implied that they may not be the real deal, like Mother Teresa. My colleagues smoothly pulled their Bibles out of their holsters to tag these guys with scripture, indicating that God's bar was set higher and disunity meant someone had to be wrong—and it wasn't 'us.'

Moments later, I was getting more peanuts at the oversized bar counter next to the selections on tap. My discipleship leader from Nigeria was there with me. As we watched the bartender pour Stella Artois and Guinness for customers, I said,

"Simon, if these guys are going to hell, then so are my parents."

"You know, Mike, I talked to the leaders of our church about it. You have, in many ways, shown to be more righteous than us, and your enthusiasm for God and your faith is contagious .. Uhh, but because you haven't committed to this church, then you must not be a Christian either. You need to be baptized into the only united church."

Everything had felt so right up until this moment, other than the snafu with the homeless man. I couldn't imagine that with all my parents had done for God and others .. that they were headed to hell.

On the one hand, I felt that I belonged and mattered to people; they even trifled over my salvation. The love-bombing from pretty women from around Great Britain was especially lovely.

I called my parents—indeed. We walked back all that I had learned about my new community. Having an outside voice of concern immediately brought to light a lot of contradictions between what they claimed and what could possibly be true. For example, this church said that only 14-year-olds could go to heaven, but Jesus made it very clear that if you did not have the faith of a child, you couldn't enter the kingdom of heaven. They were made right to be with God contingent on coming of age. There were scores more of these internal manipulations of the Biblical scriptures to suit their purposes.

A few weeks later, one woman from Nigeria had disappeared from the church. She was the women's leader in my weekly group .. the one whose house we'd visited during the Mother Teresa conversation. I asked my leaders. They had very vague answers and shrugging shoulders. I pondered the lackadaisical responses and suddenly got suspicious. I thought about the energy these folks had to bring me into the church and bring others. The homeless man came to mind. This chafed against the lack of concern for the safety or well-being of someone we knew very well who had apparently left. It wasn't a race issue. At least half of the congregation was Black, and so was one of my leaders.

I had been invited to visit the head of the church in the UK. It was a global movement. His wife was Indian, and he was, well, a white British man. When I arrived at his house, his eyes were a bit bloodshot after a night of playing a turn-based computer strategy game franchise that I, too, have had thousands of hours playing. The game's moniker is "Just One More Turn." It seems that he had a few too many turns that morning. When I expressed my reservations about simply writing people off outside the church regarding salvation, he said that he used to think exactly like me and invited me to a Bible study later that week.

One night after our discipleship time, I sat down with my discipleship leaders on a bench in the Kings Cross Underground station and spelled out the reasoning my father and I had concluded during our phone call. From the scriptures that we all claimed to believe, I started pointing out many of the conflicting statements the church believed in that weren't in line with what they said. And that was it. Like with the Nigerian woman, everything ended.

No one called. No one spoke to me. The interested ladies. Gone. I had no friends in the UK at this point. I visited the church a few months later and got an irate parishioner when I openly admitted to having serious questions about their beliefs about baptism.

With a feeling of disenchantment and anger toward God, I had to start my London life over. I started hanging out with my coworkers at places like the Barley Mow.

A following weekday evening after work, I walked into an old church that looked like a cultural landmark not far from work and within a stone's throw of history. I started perusing the pamphlets they had in the welcome area and picked up a brochure that was ominously titled "The ICC and Why It is a Cult." Recognizing the name as the church I had just been involved with, I paged through it and took it home.

A month later, I walked into this new church at a welcome luncheon for folks considering becoming regulars, and no one said 'hi' and barely acknowledged me. Groups of people were bunched up like grapes or bananas, and I was the one without a stem exposed and about to rot in the corner. But I was so relieved to be genuinely ignored!

What I didn't know was this was one of the most known Evangelical Anglican churches around the world. It was John Stott's church.[42] [43] Before he passed, I heard him preach, and he'd fill the place and the basement where people would watch him on screen—of course, others would watch from home.

I joined a group and met some amazing souls. None of them would have said hi to me at first. They were sometimes rude. They would give me a very hard time for putting sugar in my tea. They invited me regularly to the pub to have a pint, and that was astounding to someone who grew up understanding alcohol to be forbidden or at least associated, rightfully, with moral carnage. They confessed quietly to regretting sexual activity with strangers. We all went to a Fun Lovin' Criminals concert, and I accidentally landed my elbow down on a girl's head, but she was either too high or drunk to care. We made sure to send encouragement and congratulations to our friend who joined the Royal Navy to wind up pregnant on deployment and a single mom. I was matched up by one of them with my first girlfriend, who taught me a thing or two that I later confessed in my drunken stupor at work to Jodie, my Mamma Mia shipmate. I met my two wonderful friends, Adam and the Beatles song, Laura, from Orford.

The Bar & Grill

I had two close friends from my church in Chesapeake, Virginia, while serving onboard the USS *Bulkeley* homeported out of Norfolk. Ryan was the youngest of several brothers in a prominent family in the Sovereign Grace Ministries empire. After I moved out of the family's converted attic, he was my roommate in my new apartment. I discovered, he was battling his obsession with 'art', sucking his inheritance dry, and failing at college. I would have ended up dead first, however, falling asleep at the wheel from playing too much *World of Warcraft*. His father was a founding figure of several churches and a key source of employment for many members, and the extended family was plugged into the church in various parts of the country. Ryan is the progenitor of bringing out my deeply suppressed love for music and musicians. He introduced me to POD, an alternative rock band that helped him in a similar way as we dealt with the idiosyncrasies of bad religion and a loving God.

Steve, on the other hand, was the token Black guy in a very, very white church. There was nothing white about Steve. He played bass, loved fried chicken, and, as long as I've known him, has followed through with a dozen other Black stereotypes placated on the Black community—outside of being estranged from it and being at Sovereign Grace with us. He championed the hot dog eating contests and absolutely loved the Boston Red Sox and New England Patriots at a time of their peak with Tom Brady and company, and Big Poppy knocking the ball out of the park or being intentionally walked to first base.

Sovereign Grace was the Bar & Grill of church empires. It was conservative but not in the same manner as PCC. For example, one of their figureheads was a guy named Joshua Harris, who wrote the book on 'kissing dating goodbye'.[44] Parents loved how his novel methods expunged the uncertainties of parenting teens who wanted to have girlfriends and boyfriends in a culture rotting with prom rape and teenage pregnancies. They had a unique marketing setup that displayed a surety of what and where we should and shouldn't be for God. It filled a vacuum for a large number of church-going Christians from other denominations looking for the 'real deal', especially when it came to family.

It was cool. They had guitars and talented musicians to headline their 45-minute worship sessions on Sunday mornings. I had to sit down halfway through them because of leg cramps. I'd also fall asleep when the preacher would start. I would wake up 20 minutes later to people pretending not to notice. I was sometimes drooling, sometimes just with a crick in my neck. Possibly, they thought I was just praying... and hungry.

The girls were allowed to wear jeans. Not sure about the dancing. I was infatuated with Beth, the oldest daughter of one of the pioneering elders of the church. They had four young adult ladies who could all win beauty pageants. Beth was probably the ugliest of them and still could take on the rest of the church. Ryan and Steve gave me a hard time about her long toes. You'll find out why later. I admitted to my fondness for her to one of our small group leaders, and he said I needed to talk to her father if anything were to happen. That's what Joshua Harris suggested from his authored pages. So, I set up a meeting before church on Sunday in one of their side offices. I always thought these big churches reminded me of corporate buildings instead of places of worship. Sitting in plush seats behind a 10-seater table with Beth's father didn't change my mind much. I felt like a salesman giving a pitch to one of the corporate henchmen at the top.

"I like your daughter, and I ... I'd like to court her," I stammered.

"I know, and I talked to her, and she just wants to be friends."

"Um... Ok."

I wasn't sure what was dating, courting, or friends in this church, but I did know I was attracted to her and wanted to go out and have pizza with her or whatever we did before $4 coffee drinks with crushed ice in them became the thing. Don't things start off as friends? Wouldn't hanging out with her exclusively help her make a better decision? She was in college and certainly old enough.

The final straw came with Jasmine. Oh, Jasmine. This girl wasn't as tall as Beth and her sisters, but her smile and eye sparkle caused the wind to blow her hair every time I looked. The problem with Jasmine was that she was shy. I showed up at her workplace one time and asked her to lunch, skipping the whole dad thing, and she said ok. She smiled with an eye sparkle, and the wind blew. I had never felt so good since I made it through the whole *Diablo II* video gaming series the second time. I sang all the way home. Then, I got a text... from her father. He said he needed to talk to me. He went on to tell me that I scared her by showing up at her workplace and that she was not interested in me but didn't know how to tell me.

Thank you, Joshua Harris.

Joshua Harris and his mentor CJ Mahaney would put on these crazy conferences called 'New Attitude'. That's actually how I found out about this church. The headlining band was the worship team from the Chesapeake church. I met some of the band members who would become friends at a more intimate small gathering on the side. The first time I went to the 'New Attitude' conference was with friends from my dad's church and the church across the river in Easton. We had a great time. I was being prospected by the beautiful Savannah Diggs until I told her I wanted to sleep in separate bedrooms when I got married. I said that my future wife and I would take turns inviting each other to our rooms.

The next time I'd be there was when I was already a member of SGC. With all the zing and boom, I thought I heard God telling me Beth was the one. When I was on the ship and admiring a sunset and the salty breeze, I thought I heard Him say Jasmine was the one. In the end, I discovered that God wasn't speaking to me at all.

My father. Of course. He quoted a scripture verse to me that suggested that our hearts are deceitful, who can know it? We often think it is God, but it's really our own ego. We are quite possibly missing out on what He really wants us to do... Love and relate to people outside my church.

I tried in my own way and tested it on poor Nikki, my supervisor and closest shipmate at the time. When I invited her to come to church, she exclaimed, "If I walked into that church, I might burst into flames."

I was at a conference, and suddenly, listening to a preacher, I got the burning desire to go out and call her, as if she was in the clutches of mortality and at any moment might end up in hell—I implored that she believe in Jesus to avoid it.

"Jesus, Sullivan, it's not a good time right now. Someone just died in my family. That's not what I need to hear."

After that, I rolled out to tell a janitor with his baby's mama regretfully tattooed on his arm. Later in life, I'd tell my wife putting my name on her back might be a mistake, because I might go and do something very stupid and unforgivable. He was the one who gave me that golden nugget. I suppose since it's on her back now, she doesn't have to see it?

Before the burning embers died within, I met with a homeless guy and another guy at a real bar and grill. The next morning, after running on the treadmill with a deep chest cold, I told another gym rat. I told them all that they needed Jesus.

Then the spirit left me, and I was a mere mortal again—afraid of getting shunned by Beth and her group. I remember hanging out with them, and there were enough seats for all but one. There was a 16-year period where I had to stand there and wonder if I was going to sit alone. Thankfully, Abby (another one) decided to accompany me, and I probably told her, "Blah, blah, blah... Thailand!"

One night at Bible study, we were asked a question from the leader about what our life was like before we met Jesus. One of my Navy shipmates from another unit, whom I didn't know well, blurts out after a moment of silence, "Going to strip clubs and fucking strangers." I could hear a dog barking in the background a mile away and Beth sucking in her gut and holding her breath. I added some triage to my embattled fellow sailor by hanging out with him the rest of the night and swapping sea stories. Steve, Ryan, and I roared laughing later about it on our way to get refillable coffee at a 24-hour IHOP. Most of the attendees were just like me; they grew up under rocks. Not a missionary kid rock, but another thick religious bubble that disconnected them from the realities of the rest of the world.

The way it worked in these churches was that you would jump from small group to small group. As a single guy, it was paramount to find a group with a decent number of attractive women. I would attend no less than eight groups in the five years I was there. I settled on a group of young couples, no singles in sight—just some empty promises from the couples that they'd "talk to so-and-so and convince them to come." I loved them. After my debacle with Ryan and his midnight forays into 'art', I decided to stay with one of those couples who had just gotten married. I lived with them for a time before they had their first baby.

Out of the small group leaders I had—two became atheists. One questioned his sexual identity, and another threatened to file a lawsuit against his brother. His brother was a former pastor of the church. I would come back from time to time because I was attending graduate school in the area and share cigars with the former pastor as we caught up on the latest with him and his family. At least I could smoke them properly.

The 'mother' church in Gaithersburg, Maryland, had leaders indicted in a huge sexual assault case that the leadership mishandled, not informing authorities and keeping it behind closed doors, often putting the perpetrator and the victims in the same room.[45] CJ Mahaney would be accused of abusing his authority but be reinstated after stepping down for a year in 2011. Over 20 churches parted ways from the larger organization as a response.[46] Joshua Harris would go on to no longer call himself a Christian after attaining a formal seminary education.[47] His next book is called *I Kissed Christianity Goodbye*.

So much for the Bar & Grill.

Pastor Mike

"Pastor Mike, *Kumusta!*"

This is a regular greeting for me here in the Philippines. Yes. Once you earn a title there, it's very hard to have it removed.

I had moved to the Philippines, newly married and in over my head with four kiddos. We attended South Cebu Church (SCC), the congregation of 'Bro Dominic,' the pastor who married Jen and me on the beaches of Mactan Island—where the DJ failed to play my favorite song to dance to. I was under the assumption that my laundry business would become an empire. We had the name La La's Labada and were working towards getting customers. I purchased a lot, and then a follow-on house and water business using credit only. I had that gargantuan water tower built to give me the water pressure we needed for commercial business. 'Bro' Dominic and the young worship band leader 'Unjun from Japan' would stay with us. Unjun was not from Japan, but he had the hands of Jimi Hendrix.

We became a fixture at SCC and got involved with the young people. I found myself a leader organizing events for the church and their leadership team. Eventually, I joined the leadership team. We had a guest speaker one night at our weekly youth events. He was from the US, and as he shared with us a message about his path toward God, I suddenly got the inkling I should move toward becoming a pastor or minister of the Christian faith. I wasn't sure if this was a 'Beth/Jasmine' inkling under the shadow of my parents' legacy, but I decided to go for it.

After making that commitment to myself, I would see my young adult ministry melt away because of a squabble between 'Bro' and the other senior pastor. I completely botched the handling of another incident involving another American, involved in our youth ministry. It broke our relationship. It was here that I also realized that blood was much thicker than water in the Philippines. Admitting fault or being self-reflective was not an option for 'Bro.' Keeping the ball rolling and people attending was the only game in town. Their family name depended on it. Our relationship was broken as well.

Adding soy sauce to already soured milk, we were in the financial throes of going broke the first time. My water filtering plant kept breaking down. As I was trying to pull off the ring clamp at the top of the osmosis membrane canister, it suddenly came off. I bashed my face with the metal top, chipping my tooth. When closing the gate one night, I got my finger caught in the hinge, yanking one of my fingernails completely off in a bloody mess. The pain associated with it was not nearly as painful as my wife's rejection of me and the financial pit we had dug for ourselves.

I left for Thailand to 'find money' and was soon accepted into Regent University School of Divinity. I wasn't particularly fond of the founder, Pat Robertson. I had heard about his Christian Coalition and the mobilization of the 'silent majority' Richard Nixon spoke of on November 3rd, 1969.[48] Among them were millions of white evangelicals and fundamentalists from the South who had historically voted for Democrats because of the legacy of the Civil War. Pat Robertson ran for president in 1988 and was pivotal in the Christian Coalition's success in dividing Congress in their favor during the Clinton Administration.[49] I was skeptical that this mix of religion and conservative politics was showing the love and kindness espoused by Jesus. I found it a bit ironic that 25% of the seminary students were Black.[50]

I told myself that if I became a Chaplain in the Navy, at least I wouldn't be a combatant or a "baby killer" as many have accused us of—but more importantly, I could retire, having already served 12 years. I wouldn't have that worried look from Jen, nor have her telling me she just wanted to go back to the forest where she came from when the coffers were empty. I needed a hybrid course that would give me the residence requirements the Navy had for chaplaincy. This allowed me to go back to the US once a semester (with the airport detainments) and fall asleep in the luxurious library study rooms. It didn't help that libraries always overstimulated me and caused me to want to run to the bathroom or fall asleep. I was also fighting jetlag. I checked out a lot of books that I never read but wanted to.

It was in seminary that I found that Adam and Eve might actually be made up. While growing up in my bubble, suggesting otherwise amounted to questioning my salvation or being subverted by Darwinism and other clear and present dangers espoused by the evangelical movement. We were strongly discouraged from believing anything other than the world being created in seven literal days. As I studied at seminary, like Joshua Harris, I started to become aware that certain sects of the Christian faith cherry-picked what was literal and what was symbolic or cultural.

I met up with old friends from Sovereign Grace. Regent University was next door, and I got free accommodations from former small group members. Steve and a mutual lawyer friend started a band called Outta the Furnace. I had a chance to see them live at a local craft beer establishment flooded with military folks. Steve and I would go to an afternoon service downtown at the new extension of our old church. We stopped on the way to visit a friend. As Steve and he smoked a bong, we had a talk about the old days and finding peace with our SGC background that had caused so much doubt toward the Christian faith.

I came back from Thailand to get fired from my job in Manila. I was still in seminary at the time but falling behind. I jumped into my startup company. I saw an inequitable world. I saw our systems failing to support meritocracy, especially when it came to finance. I created a system that would evaluate simple purchasing data to surmise someone's trustworthiness, which could then be displayed to other entities to reward them for their financial management skills. Rather than these systems stealing what little people have, disguised by the experts as risk premiums, our system lowered the risk of doing business, thus saving money and cutting out middlemen. My 'blue ocean' idea was to specialize in providing a better picture of the data we humans can collect now to help us overcome our biggest challenges. I started with a fintech MVP (minimum viable product) to combat a rigged system that was filling up only the coffers of the rich and the oceans with plastic and fast fashion.

In Cebu, Philippines, with my fresh plans for my startup at hand, I met a young lady named Debbie, the eldest daughter of two doctors. Debbie had just come off a negative experience working for a local startup in digital job advertising. I'll never forget how enamored I was by someone who was willing to stand there in the hot sun in the motorcycle parking lot and never stop talking. I jokingly call her 'Twinney.' We have the same annoying procrastination habits and fears. Our similar personalities prevented us from working at the speed necessary to make our great startup idea bloom. However, something far greater was born.

One night, she got up to share during a New Year's Eve church event. I was broke, depressed, and wondering if my family was going to hold it together in our current iteration. She talked about how I was there for her in a season of her life when she needed mentoring and encouragement as she navigated preparing for marriage and deciding on her future trajectory. Furthermore, her parents, both irreplaceable members of the larger Evangelical Christian community in Cebu, became my Filipino parents. Their care and prayers for me over the years have tattooed my crazy life with fortitude and peace. They often spoil me with fancy dinners on my return to the Philippines as if I were their own son. They had a son, making gobs of money as a doctor, but they cherished my role in their daughters' lives. Yes, the youngest, who also became an MD, we, too, stopped for designer coffees and discussed her Twitter addictions and lack of dating options.

When my father left me with 80 bucks and promised to pray I'd find a job, I never considered what would happen next. I had long since failed out of seminary and got into a disagreement with my probationary status as a Divinity student, but I continued as a minister at the church I was at. I had a new church family of people who loved me and depended on me each week. The church was almost 100 years old, the worship was at least 500 years old, and there was no air conditioning on a tropical island near the equator. But something very powerful was sprouting from my heart.

I was asked to teach the story of Genesis at the local Sunday school. Having my own doubts about its validity, I dove in and studied what people have been writing about it for centuries. I studied it as if I would still graduate. I discovered that the story of the 7-day creation is about God's daily provision each day of the week. The Author nicely spread out God's handiwork of creation over six days, and on the seventh day, He rested, denoting our need for self-reflection and worship. We all know that an omnipotent God doesn't need rest. It wasn't for God. It was for us, resting on His provision for our life, trusting that He would be faithful to His people. He put Adam and Eve in a garden and asked them not to touch the fruit of the tree of good and evil. But it was pleasant to the eye, and they ultimately succumbed to their fleshly wants rather than looking at all the other things: a protective garden, endless fruits, and a job to care for the planet that God had so graciously given us.

At this time, on my way to work, an angry taxi driver mistook me for someone of lesser means and chased me down and punched me in the head in the middle of traffic one day. When I refused to take the bait, not wanting my wife to lose two husbands, he shoved my head one more time as I got back on my bike and said,

"You have an ugly bike."

I would drive that 10-year-old ugly bike each morning from the southern suburb of Cebu City all the way up to Mactan Island to teach English for that good ol' 800 dollars a month. On one side, I saw the mountainside jutting up on the left, and on the right, the blue sparkling expanse of the Cebu Strait, reflecting a new sun groggily coming up over the horizon. It reminded me of the verse in our scriptures, in the book of Genesis, of God separating the land from the water to create a place where we could live.

I saw a cat in the middle of the highway one morning, gripping the road with fear, waiting to get flattened by high speed and rolling tires, carrying the restless along on the broken asphalt along the shoreline. It was me. Watching my neighbor's houses go up, flowing from money abroad. Watching these less-than-ideal startup businesses perpetuate while my brilliant idea floundered because of no investment. Terrified and scared, I asked, "Why not me, dear God? What am I doing wrong?" I turned back to help the cat but he was gone—thankfully not flattened. I wouldn't be either.

My wife was making 300 dollars a month and commuted two hours to work each day. While she was arguing with Australian first-world eBay customers about their 5-dollar discounts, where they failed to read the fine print below, I was learning from all the most successful corners of Asia in our tiny boutique English Academy, Philinter.

I would go on a Wednesday evening to the church to teach a young people's Bible study. Sometimes, no one would be there. Sometimes, seven would be there. It didn't really matter. What was planted were the seeds of awareness that I was gifted with young people. I made them feel valued and appreciated. I was the drunken master of pumping enthusiasm and hope into a fledgling group of unlikelies like Ryan and Steve. It happened at SCC. It happened in Korea, where I was no longer 'Pastor Mike' but 'Mike Teacher.' It was in Korea, where I was formally invited to create synergy and offer direction to the many young English teachers in and around Cheonan. That's where I met *mi hermanita*, my coffee buddy, and the rugby goddess.

During my fellowship for the US Department of State in Türkiye, I'd regularly conduct Q&As when introducing myself to a room filled with young guns. It was a way of building confidence and rapport among the students. One of my college freshman asked me what my purpose was in life. I chuckled.

I thought of the number of failed attempts at life I had, but without a doubt, I could answer a question most of the world could not. I said,

"To make people feel valued and heard... Especially young people like yourself."

A Call to Prayer

Every morning for two years, I was accosted by the Muslim call to prayer in Türkiye. Before the break of dawn, the Muslim call to prayer rings out. It has a schedule based on solar movements, so the times change in sequence with the day and night.

As a podcaster, it would never fail to have the imam burst out to interrupt my interviews, and after a while, I included them. After all, my podcast was ultimately about the intersection of multiple worlds that many of us grew up in. Why not add another to it?

I asked my students if it wakes them up in the morning. They shook their heads. Immediately, my student, Muharrem, hands locked with a beautiful woman wearing hijab, says, "That's because you didn't grow up with it."

After they are done with their libretto, I lean over and click on my Bluetooth speaker to play my cool Christian contemporary worship music I learned from SGC that spills out sentimental feelings from an accumulation of years of being in and out of dozens of churches. It reassures me of God's presence and His faithfulness to me. My neighbors, in turn, I think, slashed my bicycle tires because they didn't like my music. I might as well have been belting out "Born to Be Wild" in honor of Brian Bradford and my failed start in college. That brings feelings of sentimentalism, too.

On my life-changing 26-city tour, one of my students asked me to stop in Konya. Konya was known to be the bastion of political support for the current conservatively pro-Muslim regime. My two students were both from devout Muslim families and wore hijab. When asked why, they both responded that God required it. One of my students had a sister who accompanied us, who was already of age and did not wear it. I named her 'silent film' because of her curious antics and few words throughout our day touring Konya. Out of curiosity, I asked my student why.

"My parents don't want her to hate it."

The pictures on social media of Iranian women all in a tirade, chanting the death of the religious leader of the country, stamping on their hijabs, came to my mind.

In my humble opinion, her parents understood something that this polarized world does not: We don't have room for people who disagree. We judge. We denounce. We align with power structures politically or just inside our congregations to make changes that will force the other side to contend with what *we* believe. Of course, the predictable result? They hate our beliefs, our God, and even us. Worse, we often raise kids who either altogether reject the chokehold we put them in or quietly and unquestioningly conform rather than have the joy of discovering who and what God might be like—have faith that God is the master of that process.

There is no denying the experiential manifestations I have had, which have led me to believe that I have a relationship with a real and present God. I am not here to dismiss your objections to my beliefs. I want to challenge all of you to consider that if you hope to convince anyone that your beliefs are valid, you may have to start by loving and relating to them.

Chapter Seven

In Between

My lover's got humor
She's the giggle at a funeral
Knows everybody's disapproval

Hozier (performing "Take Me to Church")[51]

In Between

The phrase 'in between' always gets a tiny smile (and possibly a giggle) from me and calls to mind the name of a gay bar in Virginia Beach. One Sunday night after church, Steve and Ryan bet a mutual friend and me to spend 10 minutes or more in there to win some money. So we strode in, and instantly, our confidence dwindled, and we felt out of place as people's gay-dar started sounding off that there were annoying and possibly homophobic intruders among them. My *nunchi* told me that we were imposters, yet no one really batted an eye in the end. The bartender didn't wink at us; they just gave us our drinks like we were tourists from out of town in a country called *In Between*. We wanted to run out, but we wanted to win our bet too. So, after getting our drinks, we ran giddily and giggling into the restroom to plan our brief stay at *In Between*. We came up with a plan to finish our drinks, then parade out holding hands and 'fake' gay pride to demonstrate to our friends waiting in the car and to the world that we weren't homophobic. We managed to win the bet and win our trophy, albeit as small and ridiculous as it was. Be offended. Be humored. Church kids living on a precipice.

Don't Ask. Don't Tell

I joined the military in 1999. This was about a year and a half before Bill Clinton and his gimungous nose left office. In fact, I served under three presidents who would all hold office for eight years. When Bill Clinton came into office, the very first federal policy he enacted in 1993 was the *Don't Ask, Don't Tell* (DADT) policy in the military.[52] What may seem absurd in 2024, 30 years later, is that this was a liberalization of the current standing in the military. At the time, the military prohibited anyone living a homosexual lifestyle from serving. This new policy meant that if you were gay, you could serve, but it meant you needed to clam up and not discuss your lifestyle with anyone, or you could get booted from the military. It also meant that they couldn't be asked or berated or accused.

Before I was assigned to a unit, I was at my technical 'C' school in Norfolk, Virginia, learning about shipboard communications equipment that I would be responsible for the rest of my career. I would take walks with one of my gay colleagues. He was in love with his roommate and needed someone to talk to about it. I was sworn to secrecy, of course, because of DADT. Because of the precarious nature of the discussion, we'd continue to meet at night after his run and sit on the bleachers of the softball field nearby.

Eventually, he told me his whole life story—his short modeling career, his hesitance at first to take showers in boot camp. For him, it wasn't a mystery why he was gay. He told me he was gay because of a weak bond with his parents and being molested repeatedly by a female babysitter at five years old. This trauma altered his views on the world and sexuality. He, by no choice of his own, steadily became sexually attracted to other men as he grew up. He had never attempted anal sex before but had some mutual sexual encounters by other means.

It was the first time I divulged some of my most closely held secrets as well about my sexual formation. I suppose Jodie (*Mammia!*) would later hear some of them the second time. It was also the first time I had ever spoken about a night of discovery I had as a child with another seven-year-old boy and a neighbor's daughter coaxing me to drop my drawers and show my stuff when I was six. She reciprocated. My piously evangelical Christian background forbade me to talk about this stuff outside the context of confession of sin.

I was a late bloomer. I was a very naive kid, and even as an adult in the Navy, I carried some of that naivety with me. Ask my colleagues about my night at a strip club rubbing a girl's feet and telling her to put her top back on because I just wanted to talk with her. I came away with a 1000-Euro bill that night as 'Suzanna,' or whatever her real name was, told me her life story growing up in the Czech Republic, getting a cage dancing gig in Lisbon, and having a Portuguese boyfriend who had no idea I was rubbing her feet on the Spanish island of Mallorca—and paying for it.

My coming of age was fairly routine; however, one late night at the dormitory, we dared ourselves to hang out naked in the girl's bathroom and try on dirty women's underwear from the hamper. We discovered my Lego companion from childhood was gifted in a similar manner as Bill Clinton. In eighth grade, Darren, the sexipade storyteller, introduced me to porn. We would scour the city on our bicycles, looking for adult material. Our parents had absolutely no idea what their missionary kids were up to. I found out later that the boy who I tussled with at around seven years old had come out as gay as an adult. I often wonder how much any of these folks remember.

My gay Navy shipmate helped me understand the life-altering nature of child sexual abuse. For me, that's why it's easy to admit to wearing girls' underwear or scurrying around Chiangmai looking for magazines of naked ladies. The shame and horror that a very high percentage of people live with. These aren't humorous anecdotes to their lives. My friend here at this time was only one of several men and ladies who would confide in me over the course of my life about their sexual past. The number of stories involving family members and a close confidante (in his case, a babysitter) is too many to count.

Another formative relationship took place in alcohol rehab.

On the very first day, while I was checking in, my roommate showed up. Mind you, we had private rooms with door locks but shared a common area. I was not ten minutes into our opening conversation when he suddenly offered me a blow job.

With DADT fresh in my mind, I was more curious than anything else. I asked him if this kind of risk-taking had worked in the past and how many heterosexual men had given him the green light. He told me it was too many to count.

Apparently, others had "thinner" boundaries than I did. I had seen my Navy roommates in my technical 'A' school, watching a plethora of prison movies that seemed to always involve normal heterosexual men engaging in sexual acts with each other, but it was Hollywood and prison—surely no one would do this in the real world except folks in the gay community. Instead of taking him up on his offer or rejecting him, I told him that I was still a virgin and was saving sex for the marriage bed. Not the same bed as her, but you know when she invited me to her room. That was true at the time. My Master Chief hadn't fulfilled her offer yet. I told him that sex belonged between two people who loved each other, not one person using and abusing another. If I took him up on his offer, I would be one more person to use him.

We would both attend alcohol rehab, and we'd see each other only briefly each week at our group sessions. All of us there in rehab would meet twice a week to talk about our troubles. When someone would leave the program, we'd have to say goodbye, and everyone would get one last word in. He desperately fumbled for words to tell me how I made him feel. He told me he didn't want me to walk out of his life. I made him feel wanted, valuable, and safe—not discarded, used, and isolated. The counselor coaxed me to exit, and I had to get up and leave the session—but he was still shouting for me not to go because he had more he wanted to share. Unfortunately, that was the last time I saw or heard from him. I hope he somehow reads this book and reaches out to me privately to connect—he and an endless number of people who have graced my life with vulnerability and trust.

It made me sad to think that many men had used him in such a way that he would, out of the gate, only ten minutes into meeting me, offer sexual services with no mutual demands in any sense. It angered me that people could be so insensitive to his need for love and acceptance. It gave me pause in the sense that we were both, for one reason or another, at alcohol rehab. I bet for the same reasons .. our desire to fit in and be loved by others. I drank to fit into the Navy crowd and landed in trouble and in beautiful Rota, Spain. He was engaging in gregarious sexual acts but also trying furiously to be loved and accepted and ended up in trouble and in beautiful Rota, Spain.

The Gays

In the Philippines, the general linguistic vernacular for those in the LGBTQ and beyond is the noun 'gay.' He's a gay. She's a gay, etc. My wife works in the hospitality and events industry. We laugh a bit because it feels like all her best friends are gays. I guess I'm her 'gay' husband? When we moved to Thailand for a short time, it was the same. When she decided to return as a non-traditional college student, I got to meet many young gay students. One of them wistfully looked at my family and openly wished he, too, could have a family someday. He was under the burden of being pronounced 'gay' and thus a lifestyle projected on him by a media machine that strips people of choices and suggests, just like me, what a person should and can be. He, too, at 18, just like me in my Christian bubble, was subjected to a world that suggested he only had certain avenues to go down, and it certainly couldn't be marriage and a family—at least not in his Filipino society. That, to me, was very, very sad.

I watched how the police shot Jen's gay friend, mistaking him for his older brother, wanted dead or alive in a murder investigation. His credibility was hinged on the fact that he was a gay man. He was funny and loved my wife like a sister—in fact, my wife called him 'sister'—she still calls him 'sister' on the anniversary of his death and birthday, reposts their pics on social media, and visits his grave.

My wife lost a trans-woman friend in the events industry to kidney failure. No family came to the hospital bed in her dying moments. In fact, the family walked away with all the money donated through a local LGBTQ non-profit and wanted my wife to take down posts of her death so that people would continue sending money for the hospital bills.

There is a very long and humorous, and not-so-humorous string of incidents when my wife first entered the events industry as an MC. She worked for a trans woman named Monique, who was quite talented and had a successful wedding planning business. Unfortunately, Monique did not know how to handle her money or success. The money often went to drugs and male prostitutes. One night, when Monique had shafted a client and gave them a less-than-spectacular event, family members chased after her with guns, claiming they would kill her. My wife had to stick her head out the window of the van to make sure they knew not to conduct a drive-by and kill the wrong person. The family of Monique continued to use her and her talents to bring money in but were never willing to address her lonely heart and her issues with drugs. They continued to hide it to protect their family's reputation. My wife gave all she had to help her. That's my wife. It hurt to walk away.

At first, I didn't like them. Many of my wife's friends made me feel uncomfortable. They were unreliable, often swindlers. They weren't my crowd. My friends, on the other hand, were all products of a religious bubble—many times self-righteous, often unable to relate to the world around them, especially with the gay community. I have fallen completely somewhere in between at this point, and I'm so glad I obliged.

Because of her, I have bonds with people I would have never imagined loving or relating to. From the very beginning, they have been in the background. I remember commenting early in our relationship that her friends were the prettiest men I'd ever seen. They were pretty. Really. I can't say I've always been waving the checkered flags for them to come into our lives. I've been guilty at times, even suspicious and judgmental. I have jumped to the wrong conclusions from time to time. But I changed a lot when I took this front-row seat to my wife's life. We didn't come into the relationship promising to have the same friends. I don't think any marriage should.

Toni

We've had quite the experience with nannies and house helpers. Because my wife and I work and have four kids, we often decided to hire help to carry out household chores or take care of our children when they were younger.

The situation would typically start out decently. Then, the helper would borrow extra money against their future salary and end up a month behind. When we'd cut them off, they would quit. We've had jewelry stolen. One helper early on bit my son and locked him in rooms. One housekeeper seemed to hate me the day I arrived after not seeing my family for two and a half years because of COVID-19. When I sent a huge box back from Korea, and we opened it, she had disdain written all over her face. I suppose I wasn't as rich as she had envisioned in her mind when she saw I sent all my used things back and very little *pasalubong*. She lasted a week longer. What was really annoying was that they would often never officially quit. They would at first just say they were sick or a family member died and they needed to go to a funeral, and then they'd never come back.

In comes Toni, a trans woman. I was hesitant at first but realized that my upbringing had skewed my opinion, making me think she was somehow more dangerous than others, and possibly I could be wrong. I gave her a chance. She almost quit after the first week when I left money in my pocket. She thought I was testing her honesty, but I am just… forgetful. Ask my 4th and 5th grade teacher.

Because my wife was busy, it was often Toni and I who would go to the kids' events at school. It was constantly Toni and I sitting on the couch watching women's volleyball. Toni loved women's volleyball. She dreamed of playing it and would often play on the seaside when given the chance. Toni became a close confidante and friend. She saw our whole lives with little judgment, and her cooking was delicious!

Christmas of 2016, when I was completely broke (and broken) because my startup enterprise failed to materialize, Toni had already foregone her meager salary for the month because I couldn't pay, but still rented a karaoke machine for our Christmas celebration. She had used her spare money from a community savings plan to do so.

When my parents arrived from the US, my dad came to my rescue and helped me pay her salary. My parents had, at this point, never met a trans person. Not only did our trust in Toni break a mold in our family, but this experience transported itself halfway around the world to an often transphobic evangelical Christian world that surrounds my parents every day.

We didn't have anything overtly sexual in nature take place or any of the 'grooming' adventures that captivate the fears and imagination of bathroom-legislating Americans. There is plenty of grooming in the Philippines, but only two house helpers we've had abused our kids, and they were both biological women. Toni, on the other hand, absolutely loved our kids, especially my youngest, who wasn't the easiest child to look after.

We had some issues. Don't get me wrong. Toni lacked boundaries due to coming from a broken home. It wasn't because Toni was trans. I wasn't trans, either.

Toni was made fun of by neighbors and even some local family members. Society was not beholden to the equality of people like Toni, being both trans and poor. Peer pressure won out many times. They made fun of her issues and problems. Toni would often end up with partners who used her, like my roomate in rehab. We had to rescue her a few times. Toni knew Jen and I loved her. That's probably why she stayed so long despite the challenges we faced with other house helpers. Toni lasted two years, 18 months longer than anyone else.

On social media, Toni and I still send well wishes. I'm thankful for her friendship and love for my kids. More importantly, I'm thankful for her shedding the stigma and fears that are associated with trans people—fears that are unnecessary.

Tarkan & Pınar

In Türkiye during the '22 and '23 school years, I had a wonderful gay student in my university classes named Tarkan. He, as a young gay man, was concerned about gay rights and LGBTQ issues. He was very open about it in a society that didn't look fondly on it. I came into class one day, and he blurted out something to everyone in Turkish. I asked him to please translate for me. He said that he was going to watch the men's netball team play and wanted to know if anyone wanted to join him. I told him I might want to go, not to ogle at the men's netball team from our university, but to find out what netball is like. I grew up being told that only girls play netball.

One of our first conversations was an admission, accompanied by a smirk and a short laugh, that his roommates were Muslim divinity students. Having been to seminary and been a pastor, this made me giggle (like a giggle at a funeral). He wasn't comfortable at first because of the lifestyle clash and was looking into changing dorm rooms. I told him that possibly he might do more for them than their religion. He might challenge them more about what love and acceptance are than anything they receive in class.

After the earthquake, Tarkan invited me out for dinner one night to meet his best friend, Pınar. He then announced that they were lovers. Not only ten weeks before this, I was talking to him about how sexual orientation can be a moving target, and one of the things I didn't like about polarizing agendas on both sides of the argument about gay rights was that they both make broad assumptions about identity and whether or not we are stuck with it for life. The truth is, there is no one-size-fits-all package. Labels are just that … labels.

He informed me that he wanted everyone to know he was lovers with Pınar, who, like a decent percentage of women, flirted with bisexuality, was now lovers with a gay man, and to be sure to include that in my social media post on Instagram. I suppose this was to ward off both men and women interested in them. The following school year, I was inundated by Instagram stories with the inseparable pair. Oh yeah, and those divinity roommates of his? He told me that he's glad to be back with them again for another year and that they've become lovely friends.

A Broken Record

While working at the kindergarten in Korea, I would hang out with young people I met at a book club on Friday nights.

I was with Todd, Dongho, and two young ladies, Evelyn and Allie, sharing coffee and conversation afterward. Evelyn and Allie both opened up about their unhappy pasts growing up. Evelyn was the more aggressive of the two. She spilled out venom about her mom, especially, and how much disappointment she had caused her family for not turning out to be the Christian 'lady' that her mom and dad expected. Allie, on the other hand, lamented about how much she was derided for being a 'big' girl and too manly to be a proper woman. Her parents had even admitted they were sorry she was not a boy when she was born.

During the conversation, Evelyn admitted to being bisexual. My curiosity got the best of me, and I broke open Pandora's box. Or possibly it was just my subconscious bias combined with a bit of curiosity. She was quite open about being bisexual, and I wanted to know what that was like. Inquiring minds wanted to know. It seemed benign enough, but when I inferred that people aren't born that way, things got ugly.

I don't remember exactly what I said, but I think I tipped over the holy grail of most LGBTQIA proponents by suggesting that environment partly shapes people's sexual preferences rather than genetics or biological predisposition.

Allie cried. Evelyn got angry and hostile. If someone had come into the conversation toward the middle or the end, they could have assumed I had cheated them out of money or punched them in the face. I tried desperately to dig my way out of the discussion with logical nuance, but no matter what I said, they fired back with angry retorts and rhetoric, accusing me of being a closet homophobe. Evelyn mentioned about 35 times that night that she had spent five years studying genetics, so I couldn't be right.

By the end of the night, I was shaken (and shaking). I was a people-pleaser, loved young people, and had, only a month before, been listening to their stories about the aftermath of Trump winning the election and the toll it had taken on them both. I had made them feel safe to share their stories despite being older and having more moderate leanings. We had built a rapport. Now, it was gone. I saw them one more time at a Korean chicken joint called Mom's Touch. There was no overt coolness from them. They greeted us congenially, but I had a hard time looking them in the eyes and soon motioned to my friends that I would wait outside. I was afraid I might trigger them one more time.

Looking back on it, I assume I hinted that *they* were responsible for their disposition. The vitriol I received in return led me to smugly admit silently that I was right about it all. I self-righteously thought, *Well, if you have no qualms about your lifestyle, why be angry at me for thinking it was your choice? Doesn't that give you more power?* And I pushed forward with my agenda to prove I was right. For whatever reason, my arguments apparently brought back a slew of baggage for both of them.

Yes, I firmly believe their childhood had most likely shaped and molded their beliefs about themselves and the choices in front of them, not merely biology. I wasn't implying they were completely responsible. But it didn't matter. Challenging them was a complete and utter mistake and burned any bridge we had built. I made Allie feel ugly all over again and made Evelyn feel tainted. I brought them both back to a time when they were made to feel that way—probably from their parents and a larger community of people who rejected them, didn't love them, and definitely didn't try to relate.

Like airport traumas, I replay this incident in my mind often. I wish I could have shared what draconian expectations were placed on me when I was younger and told them about the teachers who made me feel worthless. I would convince them we were the same. I didn't live their lifestyle and may not fully agree with their opinions, but that didn't matter nearly as much as empathizing with them.

Queer

My wife had to say goodbye to a third gay friend, dying early .. most likely from an actual disease, but I suspect additionally, from loneliness and the gaping holes her family left her when she was a 'him'. I reflect on the real problem. It's not being gay or trans.

I don't think they are suffering from anything particularly unique other than being alienated. Their actions on the outside look queer or odd because of their orientation, but on the inside is a problem that we all have. We can't completely relate to these experiences they've had, but there is no reason for them to be further isolated if we uncover that truth. The only way to uncover that truth is to be close enough to know it. That means knowing their stories. My wife and I know them because we care about them.

In Between. It's such a great name for a bar. I always wince at the name LGBTQIA; as important as it has become on the road to a more inclusive society, it's hard to say, for one. It's unnecessarily cumbersome and often fails to achieve its goal of avoiding negative stereotypes about people's identities. Like the term 'comfort women', it paints an unimaginative picture of the people in this community that I have grown to love and relate to. It feels overly clinical and impersonal, distancing us from them. That can hardly be the picture painted for any group of human beings I've encountered. Based on my interaction, their desire for affection, intimacy, and pleasure isn't much different than anyone else I've met outside their 'labels' or 'categories.'

I constantly shook my head then, and shake it still today realizing that our society actually embraced a policy called *Don't Ask, Don't Tell*. Inhuman. Hypocritical. I stand on the conservative end when it comes to all things gender and sex-related, so how could I manage to build such precious memories and bonds with these folks? Isn't it capitulation and cooperation with their agenda if I choose to put away my personal feelings or ideas for a moment to treat them like human beings? No. No way. Why are they so important to me? They need us. And we need them. Toni, my students, and my wife's professional community and beyond taught me a rich lesson. They aren't a meme or a reason for your political plaudits. Merely waving rainbow flags around or disparaging people who do won't move the needle to make our world a kinder and safer place for all.

We need to stop treating them like there is something more wrong (or right) with them than us. They aren't the 'other' as much as you may think they are. Like all of us, they are somewhere in between.

Chapter Eight

Crossing the Colored Chasm

I see no changes. Wake up in the morning, and I ask myself,
Is life worth living? Should I blast myself?
I'm tired of bein' poor, and even worse, I'm black.

2Pac (performing "Changes")[53]

Black People

During my one-semester stint at the very conservative bastion of Christian fundamentalism, Pensacola Christian College, some college friends and I arrived at the bank on a Monday to handle some of our business.

A middle-aged Black woman was standing nearby using the ATM, observing the infuriating nonsense taking place before her as three white guys were scratching their heads and peering into the glass, wondering why the door was locked.

"It's Dr. Martin Luther King's birthday," she said, shaking her head as she moved past us, probably to avoid saying what she really wanted to say.

I was shuttled out of my very white world early in life to Asia. I have no memory of Black neighbors, classmates, or significant people in my life as a child—not even in the restaurant I worked at in Phillipsburg, NJ, as a junior in high school. The Black kids were all in Easton, PA, across the river. I think there were possibly three Black kids in my whole elementary school as well several years before.

When I arrived at PCC, I was utterly oblivious to the white evangelical reaction in the Deep South to the integration of Blacks into white society. PCC and Bob Jones University were founded on the undergirding premise of Deep South racial conflict. They received no federal funding as a means to press an agenda that often involved segregationist ideology that mixed couples were not God's ordained world.[54]

When I was in the Navy, living in Chesapeake, and was finally allowed to move off the ship because of my rank, I'd get my haircut at a salon for Black ladies. I had no idea I was the only white male to walk into the place at all. No idea. They never said anything. They just cut my hair, and I'd pay my bill, tip, and roll out. It was the one closest to my house. I wasn't there to apologize. It had been purely an afterthought that there was a raging chasm between our worlds.

They couldn't possibly get away with doing the same things my privilege gave me. I couldn't figure out what all the Black car salesmen were looking at when I traded in my Black Impala SS that got me my vacation in Chesapeake City Jail. At that point, I had no idea that a white man under 50 wouldn't step into a car like that.

My disposition bought me precious time with scores of Black folks I served with and connected with over the years. In conversation, I blame it on not growing up in the United States, but I think I'm being modest. I have plenty of missionary kid friends who live status quo distance from the Black community. Possibly, something else that I grew up with aided my cause.

My Dad

I suspect that something was 'someone'. Obama gave a speech that moved me to vote for him in 2012. He was speaking from one of the grassroots churches that supported the work he did early in his career. His career started as an NGO lawyer in the city of Chicago. It's hard to believe he ran against probably the two best Republican candidates of all time, John McCain and Mitt Romney, and won. It's very improbable. He talked about the importance of fatherhood and how communities can't live without it.[55] My dad crossed party lines to vote for him in his first election.

When my parents were in their twenties, and my dad was seeking his first opportunities for Christian ministry, he started a youth group. A story that is on repeat in my head when I think about religion and race is an incident early in my dad's career as a minister. He was running a youth group and had many Black kids from the neighborhood attending—worshipping, singing catchy songs like "Do Lord," and clapping. This was all in the basement of a Baptist church, and the pastor asked my father to stop them from clapping because when Black people clap, according to him, they 'bring out the devil'. My father had to move his ministry somewhere else. I discovered later that this wasn't an isolated belief.[56] At PCC, I remember discussing these sentiments with a high school classmate and friend sharing

131

the same dorm room. Beats from Europe were ok. Definitely 'devil'-free. Bang on the congas or foot pedal bass at too fast a clip, and it was from the Dark Continent and the minions from hell for some reason.

When I was a junior in high school, at the Christian high school where my dad taught, there were no Black kids there, despite the decent-sized demographic of Black and Hispanic people in the Lehigh Valley. I heard a lot of derogatory references to the Black community, among others, which puzzled me at the time, but I was too busy chasing Chrissy White to pay much attention.

When my dad was a pastor at a Baptist church with middle-class parishioners in New Jersey, he was chastised by the elders because he and the youth pastor were bringing in lower-income families. It was unsaid at the time, but the frequenting of Black people to our church was starting to scare some of the long-time members as well. In an area with a history of the KKK, most Black folks settled across the river in Pennsylvania. When we did a youth event and spoof on the Jerry Springer show and invited my father to give the gospel message at the end, the event was riddled with bullet holes of dissent from many. It was the first time Black family members of some of our youth came to our side of the river. My father eventually resigned under protest, and his youth pastor was drummed up on 'charges' of irresponsibly allowing kids to jump into a lake that forbade swimming.

He doesn't claim a tall place in my life, but he has one. It's easy to see, thus far in my story, how much trouble he has had to pull me out of. He would play *Earl Weaver Baseball* and *Lode Runner* with me as a kid on the computer when games were first becoming popular. He wasn't huge on gifts (that wasn't his love language), but he was the steady provider for our family and always figured out a way forward. He and my mother worked through some challenging marriage issues. They were willing to walk away from their missionary legacy to get reacquainted with their kids, feeling overworked. He has continued to inspire many after retirement, with my mother providing grief counseling to folks who have lost loved ones. He and my mother have an enormous network of folks they have touched. It's hard to believe he suffers from feelings of inadequacy similar to mine, looking at all they have accomplished together.

In a time when racial reconciliation wasn't a political buzzword, my father showed me that God's love extends beyond the boundaries that people—whether in church or society—try to erect. It's from him that I learned the power of crossing those bridges.

Mark Mother Fuckin' Donald

The Navy provided me with a crash course on the kaleidoscope of American society. We all wore the same uniform but came from vastly different places. One of my shipmates hadn't seen a Black person until he was nine. He was told Black people didn't know how to swim, so how could they be in the Navy? He was from Idaho. I embraced it. My Black shipmates were integral in reacquainting me with the society of a country I barely knew. Most of this experience came on the USS *Bulkeley*.

I tried not to because I 'hate TV', but we all watched *Family Guy*.[57] My supervisor, IC1 Williams, was Black and watched it as well. He was a quiet man, but one night, when my supervisor, Nikki, and I snickered about the episode where a dog kept barking at the character Cleveland Brown, he admitted to being a bit offended when we'd come in and suddenly bark at him. One time, when Nikki was getting something to eat in the ship's store, the guy behind the counter, who was Black, said to her with a huge grin on his face, "You want some chocolate?!" Along with "Blah, blah, blah … Thailand," that one became a regular joke as well.

Radio—that was the compartment where all the ship's external communications were controlled. I spent an enormous amount of time there because the equipment there was my main responsibility (besides serving potatoes to officers and cleaning the passageways). Most of our radiomen were Black, and some of them were women. As the Navy modernized while I was on active duty, their rating was changed to Information Systems Technicians or ITs. There was a fiery Black IT2 who fought with me one night because I mishandled the cryptological keys meant to keep our communications secure. I loved her! She probably retired as a Navy Chief by now. It was down in Radio where we'd spontaneously start dancing to "Superman that ho" in the middle of duty or spy on what people were doing on their computers around the ship. One night, this backfired. We were spying on a shipmate in my division and suddenly saw he was perusing gay porn and male dating sites. All of Radio went silent. This was during DADT.

I had a few Black shipmates in my division besides IC1 Williams. The one that had the most impact on my life was Mark 'Mother Fuckin' Donald. That's what we called him on a night on the town. We both were electronics technicians on board. I was a 'comms' guy. He was a 'radar' guy, primarily responsible for navigation radar maintenance and repair, while I was down in Radio dancing to "Superman" or finagling with antennas on the mast.

I can hear his voice raise in tone, "Sullivan!?" as he shook his head, half snorting and sighing at me. I hadn't talked to him for almost ten years, and suddenly he called me in the middle of the night with a cup of something in his hand—he was a bit sauced but informed me that he'd been following my life on social media and was super proud of how I turned out. I can't remember if I said it or not to him, but he's part of the reason.

We reminisced about the time he and I drove seven hours from Norfolk, Virginia, to visit my parents in Pennsylvania. He was the only shipmate in my whole Navy career to enter that hallowed establishment.

It had been a while since Mark had called. He had retired already, and I had been out of the Navy for more than 15 years. He would occasionally call me at odd hours in his early morning. Since I was rarely in the same timezone, there was a chance it would be convenient for me to answer the call. He typically had a few drinks before ringing me up. One night, during his phone call, he gave me that old, sheepish laugh we grew to love in our time together.

"Yeeeeahhhh, I'm workin' for the Feds. Can you believe it?"

He announced he had just been hired as a retired vet to work as a civilian contractor for the Air Force. Federal civil service still made him cringe.

A couple of MMFD (Mark Motherfuckin' Donald) stories I retell constantly involved clubs and drinking—two things throughout this book that you can see I don't survive well. When visiting ports, it was required that we go out in at least pairs. It was called the 'buddy system' to mitigate the risk of people taking advantage of visiting sailors. There were plenty of instances where people took advantage of us, but at least we were taken advantage of alongside someone else. Mark asked me if I wanted to go out to a club in Savannah, Georgia. I agreed. He took one look at what I was wearing and told me I needed to change. He put me in one of his button-down shirts and a pimp hat, and we rolled out. I was the only white person there the whole night. At one point, as a young gentleman was hitting on a Hispanic shipmate of mine, I piped up that he needed to lay off; he looked at me and said, "You're white." I put on my white-man badge and continued out onto the dance floor that night and never looked back. I remember being tempted my next free night to try a more white-man-ish thing to do and go to the wet t-shirt contest near the local college. Nah ... I savored my night, pimped out in Mark's outfit, shaking it off the whole night as if Taylor Swift were Black too.

Mark recognized some of my inhibitions and conned me into a strip club in Glasgow, Scotland, one night. There was a group of us. We pretended to be wealthy, and I was their pilot. I chatted with the waitress all night, too scared or too stingy to do anything else. She was studying city planning at a local university. Another night, he and I were at a bar, and we traded shirts—I wore his "Vote for Obama" shirt ... and he wore some shirt that advertised I was very white, but we both walked into this honky-tonk Virginia bar to catch some odd looks. There was no money on the table.

I preferred to stay away from excitement in my home port and chase church girls like Beth and her long toes and Jasmine with the eye sparkle. One infamous night, the only night I went to a club in Norfolk, I decided to go out with MMFD and Tina, Mark's supervisor, who tried to push me down a load of stairs in Savannah; we met a few more supporting cast members and headed into a bar.

I had too much to drink in a similar manner to my alcohol incidents in London—I oozed off the bar seat in a similar fashion. I staggered after the group when they had decided to bounce to an adjoining establishment. But when I got to the door, the bouncer wouldn't let me in. He said I was too drunk. He was probably right because when I stood outside, I suddenly had the urge to vomit my insides out, and the only place I saw to do it was over the balcony onto shoppers and partiers alike down below. I can still hear their screams as I shared what was left of my celebration with them in a waterfall of Hooter's wings and mixed drinks. The cops showed up ... and that's when Mark Motherfuckin' Donald came out of nowhere and implored the cops that he would just take me home. He called a cab driver friend of his—I continued to try to spread the love again out the windows of the cab but was spreading it inside instead and on my face as the wind whipped it back in. Mark told the driver he'd clean it up.

When we made it pier side, our ship's gangway was past the security post and about 300 yards beyond that. I got out and immediately just crumbled to the ground. I couldn't get up. I told Mark to leave me there. I wanted to die or sleep or just lay there. He knew I had been in trouble with alcohol before. He knew that I couldn't afford to be caught by security one more time.

"Sullivan. SULLIVAN! Get up ... The roving watch is coming."

He willed me to get up, carrying and dragging me through the pier gate. We stumbled 300 yards to the gangway stairs—a lot of stairs—and onto the quarterdeck, coaxing me to stay alive to convince anyone concerned that the situation was under control.

Navy policy dictates that we have to make it on board under our own power; otherwise, we can be punished. I was well under the bar, and that was the second time Mark Motherfuckin' Donald carried me ... like the *Footprints in the Sand* poem, to safety.

Mark always knew that I didn't know. He treated me well and embraced my naivety about the world that he lived in, growing up poor in Cleveland as a Black man. I didn't initially see how much Mark's experience as a Black man shaped his world compared to mine. But over time, I came to recognize the chasm between us— the privileges I was afforded as a white man that Mark could never take for granted.

Mark was more than me. Outside in the real world, if he'd thrown up over the balcony to the horror of people below, he would have lost his Navy career with a misdemeanor on his record. I could recklessly and clumsily be rescued in part because I was white. He rescued my career more than once. Despite having flaws of his own, he looked out for his naive white brother and shipmate. I don't know if I can ever repay him. I can only tell his story here.

JonBenét Ramsey

I was in rehab in beautiful Rota, Spain, and one of the requirements was for us to write and journal. In reflecting on my past, I wrote a piece about the time I had recently arrived in the US from Thailand, when the six-year-old beauty queen JonBenét Ramsey was murdered.[58] At about the same time, I was reading our local newspaper and read about the horrible murder of a 13-year-old Black girl named Richezza Williams in the poor part of Easton, PA. She was tortured with hot fireplace pokers and sexually assaulted by three men before being killed and left in a box in the local cemetery.[59] One of the perpetrators is still at large to this day. JonBenét was in an upper-middle-class home. In contrast, Richezza had run away from Long Island, her mother had a history of crack cocaine abuse, and her parents were not together.

Richezza's murder was brutal but did not make national headlines. She was, after all, running drugs for the crime outfit her murderers belonged to. Like the Ramsey case, it remains open. In my reflection, I highlighted the disparity between the media sensation around JonBenét's death and Richezza's. Richezza's death reflects a much greater societal issue than the mysterious case around JonBenét, but you wouldn't think that based on media coverage and the outrage from the average citizen (where it matters). I wish I had more details on Richezza's case, but unfortunately, the online search results are few. Collectively, if we were to say that lives matter—all lives—we would instantly garner the resources necessary to save people like Richezza, but we don't. We spend our lives centered around the activities of a few notable celebrities. Their murders matter more. My friends, years earlier in Missouri, irritated with my blabber about Princess Diana, may have seen where I was coming from. I'm not so sure.

There are so many little candles in the wind being snuffed out by forces far greater than their economic or communal fortitude. What little they have is exposed and easily robbed by violent men like Richezza's killers, and the country doesn't blink—perhaps because of the lack of excitement about just another drug-related death that has long ago tired in the news. How many Black girls' lives go missing today without the intrigue of upper-middle-class status to keep people watching at night?

Seminary

Part and parcel of my life has been the erratic and spontaneous career turns I have made throughout my time as an adult. I often have the nightmare of wondering if people think I'm lying about my life. I was a fantastic storyteller as a kid. I told lots of interesting stories to my friends that never happened. Kenton knows. I grew out of it eventually—well, not the storytelling bit. These are all true.

The political irony of Regent Divinity School being 25% Black in Virginia Beach gave me hope. That hope faded a bit on my first day of face-to-face classes. I flew from Asia all the way to the East

Coast to attend a session in 2015. I was walking across the public road from the Burger King across the street when a jeep with oversized wheels and an oversized Confederate flag flapping behind it bore down on a Black woman driving a compact sedan in front of him. He was upset with her speed, screaming profanity and calling her an ugly nigger, blaring his horn. I stood on the side of the road, incensed and startled. Having grown up bullied, moments like those cause my muscles to tense up and my brain to suddenly drain out. I stood there frozen for a moment. For the rest of the week, I imagined myself chasing him down and... just chasing him down. It brought me back to other moments where I felt powerless in the face of bullying.

I then walked into a class of almost all Black pastors and a Black professor. It was a class on urban ministry with Dr. Antipas Harris. He was a well-decorated theologian who had grown up in the Southern countryside. He also wore amazing suits and bow ties to almost every event I've seen him in. He looked good in purple too, and his shoe choices were top-notch. Since he was in a cross-cultural marriage as well, we'd have awesome talks about what it was like to be with a fiery and spirited spouse from another land.

He was the founder of the Urban Renewal Center in Norfolk, Virginia.[60] During our sessions together, he brought in various guests doing work in the local urban setting of the Tidewater area in Virginia. One of those guests was a local Catholic priest who ran a therapy group. In this group, people had to come clean about their problems with bias, prejudice, and outright racism. All who attended would admit and disclose the thoughts and actions they carried out because of their fears of people not like them. The premise, explained the priest, was that we all have internal biases against those we are not familiar with. They might represent a group that has mistreated us or loved ones in the past. He felt that if we could all look each other in the eye and cough up honest reflections as a community, this would provide the means to heal a divided world. At this stage in my journey, I hadn't fully realized what that meant for my classmates and my professor, but the bonds that grew during that time would be one more stepping stone in the right direction.

I forever cherish the special gift given to me by my classmate, the reverend at a church in the local area of Portsmouth—a fat cigar! It was bought from the same store I'd hang out in with the former pastor of SGC.

Jordans

While in Korea, I joined a group of people who would provide food for the elderly poor in Cheonan. The government offers minimum care, housing, and stipends, especially for its eldest. Homelessness was rare, but they often had difficulty making ends meet. We were part of an effort to provide a tasty hot meal for them on weekends. I served regularly with two Black women, Makiba and Carla.

Carla was from Cape Verde. She was, indeed, an African American and spoke Portuguese and English. Her English was from the Bronx. She was a disabled vet who served in the US Army for four years. She was 50, running every day, and doing hikes with the *ajusshis* (아저씨). My favorite story of hers was when she dated an NFL player. I asked if he was any "good" with a wink. She answered with a laugh, "I'll never tell." She connected well with Koreans. They embraced her. She had picked out 'favorite' members of our regular weekly crowd and would be out on the floor conversing with them and giving them shoulder squeezes and hugs.

A group of us would pile into Carla's tiny car and stop at Subway to get sandwiches. It became a tradition. We'd talk about politics, women's rights, and the recent unfolding of the killing of George Floyd. She whispered to me one day, "I'm sorry, but I can't relate to most Black Americans when it comes to their experience." Similar to Bee's family making America great, she and her family were immigrants.

Makiba and I talked a lot. One time, when we were at a friend's birthday party in Seoul, after a vegetarian burger meal, we sat out on a rock at Gyeongbokgung Palace, one of five grand palaces from the Joseon Dynasty and probably the most visited because of its location in Seoul. We were there because it was our friend's birthday, of course, but also the Queen's Garden was on display for the first time. This was where the Queen would 'hang out' with her male Royal consort. She would go down in history as never 'telling' either. The others were very busy getting pictures in, but Makiba and I were pretty satisfied staying put and gabbing.

She would tell me about what it was like growing up poor and Black. When I complained about my son's obsession with getting a big bike or the right pair of Jordans, she was on target to understand why my wife and my son were fixated on particular symbols of material arrival. Attaining them was the distraction necessary to ignore the enormous gap between those who could easily buy more than one pair of shoes or wheels. Banks would float loans with no problem, but for her family and mine, it was a distant dream. A dream to drown disappointment in. My wife and I have moved on to building resorts and traveling to Europe to drown out our day-to-day when my son finally had his Jordans, and we had a beautiful Hyundai Tucson in our driveway. Maybe it isn't so different even when you aren't poor.

One particular story Makiba told me was of her family's challenge with old habits that were hard to break. They would repeatedly wash their meat thoroughly before using it. They washed it very, very thoroughly out of habit because, in the past, they were not sold the same meat white people were sold. For generations afterward, even when it was the same meat clearly sold to white folks, they washed it thoroughly, showing the lingering effects of generational mistrust—the same mistrust that brought sighs from Mark Mother Fuckin' Donald when he had to work for the Feds one more time.

Columbus Day

When stationed in Singapore while in the Navy, I was part of the diversity committee where we put on events that celebrated heritage from around the globe. One day, I asked a question that possibly other white Americans knew not to ask, but due to living under a rock, I asked why there was no month celebrating Irish contributions to society. Even Italians hijacked Columbus Day to make it a holiday around the country. St. Patrick's Day was not a public holiday, and I found that a bit terrible. I uttered this, and you could hear the distant buzzing of weed whackers over the giant green crabgrass hills in Sembawang. In my view, I saw there to be whole months in honor of Pacific Islanders and Asians (all 5 billion of them mashed together), Hispanics, and, of course, Black History Month. Women had their month, and now we have Pride Month, too. What happened to the White Irish guys? What about Eastern Europeans? Surely they could use something, too, right? Not even the Jews got a day off.

When discussing heritage, I tell people that my German-American great-grandfather was in the KKK. In the North, in places where Black folks didn't reside, their efforts had nothing to do with them. In fact, it had little to do with color. It had to do with a more nuanced pallor or identity. After all, Nazis weren't gassing Jews for the color of their skin or even for where they came from. Catholics and Jews were a menace to society, many thought. Irish folks were very Catholic. Instead of harassing and stringing up 'coloreds,' it was recent immigrants from Europe that had something to worry about when it came to racism and hatred in this region.

To humor English students learning the imperial language, I ask the question at the beginning of class: Why do we all have to learn English? They give pragmatic answers like it's the lingua franca, or they want to travel. I tell them… because the Germans lost the war. The French lost the war. The Russians lost the war. "The sun never set on the British Empire." The greatest empire the world has ever known spoke English. They were the victors of both world wars and a number of others. The United States, a former colony, would go on to replace it as the world's superpower.

Did you know that Ireland was the first colony? Due to rich British landlords scooping up the land, Irish people were forced to work what used to be theirs, for very little in return. British landowners utilized the land to provide agricultural needs to the mainland in England and beyond.[61] The main staple left for an average Irish family was potatoes. They grew potatoes largely to keep themselves alive.

A rare bacteria came through and started wiping out all the potato plants, leaving Irish people with nothing to eat. Their rich landlords, wishing to protect the profits, continued to export livestock and vegetables to the mainland. The British government largely turned a blind eye to the plight of the Irish. From 1845 to 1849, over one million, they estimate, starved to death. Over one million Irish people, in the desperate hope to stay alive or feed their families, spread far and wide all over the globe, as far as Australia, South Africa, Canada, and, of course, in Senator Obama's words in 2004, a magical place, the United States of America. It's a devastating mark on Ireland and Irish history.[62] It's my dad's generational legacy. It's the reason I'm an American. I'm proudly an Irish American.

I did not own slaves, and neither did my ancestors—quite the opposite. My ancestors were the first to be under the yoke of British power and suffered immensely because of it. On my German agrarian side, they worried about white people who represented their Old World enemies. I found it infuriating to be thrown in with racists just because I have white skin. As much as race is a human construct, so is the justification to judge me for the color of my skin.

Heritage

In Cheonan, South Korea, I found a Nazarene Church to attend. We had our church services in a conference hall with stadium seating and a stage. Our agreement with the university was that we could utilize the hall and the side classrooms for our services each Sunday. I was involved with the church band, which we typically referred to as a 'worship team,' in charge of leading the opening songs we'd sing.

We weren't quite as cool as Sovereign Grace, but close. We had a myriad of characters that would come and go and be a part of playing the drums, piano, bass, and lead guitar—sometimes a violin or viola. Our stalwarts, Adam and Ashley, were English teachers at the university who had been there for a decade. They took turns leading each week. They'd do lead vocals and acoustic and sometimes electric guitar. Along with Ryan from SGC, these folks brought out the musician in me. By the end of my time in Korea, I played the congas, harmonica riffs for special events, and sang background vocals.

Chanel shared soundboard duties with me. She was also a closet musician, having grown up playing the clarinet. She eventually learned to play bass and would alternate with another on stage each week. We'd have to set up, practice, and perform all on the same day, so our mornings were busy. But Chanel and I would catch a few moments to talk. We'd sit in the back behind the church soundboard and catch up on each other's week or ponder a deep theological thought.

Chanel was a Black woman in her early 30s from Detroit, who, along with the trio making America great again (*mi hermanita*, my coffee mate, and the rugby goddess), became like family. She was married to a Korean man. Like Debbie, I had the chance to be a part of her formation, newly married and working through some tough demons of her past. I suppose therapists like 'Dr. Zang' are qualified to help people through their personal struggles, but I've discovered that having trusted friends alongside can make a world of difference. The mutual trust and transparency I would have about my own past and current struggles drew the next generation to me. Authenticity often wasn't seen in the other aspects of their lives at work, in their families, or in their church. The power of just throwing up my hands and saying, "I don't know if hell is real. I've never been there... But the Tutsis in Rwanda have." Those one-liners may not have been popular with the pastor and may have alienated my chances to share the pulpit up front on a Sunday, but they were exactly what young people needed to hear.

I felt safe enough one day to ask Chanel about race. I tried the same line on her that I said at the Navy diversity committee meeting, where nigh a pin could drop without notice except for the laborers cutting the grass.

"Well... at least you have a heritage," came the response.

Her words made me realize just how much of Black history I didn't fully understand. Through Black Chattel Slavery, their heritage was completely wiped out over 250 years. They had no idea what part of Africa they came from. They had no linguistic heritage or religious heritage. They were kidnapped, chained up on boats, and sold like animals to work for the European colonists in America. That was their start in America. Their legacy *is* slavery. That's all they know. Their women were forced into having sexual relations with men based on reproducing more robust and stronger slaves to produce economically for the slave owner. This was condoned, celebrated, and, worst of all, justified on a grand scale, including using religious texts and church catechisms.[63][64]

Can you imagine? No... even they can't... thankfully, but only three generations removed, that was a reality. When most of us go back three generations, we are referring to a rich heritage of some kind. It may have involved persecution, or in the Irish case, utter devastation... but it didn't erase our culture. We had identity moving forward. Even Hispanics have a great deal of heritage that they bring with them despite colonial overlords. Those who come from indentured servitude, such as President Barack Obama's grandfather, even have their heritage retained. It has repercussions, but not to the extremes that chattel slavery has had.

And to think, I was repeatedly told by my conservative community that it was their moral problem to fix. I had been told repeatedly that they were lazy and sucking up welfare benefits. I was told that their cries for justice were communism, not Christianity. In reality, the highest percentage of conservative, orthodox Christians per racial demographic is Black.[65] My history books failed to explain the serious failure of American society to recognize and correct a wrong. And worse! It took a war and over 600,000 American deaths to try to bring it to an end. Not only that. They were given freedom only to see those freedoms get stripped away by a political agenda to hold on to power in the White House. With the removal of Union troops from the South, hateful and angry white southerners, left with burnt-down cities and no future, used the democratic process to establish Jim Crow laws and blocked votes to people who couldn't read. Of course, they couldn't read! They were treated like barn animals for over two centuries! You would like to think that Black folks who moved North were welcomed with open arms. They weren't. Along with the millions of other immigrants fleeing their countries in the 'old world,' Black people had to compete as if they were foreigners from another land. They were! But they didn't choose to come there at all. No property. No education. No heritage. A legacy of torture for 250 years for the economic benefit of the United States of America.[66]

Like Makiba and her family washing the meat. Like Mark telling his daughter that she will have to work three times harder to be taken seriously, even as a fresh college graduate in 2024, and his sighs that he is still chained and bound to work for Uncle Sam to help her make it happen. It all suddenly made sense to me that day, with one simple phrase from a trusted friend—a forever sister of mine.

Social Media

One day, in frustration, Chanel was quietly listening to a mutual friend and me muse about why Black and White Christians diverged politically. She disclosed that she really didn't want to get into it but shared a YouTube link for us to watch that helped us understand the dynamics behind Black Christians and why they voted the way they did.

One of the shocking diverging paths we've seen with social media is the siloing of views. What was supposed to be a democratization of information has now turned into ideological warfare carried out online. Not only are there bad state actors involved in manipulating audiences, but algorithms are designed as profit-making machines to increase screen time and views, reassuring us that our views are the right ones. Nothing was more poignant than when a friend of mine informed me that George Floyd's death was a hoax and sent me a bunch of YouTube videos to prove it. I had just finished reading an article about the grassroots organization that George was a part of.[67] Having turned his life around after leaving prison in 2013, he led community projects at a church in Houston. Looking for work, he moved to Minnesota. Suspected of counterfeiting, which has never been proven, he was arrested when the employee of the grocery store demanded he give back the cigarettes he bought.[68]

I got curious. I started to read about cases of Black children being gunned down outside on the playground or in Walmart. I began to read about data suggesting Black men are seven times more likely to go to jail than white men. 1 in 4 Black men are likely to do prison time.[69]

With social media access, Michael Brown's murder inspired the #BlackLivesMatter movement. What used to be just a number flashing momentarily on WPHL Channel 17 news, "13 killed in a gang brawl in West Philadelphia," had tangible and real lives. The one that crushed my spirit was watching the Philando Castile video from the live Facebook feed of his girlfriend in the car, with her 4-year-old little girl in the backseat. He had informed the police that he was reaching for his license and that he had a gun in the glove compartment. The cop shot him seven times. That little girl, watching the whole thing, including Castile bleeding out in his car, pulled over for a broken taillight.[70] The cop was acquitted of a sentence for second-degree manslaughter, but the family was eventually compensated through a subsequent wrongful death suit against the police department and the city. Breonna Taylor's death revealed a completely blank police report, despite seven police officers and 32 shots fired into the apartment, killing her and the assailant, who, by all intents and purposes under the law, had a right to defend the home, unaware that the police kicked down the door in a no-knock warrant issued under a suspected drug operation.[71]

I started to dig. I started to watch. I started to learn about Black history and the turmoil and quasi-citizenship that Black people have lived with almost their whole history in the United States. No, I didn't own slaves, and neither did my ancestors... but if ever the cliché mattered that doing nothing or saying nothing is worse... it applies. In my inner conscience, I cannot move on. I am a father. I have children who are brown. I have children who are looked at by a large percentage of the world as people to be exploited simply because they are not one of them. The plight of Black people in the United States should matter to everyone. As leaders of the free world, how can we Americans protest human rights violations halfway around the world in our Ivy schools yet ignore the ongoing suffering within our midst?

But Mike, how can I be assured that your information isn't fake or duped on YouTube? Where did it come from? One could say that I was in a wormhole, right? That the YouTube link I obtained from Chanel was a hoax or fake news. I've tried my best at making sure that's not the case. Media literacy is a skill that all should possess and should be taught in school. Being skeptical or curious isn't a threat to one's way of life. It's having the intellectual honesty to admit that we don't want to believe what we hear, but it could be true. What is missing from much of our exposure to social media is critical thinking or questions that thoughtfully poke at our closely held beliefs. That's what makes it dangerous. They are very short videos and usually appeal to our senses, and those are directly connected to our emotions. Like Golden Arches or the Nike swoosh, they move us in a particular direction.

But Mike, AI should help us, shouldn't it? I laugh! It's much worse now with AI. Not only do we have high-power photo editing in the palm of our hands, but we also have bots scouring the internet for results and compiling them into neat, well-organized paragraphs that don't even need a real narrator for one's content. We have lifelike voices narrating complete, eloquent falsehoods—worded confidently enough to assume it is all true. A few easy tests show that the onus is on the one seeking the information when they prompt AI for searches. AI is in its infancy and cannot be depended on wholly for the truth. The patient journey of discovery and intellectual honesty that has brought us all these amazing tools is needed more than ever in our everyday lives if we are to build needed bridges with communities different from our own.

The video Chanel shared with us was from a show called the *Holy Post* that started in 2012 by Phil Vischer and Sky Jethani.[72] Phil Vischer is the co-creator of *VeggieTales*, the most successful direct-to-video series in history. It was designed to provide a moral message through humor and catchy songs to children via anthropomorphic vegetables. He was the voice of 'Bob the Tomato' and the narrator of the video Chanel sent us. Revenues of Big Idea Productions, the company behind *VeggieTales*, skyrocketed from nothing in 1993 to selling over 175 million copies until bankruptcy in 2003.[73] *VeggieTales* became an icon of the white evangelical Christian world about the same time as the Christian Coalition was building its fervor and voter base to oppose the liberal pushes of the Democratic Party. I started to investigate upon seeing his voice and face behind an explainer on how the Republican Party may have been the party of Lincoln that freed the slaves, but it was also the party that sold them out in the end and left them at the mercy of Jim Crow et al. It was fascinating to see an icon of the evangelical world 'switching sides,' as it seemed. Here was a conservative icon defending the Black community. What else did he have to say? I would have never followed that trail had it not been for my trust in Chanel. She wasn't an evangelist for the *Holy Post*, nor did she care about Phil Vischer. But she was Black and from Detroit. Her lived experience and friendship brought me legitimate and well-researched media sources that challenged my beliefs about her community.

Tupac

Tupac Shakur didn't get a chance to sing this chapter's song to the public.[74] *Ratatatat...* and he's gone, just like Huey.

Having grown up among worlds, I've never had the confidence to tell people what my favorite music was, let alone utter a favorite song.

"I like all kinds of music," I'd answer, secretly jealous of people who knew their favorite genre, the lyrics, and the musicians they followed.

Now, without hesitation, I say, "'*Changes*' by Tupac." Regardless of the reaction I get, it offers me an opportunity to tell a story about a Korean engineer from Hyundai Motor Corporation who was my student. In college, this song caused him to stop and think about the world he lived in and make fundamental changes in how he interacted with other people. When given the chance to speak on the last day of class before heading off to Hyundai's automotive plant in Türkiye, he shared this with his classmates and me. In light of the LA riots and their impact on Koreans, this was a necessary risk in his mind to challenge his peers in an unlikely setting.

I put it on my Spotify playlist, and it soon became a go-to song to deepen my love for humanity, for my brother... for my sister.

I got love for my brother, but we can never go nowhere
Unless we share with each other
We gotta start makin' changes
Learn to see me as a brother instead of two distant strangers

And that's how it's supposed to be
How can the devil take a brother, if he's close to me?
I'd love to go back to when we played as kids
But things changed, and that's the way it is

Tupac, we have seen a Black president. It doesn't have to stay the way it is.

Part Three:
A World Away

One love, one blood
One life, you got to do what you should
One life with each other
Sisters, brothers
One life but we're not the same
We get to carry each other, carry each other
One

U2 (performing "One")[75]

Chapter Nine

Crime and Punishment

Didn't have to blast em', but I did anyway
That young punk had to pay
So I just killed a man
Here is something you can't understand
How I could just kill a man

Rage Against the Machine (performing "How I Could Just Kill a Man")[76]

An Empty Safe

You will hear laughter that quickly fades into a sad silence when we look at our wedding pictures from our special day years ago at Bluewater Maribago Water Resort on Mactan Island. Our chief sponsor at our wedding, and conduit to the mayor of Talisay City marrying us, was our Barangay Kapitan of Lawaan III, 'Mommy Delia'. She is there in the pictures and the videos, next to her then-boyfriend, Dean. You can imagine a barangay as the local district, and the Kapitan as the council chairman with her counselors who conducted various affairs of the community at the lowest local level. Lawaan III has been our barangay, and it has been for Jen since she gave birth to my eldest son. 'Mommy' Delia eventually married Dean. Dean was her second husband. Her first died of a common demise for men in the Philippines: unattended 'high blood' as they call it or hypertension, with a resulting heart attack.[77] Dean was from America, a retired Filipino-American who had served in the US Marines.

They both could be found down at the local casinos, gambling her business or the barangay's budgets down the drain. Unfortunately, she died of cancer, leaving Dean, the ex-Marine, surviving with the remaining two stepkids. My wife was close friends with her son Jeb.

While in the luxurious confines of Hyundai's Paju Training Center, a stone's throw from Kim Jong Un (김정은) and the DMZ, I was opening a pre-departure news briefing for my Korean executive and senior engineers in my English boot camp course. My wife pops in on chat, sends me a link, and tells me to check the live news on Facebook. The city SWAT team had arrived, along with scores of other police, and had Dean surrounded in his house.[78] [79]

An evening before, a fight broke out between Jeb, his stepson, and him. The acting Barangay Kapitan tried to step in as a mediator. The fight was over an empty safe that was supposedly holding millions of pesos of inheritance that rightfully belonged to Jeb and his sister. In the morning, Dean took his revolver and chased Jeb down to kill him. The Barangay Kapitan went to convince Dean to change his mind, but Dean killed both of them. He proceeded to burn tires in his house to act as a smoke screen, preventing police visibility, and opened fire on them indiscriminately with a fully automatic machine gun. This sent my oldest son ducking behind our gate and into the house as stray bullets riddled our narrow street.

A reporter was standing on the corner behind the half-constructed Catholic chapel, sending live footage not 30 meters from my home, showing the carnage unfold—while I stood worlds away, in a country where the news of the day is some rascal knocking the head off of a snow sculpture of Elsa in Daejeon (대전)—I could hear the gunshots, see the smoke, and watch uniformed, fully combat-ready police crouching fearfully behind the concrete barrier.

The police claimed a sniper got him in the end, but autopsies suggest he asphyxiated himself on the smoke and passed out first. We have his face amongst our cherished memories, sitting there passively, observing the unlikely union of Jen and me.

Maldwin and Maslow

One hot, steamy afternoon in our first year of marriage, back in 2011, we suddenly became aware of some flashing blue and red lights outside. We hadn't moved to Lawaan III yet but lived across the S. Coastal Road highway in a gated community called Fairview Village. We were taking care of my wife, Jen's teenage half-brother, Eves. We were afraid Eves might have gotten into trouble with the law. Jen startled me by suddenly shouting and talking with two gentlemen, grinning as they climbed out of the police cruiser. It was her two cousins, Euwin and Maldwin. Euwin was a local cop for the Talisay City Police, and Maldwin was a known drug dealer and contract killer. They hadn't seen Jen since we got married. They were curious about the turn of events that brought Jen out of Crusher to a gated community.

Crusher was the birthplace of my three adopted children. It was a riverside neighborhood in Lawaan III. People from the countryside would move onto these lands illegally and build elaborate networks of homes close enough to find city jobs to sustain their lives. The vast networks of families making a living near the city amounted to putting stakes in the ground like settlers in the Wild West. Their ability to perpetuate that existence wouldn't guarantee an expanded lot, but possibly a second floor made purely of wood, tin, and, if fortune really smiled on you... concrete. Canals for drainage were agreed upon by the fledgling communities, and eventually, running water would be installed by the local government, which was interested in gaining votes and influence. Once someone was a registered member of the barangay, they could start getting other things like driver's licenses, school registrations, and other signs of making it past the poverty line. Tangling meshes of electricity wires and cable internet capacity have now reached all of these places. The land was 'owned' by rich dynasties that quickly moved to draw up lines and make contracts for unclaimed land as the Philippines was passed from one colonizer to the next. There were occasional surveys and rumors that a college would be built in Crusher, but it never materialized, often for fear of backlash.

Crusher was also the place where my mother-in-law, Lola Thelma, lived. She owned a store. Her first husband, Lolo Audie, the father of Jen and three other siblings, had long moved on and had multiple family restarts with three other women. He was still technically married to Lola, but due to draconian divorce laws tied to the Catholic Church, it wasn't feasible for most people in the Philippines to get divorced. He was a mid-level crime boss in Mactan, across the channel near my English academy and the airport, close to where we got married. He had a long history of criminal activity. It finally caught up with him when he was indicted for a double homicide, which he claimed was self-defense. He spent two years in prison but was eventually released because no one wanted to come forward as witnesses.

Lola Thelma (my kids' grandmother) lived with a loyal man, Papa Vin, and they ran the successful Sari-Sari store for over 20 years, becoming the bulwark of stability for Jen and her siblings. Lola Thelma's sister, Mama Sali, lived a few houses up the hill behind her. She had three sons. One of them was Maldwin, the contract killer.

Long after his visit with us, Maldwin was involved in a drive-by attempted murder of a local senator who was trying to push another plighted neighborhood (besides Crusher) off government lands. People had pooled money to get rid of him. Instead, the senator's wife, who was in the driver's seat, lost her life. Maldwin wasn't caught but eventually surrendered to the police over gun-running charges. His sentence was for six years only. None of the deaths he's responsible for have been proven in court.

Mama Sali (Jen's aunt) had three sons: Maldwin, Lovewin, and Kuya Benjie. She was such a jovial woman. She always, without fail, had bright red lipstick on. When my wife would complain to her mother about our money situations, her mother would tell her, "*Dai*, you just wear lipstick (like her sister). Everything will be fine."

Not long after I married Jen, I remember stumbling up and down a mountainside property we had purchased near my wife's maternal home and watching Mama Sali fly up and down with grace in her rubber flip-flops.

About two days after my second stepson, Whejee, was born in 2003, Mama Sali's second son, Lovewin, was imprisoned for killing his father's cousin, Eddie. Eddie was a big man who bossed people around while standing in line to get water from the local well. One night at about 2 a.m., after a night at the disco, Lovewin and Jen's brother, Dodong Rodel, accidentally leaned against Eddie's tin house, waking him up. Eddie came out with a machete, threatening to kill them. He had a barbecue stand. BBQ was a common foray into generating extra cash and food for the family. Throughout the backstreets of Cebu and beyond, at about 6 p.m., you can smell the sweet scent of marinated pork, chicken intestines, and chicken skins roasting over a grill with a coal fire beneath.

Lovewin saved money by acting crazy and begging off people in the marketplace and got Rodel's gun from the pawn shop. He walked up to the narrow alleyway by Lola Thelma's store and Mama Sali's house and shot Eddie in the chest with a number of BBQ customers standing in the immediate vicinity. He then walked past all the gaping mouths and crying huddled masses, grabbed Eddie's head, and shot him in the back of it to make sure he didn't survive.

My wife and Lovewin were born only five days apart. My wife, about to give birth the following day, asked Lovewin, before he ran, why he did it.

"If someone tells me they will kill me, I will kill them first."

"Do you have remorse?"

"No. He wasn't a good person and didn't deserve to live."

He hid among relatives in the provinces (countryside), but eventually, they all told him he needed to turn himself in. Euwin drove him to the police station. He was eventually released from prison, pardoned by the president for good behavior. Before Maldwin got put away for guns, Lovewin joined us for church and eventually played the drums for the church band for a while.

Unfortunately, Lovewin's last days in daylight came when he killed his niece's husband—Kuya Benjie's son-in-law, JP. While on parole, he was continually harassed by the police because of local robberies reported in the area. He knew it was his niece's husband, JP. He told JP to please stop robbing, at least in the area, so he wouldn't be harassed about it each month when he showed up for parole. Not three months after Lovewin was released from prison, JP snatched a wallet out of a teenager's motorcycle box, and that was the last straw.

The oldest son of Mama Sali, Kuya Benjie, was a barber. He had worked very hard cutting hair for almost nothing and saved enough to provide a home for his wife and kids and a motorcycle alongside the road in Crusher. While I was in the midst of one of my many financial dilemmas as an entrepreneur in 2016, a cooking fire spread from one house and swept through the crowded, mostly wooden structures, taking it all away. Jen and I didn't have much to give, but I was compelled to give what I could to Kuya Benjie. I asked God why He would allow what little this man had to be taken away in moments.

Only four months beyond Maldwin's visit in the police cruiser with his cousin, we celebrated our first year of marriage. We had a huge Christmas celebration at our home in San Jose Village soon after moving there. Towards the end of the party, when our church friends had gone, my wife had invited her cousins to come eat. I watched Maldwin across the table, sucking down pork lechon, spaghetti, and fruit salad. With my anger issues at the forefront of my mind, I said to him,

"If I had lived the life you have, I would probably be a decision away from doing the same things or worse."

John John

John John (John 2x) was my wife's bestie. He was a handsome gay man who made his living by flitting around with foreign men interested in adventure and romance in the Philippines. He'd briefly come back from his excursions with his boyfriends to visit his mother in Crusher. Of course, he would stop in to see Jen and her new family in our home in San Jose Village, behind Crusher at the foot of the hillside along the river. I'd see him arrive and hear my wife shout and laugh.

"Sister!" she'd exclaim, followed by a hug, then a loud, boisterous cacophony of more laughter and stories of his time at various luxury beach resorts around the country. Before I met Jen, he'd always let her rest, take care of the kids, and clean her tiny house over the canal. He'd take her out for food, and they'd sing karaoke together.

Jelo, John2x's older brother, and his father had fallen on hard times and were enlisted into a criminal group that planned one of the most elaborate robberies ever in the region.

The Philippines has Super Malls, behemoth shopping complexes that dwarf the average mall in Western countries. Despite being surrounded by squalor and having a limited middle class, these malls provided secure shopping, dining, and countless other services for thousands of families. To do this, they hired an enormous number of security guards. The super mall closest to our home in San Jose Village was SM Seaside, a large circular mall the size and shape of a giant alien mothership, seemingly here to make peace with another world. Before the mall's official opening, while construction was still going on, these guards were paid in cash instead of through bank transfers, and this money was on its way to SM Seaside.

On May 18th, 2015, the chief of security was in on the robbery and informed the assailants where and when the money would be transported. Jelo and his father drove their armed accomplices to the scene, and one of them pulled a gun and told the young lady to give them the burlap sack holding the money. In a panic, the woman refused and tried to flee, and one of the men shot her. The panicking drivers sped off with no cash, now murderers instead of mere thieves.

Jelo, being one of the drivers, was now wanted dead or alive for his involvement in the murder. The neighborhood was told to call the police if Jelo appeared.

Unfortunately, John2x, oblivious to all of it, having returned from an excursion with a rich foreign paramour, went to visit his mother the day after the robbery. She wasn't home, however, so he waited there for her to return. He looked a lot like his brother. Neighbors called, and the SWAT team moved in. They knocked, and when the door opened, seeing who they thought was Jelo, despite John2x's protests, they panicked and opened fire. Someone in hiding yelled, "You shot the wrong guy. He's the gay (brother)!"

The police retrieved a confiscated gun from their vehicles, pulled the trigger, let a bullet hit the door, put the gun in his hand, and reported that he shot first. The neighbors knew the truth but were silenced out of fear of reprisal. It was surreal to visit the wake in their tiny home, everyone knowing the truth, but it was left to neighborhood whispers and buried with his body in the grave.

My friend from church was a chief investigator from the Cebu City police department. When I told him they shot the wrong guy, he looked up the intelligence on the case and informed me that it was highly unlikely the police had such a gun on them that they planted on John2x.

A very famous and frightening criminal network from Ozamis, the hometown of John2x and Jelo, on the southern island of Mindanao was behind the failed heist. They would go on to rob four jewelry stores in an hour, stealing 15 million pesos worth in another famous case. Considered untouchable, especially in Ozamis, the Duterte adminstration would later send his elite police forces in to the mayor's estate and confiscate millions of dollars of cash and drugs.[80]

The police had no idea there were connections with the head of the security detail at the mall at the time. So how did I know?

During John2x's funeral procession, Jen called Jelo.

"You killed your own brother! It's all your fault he's dead," her angry words cracked from the weight of sadness and grief.

Jelo confessed everything to my wife, thinking his days were numbered. Like Maldwin, he was arrested a year later for a completely different crime because, of course, the police had already killed 'him'. There was no wrongful death incident filed. The police labeled John2x as 'Jelo'. Case closed. Jelo became 'John2x' and had a nine-year sentence and would be released in 2024. Sometimes the prison guards would mysteriously come up with enough money to buy themselves nice homes and cars. During the jewelry store heists, strangely, Jelo's communication with Jen on social media went silent.

You will notice there are no references for this case. It has been scrubbed completely from the Internet. SM is the largest asset holder in the Philippines, having its own banking subsidiary Banco de Oro (BDO) and property investment arm. They own 26 billion dollars in assets and can afford to have their 'failures' eliminated from view here in the Philippines.

Duterte

Rodrigo Duterte, a criminal lawyer, became mayor of Davao City, located at the bottom of the island of Mindanao in the Philippines. He was famous for cleaning up the town, instituting strict laws, and making Davao the safest city in the Philippines. In a country rife with endless collaboration of institutions with lawlessness, these actions really appealed to most Filipinos. In fact, when he ran for president in 2016, he defeated his closest rival by over six million votes.[81]

My wife had been an MC for some of his rallies in the area, and she was a huge fan. With the killer of her first husband still running free due to the failure to bribe the local police, Duterte's sharp warnings to criminals resonated with her and many others.

His police forces grew in size. They were told they could keep the money they confiscated from drug dealers. They were given the green light and the equipment necessary to tackle well-armed and well-protected drug syndicates in different corners of the country.[82] One of those corners was Crusher.

When Jen first met some of these elite police details, they started asking her questions about names in Crusher. My wife knew many of them, like Jelo and her cousins. Soon, she earned favor with them, and they began calling her regularly to double-check on names of interest. Sometimes, if my wife was worried they might kill someone, she'd call the wanted person and tell them to take their shirt off and walk out very quickly with their hands on their head because the police were coming to get them. Those who didn't act quickly enough wound up dead.

In 2019, Crusher grew quiet, and some of the drug operations started moving into legitimate neighborhoods like our own, San Jose Village. It was suspected there was a meth lab in the house catty-cornered to ours, and the police wanted a two-story house to monitor the situation. So they staked out in one of our bedrooms and watched the times cars would arrive and 'packages' and people would leave. Our neighbors were spooked and tried to clean up and move to another location around Cebu City, but Jen reported their departure, and they were caught with all their equipment and remaining stash of *shabushabu* (crystal meth).

Without warning, one day, very tall, Tagalog-speaking elite police members came out of the woods on the hillside behind our home. If they came across the river on the walking bridge or the only entrance from the highway, spotters would sound the alarms. There were at least 20 of them, and they told Jen and the kids to hide in the kitchen, which had concrete walls and no windows facing our neighbor's house on the opposite side of our property.

They raided the house and took one of the drug dealers upstairs. Jen left the kitchen and ran upstairs to watch, hiding in the same place where the stake-outs had been staged the first time. The man was held by his neck, and the men were shouting at him to give up information. The man pleaded for his life, denying any wrongdoing. Within seconds, one of them raised his gun to the man's head. Jen dropped her head down, hiding her face in time, so she wouldn't see. She heard the gunshots.

Meanwhile, my youngest son's tears started to well up—not from fear but from sadness. He knew their names and faces, and they greeted him each day when he went out to play. Not anymore.

The house was left abandoned, and three bodies were dragged out and flopped onto a pickup truck, leaving large trails of dried blood for weeks. My kids would run past the house in fear each time they had to come home from anywhere within walking distance.

Jail

"Thank you, gentlemen... if it weren't for you guys, I wouldn't have a job..."

I thought to myself, sobbing in the parking lot with my parents looking on, *Wouldn't it be nice if you had to find another job?* That's the world I want to live in.

Jail. It was a super spiritual place. There were pastors there. One of them was caught dealing or using heroin—I don't remember. He had the whole New Testament memorized and knew that his prosperity gospel was what got him in there. He admitted he got greedy and lost his way. Another newcomer, halfway through, was a youth pastor from the Rock Church, about three miles from SGC. I passed this huge emergent mega-church all the time on Kempsville Road near my home. Again, illegal hard drugs. We had no less than two Bible studies a day at times, and as I said before, we recited the Lord's Prayer loudly while holding hands in a circle every night out in the basketball half-court where I'd do my exercises.

My cellmates—one was on probation and failed to pay child support, landing him six more months of jail time. When he went to court, his baby's mama told the judge, "I want to see him rot in jail." The judge politely informed her that he couldn't pay child support if he was rotting in jail. Some of my cellmates would lie awake until morning, reciting page numbers from comic books they remembered from childhood.

Another one of my cellmates was a former Air Force mechanic. I hadn't been aware of conspiracy theories about the CIA and Black people, but I soon was informed that the feds were still out to get them. I was skeptical. One night, when he told me my ship could tip over and turn 360 degrees in a storm and still end up upright, I made fun of him. The other guys had to hold him back until he cooled off. The only other white guy in my cell (there were ten of us) was guilty of violating a restraining order. He had popped a Valentine's Day card in the mailbox, which was evidence that he had been within 100 yards of his wife and daughter.

My most famous bunkmate was a guy who had run several businesses as a government contractor for local military installations—cleaning, construction, and other odd jobs. He said it was amazing money; however, he and his colleagues would end up blowing it all on soft drugs, alcohol, and women. Eventually, the cops caught him twice with a few ounces of marijuana in his car, and now he was facing a year of jail time. He was hoping to breathe fresh air after a few months in a work program so he could at least work and be outside. He had a U.S. patent on a safety straw and was hoping to connect with a fast-food chain like McDonald's after he got out.

Like my chicken bullies, there were a lot of offenders coming from prison systems. One of them had been in and out of incarceration since he was 13. Another man had been in prison for ten years and was doing the last part of his sentence in our non-violent ward. He had a warm heart and huge shoulders. One night, a young teenager was admitted to our ward. He didn't speak any English. My big-shouldered friend and the chicken bullies interpreted what had happened. The kid was 16 years old and fresh from the border. He had only been in the country a week, illegally.

I watched them throw someone into our ward who was addicted to hard drugs, jailed without any medical treatment, and left to go through withdrawals with us.

One guy I talked to was serving the remainder of his prison sentence for a federal crime. He lived in New York City. He had seven kids and lived in a humble part of town. His neighbors had picket fences to keep people from walking through their yards, so people would take a shortcut to the street behind his home through his property. He would look jealously at their fences, dreaming of one day being able to afford one. Constantly, members of his community would whisper in his ear that one or two drug deals would give him that fence. He shook his head each time until, finally, he gave in. Unfortunately, it was a setup—an FBI sting operation. He was dragged into federal court and sentenced. Now, after seven years, he was a few months away from being a free man.

I got up to share one night, a week before I was released. I suddenly felt led to do so. I can't remember what Bible scripture I read, but I remember telling them that meeting all of them had helped me fully appreciate what a privileged and naive person I was. I had no idea what hardship looked like in my own country. I was seeing it. I told them I'd walk out with one of the best jobs on the planet. I wasn't faced with the enormous uncertainties associated with being a felon. My crime was a class 1 misdemeanor. It was as if I was given a special ticket to see a part of society I would never have seen otherwise. I suddenly bore the responsibility of letting others know.

Free Drinks! Free Women!

As I said, I had a lot of firsts in the UK. Another first was getting robbed—twice.

Jeff, a new sailor, joined our division, and I felt it was my calling to take him downtown. Now, for whatever reason, the saying *two heads are better than one* didn't apply to the two of us this evening—at least not the heads with the noses and eyes on them. As we were strolling down the road, a young woman with a tight crop top, short shorts, and blond hair was standing outside her establishment, advertising free drinks and naked ladies at a strip club. Did we deliberate? Nope. We went right in.

We were accosted by a dimly lit waiting room with a very tiny stage, no larger than an American-sized refrigerator, with red lights above it—the red lights that made what we call the red-light district 'red.' Along with it, there was very loud music. A woman came out and asked us some questions. We couldn't really hear her, other than, "Are you here for the show?" Or something similar. Maybe. We nodded. A moment later, a woman (not naked) stepped into the caged stage and danced to the song for a few moments, then left. Her dance was nonchalant, as if she was dancing shyly on the sidelines, holding a drink at a club. Then the music stopped, and the woman who asked us some questions in the beginning came in and asked us to pay. Of course, we were stunned. Pay for what? Where were the free drinks and naked women we were promised? The woman told us that we both agreed to pay 700 British pounds for the services. Jeff looked ill, and I turned a turnip color and proceeded to argue with her. Then, a very big Black man stepped up. I thought Jeff might need some medical attention in a moment, but instead, with my amazing EQ I'd shown off in the Navy a few times, I turned and repeated to the man towering above us what I said to the woman, as if he didn't hear it the first time. With my voice rising in tenor and volume, I pushed a bit further by calling them all frauds, looking up at his face.

This gargantuan man then looked at me with eyes of almost compassion and jest. With academic verbiage, he began to undress my intellect.

I can't, for the life of me, remember what he said, but he gave a very eloquent lesson on the capitalist system, the free market, and how they had a right to charge whatever they wanted—especially since we fell for it and agreed to it. We were the wrong ones here. Not them. I was almost tempted to ask him what university he taught at.

I only had about 50 pounds on me, and my new shipmate had about 100 (and 300 more hiding in his shoe). We told them that 150 was going to have to be enough. The blonde who called out to us earlier came rushing down the stairs, asking how much we paid. The whole time, another equally large man was standing in the shadows by the entrance, blocking our path if we decided to run for it. They let us out, but not before we were completely schooled in economics. I passed by the place not even two days later and found it a gaping hole—not even doors to the place remaining.

My second time getting robbed came while I was on my way to a New Year's party in Whitehall at a friend's house. I was on the overground train, found a seat, and called to let them know I was on my way. I put my phone into my right pocket. A kid who couldn't have been more than 15 years old, South Asian, was sitting next to me. The train announced the next stop, and he got up. A few moments later, I patted my pocket and realized my phone was not in it. I knew the kid must have been a pickpocket. This was nothing unusual in London, but it was my first time. I got up, grabbed the kid's jacket, and said,

"Give me back my phone. I know you have it. Give it back."

He pulled out four phones from his pockets and said, "I don't have your phone." Indeed, none of the ones he pulled out were mine.

The train stopped, and the doors opened. He started to walk out, and I was still holding onto his arm.

"I know you took my phone. Give me back my phone."

Then, a white woman with the Queen's English appeared out of nowhere and said, "He doesn't have your phone. In fact, should you provoke him, he will summon his five Bengali brothers from the neighborhood and give you a proper thrashing."

"I know he has my phone, or else he passed it off to someone else."

Suddenly, the 15-year-old kid pulled out a box cutter. Feeling more bemused and mystified by the Queen's arrival than afraid of the knife, I let his arm go, and he ran off.

A man in a long black wool trench coat, with equally posh language, appeared out of nowhere and repeated that the kid didn't have my phone. The two of them drifted away, leaving me on an empty platform with empty coat pockets as well.

I got to my party without my phone and filed a police report. The following weekend, there was a huge raid, and an underground criminal ring was busted for using young immigrant teenagers to pickpocket unsuspecting people like me to steal mobile phones.[83] My British friends (the rude ones who tell me I'm gross for putting sugar in my tea) were convinced that I had some pull with the government, working in the US Navy. I didn't. It was a coincidence.

Black Friday

In 2007, I attended a Thanksgiving party with a family from Sovereign Grace Church. Afterward, I was invited to my first sit-in for Black Friday outside Circuit City that night. Circuit City was a box-top strip mall electronics and appliance store chain before going bankrupt during the financial crisis of 2008.

It's well known globally, thanks especially to social media, that Americans take Black Friday very, very seriously. We regularly see scenes of shoppers completely losing their grip and getting into full-on WWE wrestling matches over flat-screen TVs at Walmart every year. I had never encountered this phenomenon before.

At about 9 p.m., still thankful and full from the enormous Thanksgiving meal that Thursday, we queued up to buy gadgets at steeply discounted prices. Many of us took turns sitting in the car to stay warm and then got back in line as we waited for the store to open at 5 a.m. I was handed a ticket at my request to get one of the discounted laptops. I was getting it for over $400 off. When we went in, it wasn't a stampede of any kind like in the viral videos, and there were no fights. I wasn't sure if I should be disappointed or not. I got my laptop and continued to browse around. I picked up a steeply discounted Garmin GPS for my car that I didn't need and a digital photo picture frame for my parents. They didn't ask for one, and I'm pretty sure they wouldn't have known what to do with it, but I felt an urge to get it nevertheless. I don't remember what else I picked up, but I filled the trunk of my car.

I then took some kids out to the mall later because that's what you do on Black Friday in America… go to the mall and fight for parking spaces. One of the doors didn't lock properly, and someone in the parking lot checked. They were able to pop my trunk and steal everything out of the back that I had soldiered through the night to possess. Needless to say, I was angry and filed a police report one more time. I hated the person who stole my things. Over the following weeks, I kept imagining catching them and exacting my revenge.

As I filed my police report, it reminded me of getting pickpocketed in England a few years before on New Year's Eve and nabbing the robber before he left the train car. He was a child of poor migrants from South Asia and part of a ring of thieves, being peddled on the front lines by an underground syndicate. When I did challenge him, the Queen's bodyguards stepped in to protect him.

Moving to the Philippines, having things stolen was part of being there. It was a rite of passage. One time, when I left my bag in a taxi coming from the airport, I went back to the airport to the lost and found to check for my bag. I was ushered into a large, empty room with white walls, with a young lady sitting at a small desk with a single book in front of her. She ushered me to sit down and asked me to put my name, description of the item, phone number, and email address. And so it went. Nothing made it to the room. They became possessions of someone else. One night, my wife's DJ thanked God for the blessings that someone had left behind a pink motorcycle helmet because his wife had recently lost hers. I can't list the number of things that have disappeared over my time there. During my time with the Filipina mafia, I had a friend of mine come over wearing my 'lost shoes' I had left at his apartment after a basketball game. He's the one whose birthday it was the night I met Jen. Headphones and an MP3 player—all were borrowed and never returned.

Generations of Filipinos have had their lives and their land hijacked by colonial forces.[84] When a white man steps into their country, many of them feel they are justified to walk away with an MP3 player. They not only steal from me but each other. That was the norm set for them by the 'civilized' West. Not only this, but it was institutionalized and christened by "holy hands." Of course, we don't think of this when we've been violated. But we should.

In my favorite book of all time, *What's So Amazing About Grace?*, Philip Yancey tells about the pivotal scene in Victor Hugo's classic, *Les Misérables*, where Jean Valjean, in desperation, steals valuable possessions from Monseigneur Bienvenu. Upon being apprehended by the authorities and brought back, Monseigneur Bienvenu surprises everyone by claiming that the items were a gift and even grabs two candlesticks and says that he forgot them.

This act of extraordinary grace on the protagonist deeply impacts him. It challenges his perception of himself and sets him on a path of redemption and transformation throughout the rest of the novel.[85]

The faceless thieves of my things have flesh and blood. Like me. I'd ponder the woeful things I had done to others, hardly out of desperation but just out of habit or greed. I have no idea why people steal, and of course, I believe it is still wrong, but... what a difference it makes when I sit back and ask myself what that person may have been through to reach the conclusion that stealing or killing a man is the thing to do.

Chapter Ten

My Ride to Work

He pulls his prayer book out of a sleepin' bag
The preacher lights up a butt and takes a drag
He's waitin' for the time
When the last shall be first and the first shall be last
In a cardboard box 'neath the underpass
With a one way ticket to the promise land
With a hole in your belly and a gun in your hand
Lookin' for a pillow of solid rock
Bathin' in the city's aqueducts

Bruce Springsteen (performing "Ghost of Tom Joad")[86]

The 22nd Floor

Remember my wife giving the middle finger to her employer in 2018? Well, I also worked for a time in the BPO industry.

The Business Process Outsourcing (BPO) industry had grown to 7.5% of the Philippine economy in 2021 and employed 1.57 million people by 2023.[87] Back in 2014, as a language consultant for the company that fired me, I was working with the world's biggest banks—HSBC, Wells Fargo, and ANZ, to name a few.

If you're a person in the English-speaking melting pots of the world, such as the United States, Canada, or Australia, chances are you will get a Filipino on the phone or in the chat function on the web if you are requesting customer service. Filipinos provided an economical alternative to first-world responders, having soft and polite voices and much lower living costs. They are tasked with a long list of responsibilities, including back office work, virtual assistance, customer complaints, and training AI to scrub social media of violent and pornographic materials. They work nights, endure 12-hour shifts, and handle up to 120 angry, dissatisfied customers per night with few bathroom breaks.

My office was in the commercial hub of Makati in the greater National Capital Region of Manila. I left Thailand, and moved there in 2014. I found the view from our 22nd-floor office exhilarating. It didn't actually do anything except make entrances and exits and finding affordable accommodations nearby more painful—but at first, it felt like a bonus to our paycheck. You suddenly felt out of place standing around with the construction workers at the pancit stop or grabbing coffee from the guy on the corner. You felt you should be opening those thick glass doors to some air-conditioned paradise with overpriced cookies and a watered-down cappuccino.

In a country where average earnings are a fraction of those of their clients, I still had trouble finding a tiny apartment remotely close to work for less than a third of my measly salary. I found a place for about $300 a month. That was what my wife would make three years later, in 2017. It was a brand-new complex. I had a one-room place with a tiny balcony for cooking on a gas stove. I would wash everything but my dress pants and shirts in the shower. I avoided wearing anything white. I slept on the floor on a thin, one-person mattress with a folding table next to it for eating and working.

My newly constructed apartment had squalor surrounding it. My driver lived in a tent-like structure on the sidewalks down the street from me. There were three-story wood structures of thin plywood and tin, leaning precariously like replicas of the Leaning Tower of Pisa. I often wondered where they went to the bathroom. The wind sometimes gave a hint that it wasn't far away. Down the street was a slaughterhouse with an unforgettable ambiance—the sound of pigs squealing their last rites and the smell of blood wafting in with the breeze.

Each morning, I would overpay my tricycle driver to take me as far as he was allowed, about 500 meters from work. I'd walk across the street into an enclave of pillared white houses with uniformed doormen behind high gates with gnarled motifs, silently signaling that the world outside wasn't welcome. I'd pass women pushing trams of kids and pets around private gardens. They were uniformed proletariats working for the residents behind those gates. From there, I'd walk through the embassy district to the clustered skyscrapers of Roxas Boulevard, next to the Stock Exchange and the Ayala Triangle. I often paused at our 22nd-floor window, watching elites helicopter around over the traffic, landing on the Union Bank helipad below.

I had four assistant managers and a team of ten employees. This didn't include the owner, his son, or his wife, who managed the more complex details of the company.

One night, leaving work a bit late, we were invited to the office kitchen for a drink. Our boss rolled out his scotch, pulled a glass from the cabinet above faster than a Wild West sharpshooter, and poured. He proceeded to call the driver, Manny, a cockroach. I could feel a fog of white supremacy filling the room as my Filipino colleagues sat there, awkward and polite. That "cockroach," Manny, had a family, a house in Taguig, and had invited me to stay with him if my rent near the slaughterhouse became too much.

I was hired by a Canadian manager, who knighted his British counterpart to take his place. He didn't leave happily. He hated our Chinese-Filipino sales manager. She had connections but didn't know our products well and came from wealth, filling a parking slot of self-entitlement. She had invited me one night to her church, which met at the Makati Sports Club on Sunday nights. I found myself squashed between two seven-foot-tall Chinese ladies with Gucci bags that weren't fake.

I got caught on social media, recommending that my former boss name a stray cat he found after her. The gossip reached her, and she cornered me.

"You call yourself a Christian," she spat.

I was a fantastic trainer. Even when they fired me, they had to admit that wasn't the reason I was getting tossed. We took paid Ubers to training assignments with our BPO clients. The client might have been ten kilometers away, but it would take over an hour to get there—traffic crawling along at a snail's pace. I could have jogged faster.

It became obvious very quickly that this company was a pet retirement project for the owner and a toy for his son and his wife. They all came from money. The cockroach comment was the end for me. I had no idea they'd beat me to the punch and drop me a few weeks later.

Scams

I had been out of the Navy for about a year, and business was not good. My laundry facility was hidden off the main highway at our property in San Jose Village, so I needed an outlet to collect laundry at a mall or elsewhere. I also needed more commercial clients.

One morning, after dropping my two boys off at Thomas Aquinas School in Linao, I continued south. The Land Transportation Office (LTO) mafia was out in the City of Naga, checking drivers. They pulled me over. Since I left intending only to drive as far as Linao, I had no helmet, no license, and no money to bribe the official out of trouble. They took my plates and told me to come to the Cebu City LTO office to get it back. When I arrived, I saw a wall-sized sign spelling out the penalties for not having a helmet—10,000 pesos, more than most people made a month. Not having a driver's license? Another 5,000. I called 'Bro' Dominic for help, and he negotiated them 'down' to 10k to give me back my plates. He then helped me (by walking me over to a building) transition my American license to a Filipino one, which ended up in the black hole at the airport behind the smiling lady with the little book in the white room.

I was broke. I was moving credit debt from one credit card to another to stay afloat. My water business was in full gear, producing about 1,000 bottles a week. But my filtration machine lacked a protection mechanism to stop the water pump from grinding itself to pieces if water failed to run through it. At $250 a pop, I went through three of them in six months. I might have been breaking even, but the problem was that I had agreed to buy the water business, along with the property and adjoining home, by paying monthly installments. I had agreed to pay far too much each month, banking on my laundry business eventually relieving the negative cash flow. Neighborhood growth started to pick up, but I really needed commercial clients, like hotels and resorts, to fully utilize the giant Electrolux machines I had purchased.

In the Philippines, the business climate was toxic. Like Eddie and his BBQ, almost all businesses were side hustles to add money to a pot shared by the extended family. Despite Filipino TV channels depicting a single breadwinner, this was hardly the case for over 97.7% of the country.[88] Even wealthy Chinese-Filipino families developed a collective system to strengthen their businesses. One might own a wholesale enterprise that would feed into a cousin's retail business.

A lot of wealth comes from abroad. Remittances from Filipinos working overseas dwarf foreign direct investment.[89] In 2023, 40 billion dollars from more than 25 million Filipino foreign workers entered the Philippines.[90] It was common for them to own businesses to show off to the community that they were wealthy, like owning a nice car or a club membership. They'd throw a sales associate behind the register and install a security camera. It didn't matter if the business was bleeding cash. If I went to buy a ferry ticket, for example, it might take the associate 20 minutes to help me. For many businesses, like food outlets, pawnshops, and mobile phone accessory shops, customer volume wasn't a priority.

Scams were rampant. My wife's industry, as I've mentioned, was notorious for scamming newlyweds. When Jen decided to become a wedding coordinator, she quickly realized the work wasn't worth the money unless she scammed customers like others in the industry. For example, they'd charge 15,000 pesos for an MC but only pay my wife 5,000, pocketing the rest. They'd promise a certain floral arrangement, but by the time the event arrived, it would be far less. It wasn't unusual to see a sobbing bride while the coordinator got arrested for failing to pay the venue or caterer.

While I was working in Korea, long after our businesses failed, my wife became a real estate agent for a company—only to watch them steal from others. One day, we visited a foreign husband and his 40-year-old Filipina wife about buying a house. I didn't catch everything said in Visaya, but Jen later told me the wife and her brother were asking for an extra $25,000 to be added to the house price, to be given back to them in cash, unbeknownst to the foreigner. My wife eventually left the company after the owner scammed another customer out of the BIR (Bureau of Internal Revenue) tax, which had been promised as part of the deal. When it came time for the customer to transfer the title, she was told to pay the BIR and had to file a case against them.

Many of my wife's old friends have survived by running Ponzi schemes, cyber-sex rings, and selling products like jewelry online, only to fail to deliver after receiving payment. One friend even scammed Jen out of jewelry, knowing her husband could pay up.

Running an honest business required leverage, government connections, and, quite frankly, often not being honest. For instance, if I wanted a 'safe for consumption' certification for food and drinks, I'd have to bribe health officials who came to my home. That's how they sustained their existence.

My wife was an MC for a very expensive event, based on the venue and the guest count. She asked the client what they did for a living.

"I worked for the Bureau of Customs for 40 years," the client replied.

I tried sending a brand-new iPhone 12 Max Pro to my wife from the US. Big mistake. Anything over a certain value required an import license and about 30 pages of paperwork. My wife had two options to keep the phone from being confiscated: either get all the paperwork done in less than 24 hours or give the customs official $100 and take the phone. Even after paying the $150 shipping fee and the $100 bribe, it was still cheaper than buying the phone in the Philippines.

The only honest businesses I regularly see are street vendors—like the lady who wanders the neighborhood selling *biko* and *budbud*, or the men hustling cold water in the middle of traffic to thirsty drivers and passengers in unbearable heat, humidity, sudden showers, and toxic diesel fumes. I once told my son, who was struggling to find a job, that I wouldn't mind if he ended up like them, as long as he was kind and trying his best. I'm pretty sure I was lying.

I had a used Japanese multi-cab truck with a 1.8-liter motor that guzzled gas like a monster truck. We had a metal frame designed to carry water bottles to customers. I eventually sold the multi-cab to cover my kids' school expenses when things got out of hand. It facilitated many much-needed moves, family trips, and rides to church.

The seven-foot Gucci women in Makati had cousins. There was a branch of the same church meeting at the Marriott Hotel adjoining the Ayala Mall in downtown Cebu City. When we were ostracized by SCC, we decided to try attending Sunday service there. The parking lot was filled with Montero Sports, Toyota Fortuners, and Land Cruisers, while we rolled up in our tiny white multi-cab with the kids in the back, pickup style. It was humiliating—especially for my wife—but that's where we were supposed to belong, because I was white. I hated it.

Weirdly, because of my white skin, no one believed I was broke. The electricity guy laughed and silently judged us. My 'rich skin' hid the fact that it took me 16 years to graduate from college. My wife melted as we walked into the bank to pay an overdraft fee for a bounced check. I don't think even she fully believed it.

Bamboo

In 2016, I was at a tech conference on the next-door island of Bohol with a terrible cold. I was staying at a hostel because I didn't have much money to attend the shiny gig at the 5-star accommodation hosting the event. My coughing kept others awake all night. One Swiss lady was particularly annoyed and proceeded to scold me as she undressed in front of me. I forgot how Asian I had become and didn't know whether I should be looking at her or looking down as she talked with nothing on but a tiny thong.

I pitched my tech startup plan to some Silicon Valley investors. They were impressed. They told me to give them a call when I had a working prototype in the marketplace. It never happened.

Debbie and I were cash-strapped and unsure where to continue with my fintech startup concept. I devised the idea that if we looked for other inventions or great start-up ideas to support throughout the region, we could generate more than just funds, but meaningful relationships going forward. After all, my prototype was about finding the relationships between financial entities, and we needed some.

In the process of getting to know the entrepreneurial community, I ended up at a Toastmasters meeting one night, which was held at the prestigious Waterfront Hotel. Due to reclamation from the sea, the Waterfront was no longer on the waterfront but still possessed the mystique of being the oldest 5-star hotel in Cebu City. A woman was talking about her father's unique invention that did something with bamboo.

Her name was Rhoda. She was a single mother, and her father, Rody Monoso, was living with her in one of the oldest hillside communities in Talisay, bordering Lawaan III. Tatay, as we called him, had his bamboo machines decorating their front carport.

They were the only known machines in the world that could crossplane bamboo. Bamboo is the fastest-growing plant on earth, with some species growing 4 centimeters an hour or 1 meter per day.[91] So much bamboo grew in the jungles of Mindanao that it would clog rivers when they died. Actually, they never died. A parent plant called a rhizome underneath the ground would continually allow more bamboo shoots to form even if you had cut the stalks down. Bamboo grew all over the world, even in Siberia and more temperate climates in North America. Bamboo is four times stronger than any wood and has a tensile strength higher than steel while being more flexible under pressure.[92,93] Tatay knew that bamboo was part of a sustainable future alongside solar panels and the hydrogen economy.

Despite growing up poor and without a formal education, Tatay ambitiously worked at every opportunity he had, from elementary school and beyond. He became a well-paid and skilled carpenter, working for his father at only 17 years of age.

He mastered many skills, including metalwork, carpentry, pipe welding, construction, auto body, a/c, motor, and drive train. He was the youngest foreman for Pacific Engineering, sometimes having simultaneous site projects all over the Philippines. With his auto repair shop, he became quite successful—successful enough to provide for his whole family.

But this was not enough for him. Gifted with an inventive mind and spirit, his whole life was filled with pondering the world in which he lived, understanding advances in technology halfway around the world, from solar power to satellite communications.

Tatay invented a wheel plow, which is now commonly used all over the Pacific region on rice fields. The two-wheeled device cleverly used the wheels to move the plow using a gas motor and cut up the ground at the same time. His invention was stolen by his business partner, and now we have a myriad of mass-produced versions made in Japan and China.

He also noticed the vastness of the forests but realized that we could not replace the wood fast enough here in the Philippines. He started looking for sustainable solutions long before sustainability and eco-friendliness were trending topics.

In continental places, wood is a cheap construction material, but for tropical islands, it becomes quite scarce and hardly renewable because of not having enough land. From his travels in the air, Tatay could see extensive over-logging and a waste of wooded resources. Today, the Philippines struggles to find sources of cheap construction materials and has to import much of its quality wood products.

Tatay looked into coconut husks and banana trees before settling in on bamboo, understanding that bamboo is a weed that grows extremely fast and can be an excellent renewable resource. Despite its potential, the problem Tatay recognized was overcoming the difficulty of making bamboo into mass-produced wood products easily for the construction and furnishing industry. Current methods require too much time and effort to be an economic industry alternative to maybe pine and oak produced in North America.

Tatay developed two types of machines. One could efficiently process and furnish bamboo into beautiful, smooth, and flat products. This machine was awarded a trade patent in the Philippines. The other could flatten bamboo for mass-produced walls, roofing for emergency housing, or more expensive-looking decorative siding.

Unfortunately, all progress in his research and production came to a halt. His family received heartbreaking news that his wife was diagnosed with terminal cancer. In a country bereft of social services and medical insurance, Tatay had to make the hard decision to abandon his dreams and support the love of his life until she passed. He abandoned his newly acquired plant and property in Iloilo to be closer to medical facilities in Cebu.

Tatay had been left to tinker with his machines, perfecting them ever since, in hopes of finding someone who would help fund the recovery of the commercialization of his processes and inventions.

When we met, Debbie and I, of course, didn't have support for our invention either. That's why we were reaching out to build bridges with others. Tatay was 76 at this time, but each day, scraping up the few resources available to modify the machines or make additions to smooth the process further and demonstrate their usefulness. He'd also make floor tiles, clocks, baskets, religious icon holders, and other things that might perk the imagination of someone wealthy enough to help him.

With a small amount of help, his prototypes could be patented in a developed country, and a small business started to demo products made by his machines. I spent the remaining time looking for a means to help his legacy survive, just to see my resources peter out and land me on the couch with my dad handing me 80 bucks and wishing me the best in finding a job.

I had since moved on to Korea and Türkiye, with his situation always on my mind. On my afternoon climb up Mudeungsan after meeting the Japanese curator, I saw contours of bamboo lining the path at a certain height. I thought of him. Through my gasps for air, I breathily uttered.

"You're not forgotten."

I would see bamboo baby wipes, socks woven in Türkiye, and bamboo groves decorating buffets at 5-star accommodations—all of them—and stop and swear to myself I'd make sure this man's legacy continued somehow. Each time I'd come home, I was at first too afraid to call Rhoda and find out he might have passed. When I finally gathered enough courage to do it, I would find him out front, still tinkering and innovating at 80 years old and beyond.

Rhoda worked for 20 years at the same casino where 'Mommy' Delia and Dean threw away her children's inheritance and Lawaan III's budget. What was feeding Tatay were the scraps of millions thrown away each night on gambling. That's what most Filipinos were left with. The scraps from wealth. Here sat a man with the mind to turn our planet upside down and contribute to solving some of the most difficult problems we have, such as reforestation and building cheap emergency housing after typhoons and earthquakes. But his inventive mind and his inventions were left to flounder in a tiny corner of the developing world.

Any approach to local investors amounted to completely surrendering ownership for money. In Western countries, known for tossing money at risky ventures, angel investors may ask for 20% tops.[94] In this predatory business climate, they had no stomach for risk or respect for those whose ideas might reap untold millions. Very few were interested in the 'blue ocean' type innovation that Tatay and I were offering. Most were very satisfied with tried and true guarantees like scamming wedding couples and betting on craps.

On one of the many visits Debbie and I would make to their home, Tatay trustingly divulged one more of his innovations. On the back of a political poster, Tatay brainstormed to perfection a prototype drawing of a perpetual machine that utilizes the force of buoyancy to generate power.

How many more Tatays are out there? How many brilliant and inventive minds are left in the corners of this planet? Developing countries are teeming with human resources. Some of Tatay's own children lived in Canada and America and refused to send money home to support his cause, leaving Rhoda and the casino there to take care of him.

Rose

Rose was one of our teachers in my section. She was a young gun at 21 years of age—fun and exuberant. Every morning, she'd arrive early with two others, and we'd huddle together, eating local delights from a street cart near their home. Each day, I would go out and eat with my colleagues at the local *carinderia*. My wife and I weren't making much money then, but it was still five times Rose and her colleagues' salaries. I was treated as a barely first-world, native English teacher, while they were treated, well… like the third world often is—like cheap labor, a commodity for those who could afford it. And the commodity? English, of course. Filipinos are excellent English speakers but reap few of the economic benefits.

Rose checked into the hospital after failing to recover quickly from a routine bout of UTI. I went to see her, hoping to cheer her up. Two of her colleagues and friends were there, along with her boyfriend and family. Even her parents, who were separated, had come together to be by her side.

She was listless, and her eyes burned with anger. With her arms tied back, she looked like a trapped prisoner with the oxygen device attached to her. Some whispered to me that she had tried to remove it several times.

I finally managed to see the doctor and ask about Rose's status. Her voice sounded mechanical, as if she were explaining her daily workout schedule to me. She told me Rose had a case of lupus that had turned her UTI into a life-threatening situation. Heavy doses of steroids were given to minimize the impact of lupus, but unfortunately, it required a lengthy stay and a drug regimen her family couldn't possibly afford.

I sat next to Rose. As a Christian pastor at the 100-year-old church at the time, I thought of asking her if I could pray for her, but the intensity of her stare frightened me into silence. With the doctor's words echoing in my mind, I froze. I stammered out a few forgettable reassurances, urging her to keep fighting, but her eyes just burned brighter. I felt God slip out of the room.

I went home disgusted with myself for letting God leave. I was disgusted with the doctor. Within days, Rose succumbed to lupus because her family couldn't afford the medication needed to treat it.

I gave her eulogy at our school. It was the third eulogy I had delivered that year as a new interning pastor. One had been for a grandmother. Another was for a fellow pastor, supposedly in good health, who died of a heart attack. And now, Rose.

All of these deaths were preventable in the First World. None of them would have occurred if they had access to the world-class emergency response systems we have in the West. Rose lived in a different world from mine—one where a treatable UTI could steal away a beautiful heart with endless potential.

The doctor had seen this play out over and over, perhaps a thousand times already. People watching their loved ones slip away in the night… with no choice. Neither the hospital nor the government had the resources to save Rose and others like her. Economics made the choice for them. My mind screamed. I had no resources of my own to help. I was helpless. My family and I were also uninsured. One incident away from the same fate, but no… my parents had money. They could instantly find resources to buffer us from the reality that had stolen Rose from us.

Rose couldn't speak to us, but I felt I understood what those glares and angry twists were about. She knew her family had sacrificed everything to keep her alive for just a few more days, and it was killing her. They had to call in favors, ask their network for more money, to buy the drugs that might give her a chance. But it wasn't enough. News of her passing came within the week.

During the eulogy, her friends were crumpled together on the ground, pulsing with sobs. Just weeks before, we were teasing Rose about a crush she had on a Korean student, sharing pancit and freshly baked Spanish bread before classes started. For me, having benefited from the best medical care the world could offer, it gave me pause. Even now, as I sit here, tears and sobs well up in me as I think of her—her smiling face is still trapped in time. I call out her name and beg forgiveness for not having the resources to save her.

Chapter Eleven

Chaperones

*There's a deep girl in the corner shop
Selling sugar for money in the dead of the night
And her soul's in the sugar and her heart's in
the mud
And she's crying with a stranger
For someone to love*

The Corrs (performing "Somebody for Someone")[95]

Suzanna

Let's bring back Suzanna. Don't lie. You can't forget her—rubbing her feet for 1000 euros and all. My shipmates never let me forget either. I'd constantly get someone asking if I'd rub their feet for money. I deserved it. If I were a fighter pilot, my call sign would have been 'Foot Fetish.'

The catwalk announcer kept calling her name to get on stage and do her strip routine, but eventually, she got permission to skip it. She was busy with me, telling her story—with her clothes on. After that famous 1000-euro night at Heaven—that was the name of the strip club at the top of the hill—I called her. We had a two-hour conversation. Yes, even after four hours of rubbing her feet and listening to her story that night. For whatever reason, she felt safe talking to me. English wasn't her first language, but we had plenty to discuss.

We even made plans to see some attractions around Mallorca, but the rain prevented us. When we pulled into Rota, Spain, for a few hours to refuel, I bought an overseas phone card (remember those??), called her again, and spent my last moments of freedom trying to relive the magic with this beautiful woman—with gorgeous feet.

There's a piece of paper with this whole story on it, but I haven't been able to retrieve it. I lost it, along with her phone number, on my way back across the Atlantic. This story didn't make it back through the double doors of Sovereign Grace Church either. What would Jasmine's father think?

I would never .. in Singapore

I would love to say that I continued only to rub girls' feet, but I made it to Asia with the same thin boundaries, and I was not so naive.

While stationed in Singapore, I was sent on training missions with the Royal Thai Navy in Sattahip, very close to Pattaya and the beach, where I first learned of God's grace. I went out with my American technical team, who were military contractors, and we found ourselves in some late-night establishments.

One, in particular, was eerily similar to 'Heaven' with the stage acts they had. It was called Angel Witch. The shows involved women with either pitchforks or angel wings—and not much else—battling on top of customers who lay down on a bench underneath, to the applause and envy of everyone else. U.S. Navy ships would pull in, filling up these establishments with sailors who were catching quick shows before their strict curfews. I, being independent of the ship's chain of command, was under no such curfew and would stay out late.

As I watched, sideline girls would accost the audience and sit with them to keep them company. During show intermissions, they'd climb ladders, slide down poles, and throw ping-pong balls at us. One girl sat down next to me. Her name was Lee. The Mamasan (lady pimp) told me I could take her back to my hotel for a price. And I did.

So that's it. I didn't lose my virginity to Master Chief, Deanna, Suzanne, or Suzanna. Not to Jasmine, Beth, or my girlfriend in England or Pennsylvania, or even Charlene, who gave me my first kiss at 23. Not to Charity or the neck-biting New York nose.

I lost it to Lee for 35 dollars that night—or maybe the night after—in Pattaya, the place of my missionary childhood and my first interaction with the U.S. Navy.

Lee felt safe with me. We had lots of laughs… and sex. My virginity became a distant glimpse in the wake of a week of activity. Lee was my 'girlfriend' for the duration of my stay. We went to the movies, saw *Kung Fu Panda*, ate out, and enjoyed local delicacies like king prawn. I even met her cousin. She was allowed 'leave' from her duties for a few nights. After all, she wasn't the main attraction, just a sideline gig. Or was she?

Whereas most girls in the bars came from the poorest parts of Thailand, like the Northeast, Lee was from Sukhothai. She looked 22 but was 30, and like many of these women, she had children. When I asked about the father, she shook her head. He wasn't a good husband or father, and her son lived with her parents.

On the last day, I woke up with a hangover from hell. Not from alcohol, but from guilt. Imagine a self-proclaimed pious Christian, a believer in saving sex for marriage, someone who had studied prostitution and trafficking in books, realizing that for about 800 dollars, I had bought myself a blissful week, losing my virginity and more.

I sat on the bathroom floor, clenching my teeth as tears streamed down my face. I walked out onto the balcony with Lee and cried. She didn't understand why. I called Kaelira and confessed everything.

When I got back to Singapore, I had suicidal thoughts. I called my parents and told them what happened. I swore to God it wouldn't happen again.

But it did. They sent me to Phuket later, and the temptation was too great. With the same contractors, we'd go out to open bars that, of course, served drinks and had patrons waiting for us. We'd play games, make drinking bets on things like Jenga, and of course, lose. They played every night, and we were drunk. If we lost, we'd ring a big bell, owing drinks to everyone there.

I took no less than three women home on successive nights from three different bars. The first woman came back to my hotel, and along the way, a water main burst. I had to carry her on my back to the hotel's back entrance. The second woman I had taken home a month earlier but hadn't slept with her. We woke up the next morning and walked on the beach. When I returned a month later, she wasn't so lucky. I bought her a ring, and we rode elephants together on one of my days off. The last woman, Min, became a real friend. We initially had sex, but later, I took her to the hospital when she was sick and insisted there was no obligation for anything. I just wanted to help. She cried. We toyed with the idea of opening a business in Phuket or investing in her family's rubber tree farm.

The one thought circling in my mind was that at least I hadn't indulged in Singapore. Back in 'squeaky clean' Singapore, I had a church, a Bible study group, and a life of discipline. Navy sailors may have had a nose for finding those parts of town, but I hadn't indulged.

At least, not yet.

Mariah Jin Jin

On August 4, 2009, Mariah was dropped off at Ninoy Aquino International Airport in Manila and given specific instructions to go through a particular immigration booth. However, the immigration official bribed to let her through was not there, and another official refused her paperwork and sent her home. The following day, the correct party was available, looked at her sham paperwork, and ushered her through.

On the other side, at Changi International Airport in Singapore, she was again given very specific instructions to avoid the police, look for a white car in the parking lot, and get in, not talking to anyone or letting them know where she was going. She did so out of fear of losing her opportunity to work and provide for her kids. She was the sole provider. Not only six days prior, her husband was shot nine times and left in a ditch, betrayed by an extended family member for peanuts. He normally carried a weapon but had pawned it two days prior to celebrate his daughter's 1st birthday.

Now Mariah was climbing into a white car and ushered into a horror she wasn't prepared for. This was her last night of freedom for months. She was assigned as a patron in a little hole-in-the-wall bar in Paramount Plaza on East Coast Road, famous for its seedy establishments, under the radar of law enforcement. Patrons were not only visiting her establishment for pricey drinks but for sexual play in dark corners of the bar and eventually soliciting the girls to come home with them for follow-on action. The girls were obliged to succumb to make extra money. They weren't 'coerced,' but with some simple math after a few days, it was apparent that without getting money from patrons, they could never pay off their instantly incurred debt for the trip and accommodations and get their passports back.

On August 10th, Filipino friends and I walked in. One of them was celebrating a birthday, and the other had just broken up with his girlfriend. I had just hit my 10th anniversary in the US Navy. My Filipino friends didn't have the money to buy much company, let alone take anyone home that night, but I did. I kept buying drinks for not one girl but many. Like other nights, my tab started to rise quickly as the night went on.

At some point in the evening, when I was good and drunk, Mariah and her friend Jeil had made their way over to me. I looked at Mariah's face. She was pretty.

"What's your name?"
"I'm Yours," she said with a smile.
"Well, hello 'Yours' .. it's nice to meet you. I'm sorry, I'm drunk. Really .. what's your name?"
"Jin"
"Hi, Jen .. "

The night rolled forward, and I had decided to take three girls home at once. Not because I was some sex maniac, but because I was a people pleaser and felt bad saying no to any of them. One of my sailor buddies had told me a story that before he met his wife, he had seven girls from a bar all in his shower with his video camera.

'Jen' had disappeared at some point, and when the night was closing, I wanted to bring her home. Jeil helped me find her and run down to the cash machine to pay back my $700 tab for the night. On the way, she suggested I only take two girls home—her and Jen.

And so that was it. Jen and Jeil went back with me to my 1900 sq ft apartment, paid for by the almighty US taxpayer. They cooked me a meal, and then the sexpectations started to materialize. In the end, Jeil wormed her way out of any intimate encounters with me by suggesting that Jen and I already had a connection. And that night, we did connect. It was awkward and clumsy. I was drunk. She was too. She was drunk and too scared to say no. Jeil stayed in the room on my computer, surfing the internet with her back to us.

They didn't ask for money the next morning. I just handed a wad of bills out of guilt. Jeil said she'd let Jen use her phone if I wanted to chat with her. They both went back to their apartment. An apartment that was locked from the outside. The girls, once they were in, couldn't get out without permission. She threw water on her face.

She stared in the mirror, wondering what had befallen her. Had she just had sex with a foreigner for money? She sat on the bed and cried. Her husband had only been dead for 12 days.

'Jen' and I chatted a bit over text and I agreed to come back to the bar again to see her. The second time, I only took 'Jen' back because Jeil had left with someone else earlier in the night. Another intimate encounter ensued.

The following morning, 'Jen' had noticed Christian books on my shelf. She had converted from a nominal Catholic existence to an evangelical Christian one. She would take her two sons with her to sing in the worship band. She loved Hillsong music and had an amazing voice. She had been promised to use it to entertain Singaporeans, but that was all a lie. She had been duped and trafficked for sex.

For some reason, she felt safe with me. We started to talk. She asked.

"Are you a Christian?"

A deep well of shame sprouted like a fountain from my heart. I hung my head, eyes upward to another dimension. "Yes," I replied, looking away.

"I noticed all your Christian books."

One of the books was *The Purpose Driven Life* by Rick Warren.[96] She had the corresponding journal to this book, and it had her prayer list. She asked me to play her favorite Hillsong tune, "With All I Am."

She went on to tell this guilt-laden fool her story about her husband being killed not only 12 days before we met the first time. When I asked her if she had kids, she paused and said, "Yes… one."

Jen had her first son when she was 16 and her second son at 18. Afterward, she tried to go back to school and work but quit.

She grew up in the jungles of Balamban, raised mainly by her grandmother while her mother, Mama Thelma, tried desperately to find money. Her father, Papa Audie, left the family when she was six years old. She would wake up each morning and look out the window for the longest time, each time expecting him to come home.

He never did. He could never be trusted, and her mother, swore to kill him if he tried to come back. One moment that really finalized things in her mind was when a typhoon came in; they were left hiding in a ditch, terrified as everything they owned blew away.

Soon, things got too difficult, and the kids had to be dispersed. Only Jen's youngest brother remained with her grandmother, and she, her sister, and her older brother were sent in different directions. 'Jen' ended up at a wealthy relative's house. They were very strict and treated Jen like a slave. She would shake when they'd return home, expecting them to scold her about some mundane corner of the large house that wasn't clean.

When she was nine, her mother let her stay with her father for a time, but her father disappeared to be with his girlfriend, leaving her with no food. She and her gay friend Randy were left scouring the streets for tins to sell so they could eat. As a teenager, Jen tried to be a house helper in the wealthy part of town in Talamban and saw automatic doors and escalators for the first time. Eventually, though, she was cornered by the man of the house, posturing to assault or rape her. She ran, leaving her things behind.

When she finally landed with the Camingawan family, giving birth to their first grandson, she finally had a bit of respite. But then her husband started to gamble on basketball games and Mahjong. He wouldn't come home and wasn't providing for his family. A neighborhood man named Phillip took notice of Jen's beauty and told her he wanted her. She refused. He threatened to come in the night and rape her and kill her. One night, Phillip was able to get his hands into their thin-walled home and grab her legs while she was sleeping. She kicked and kicked until he left and, on another occasion, poked her back with a stick through the very thin walls of their room above the canal. For two torturous years, she couldn't sleep, waiting for this man to come back.

She then got married to the father of her two sons soon after joining her new church. She had her daughter then but knew that she had to find work. Someone offered her work in Manila, so she flew there. Unfortunately, instead of finding work, she found a mamasan, a trans woman named Apple, who, instead of pawning Jen out for sex, kept her around to make her laugh. Jen was funny and good company. Eventually, though, the stepfather of Apple tried to assault her, and she ran away and stayed with a relative of her father.

In the process, Apple must have shared Jen's phone number with a woman named Rachelle, who worked to recruit women into bars in various hotspots such as Singapore, Hong Kong, etc. She pretended to miscall Jen, built rapport, and then offered Mariah an F&B job in Singapore. Apple, several years later, was thrown into prison for running a cybersex ring with minors.

Before I brought her and Jeil to my home on August 11th, she had spent five days in the corner, crying and wanting to go home. She had lost her husband and her freedom, and she was stuck in Singapore, expected to service rich customers with company and sexual favors. So she finally capitulated... with me.

Terminal 4

At first, I had trouble continuing this, but Jen grew in my mind. She was a mother grieving the loss of her husband, living in this horror. Her voice was soft, she was beautiful, and she had tenderness. Suddenly, I was smitten and felt like I needed to find out more. We had the same faith, and there was a growing belief that we were meant to meet.

Just like on the bathroom floor in Pattaya, Thailand, surrounded by security, money, great friends, and family—I tossed and turned all night, gnashing my teeth, staring at a dark abyss that would be my life if I didn't figure out how to set her free. I knew the sex had to go.

I tried going into the bar to visit her from time to time. She genuinely liked me and was relieved that I could come and visit. Instead of getting drunk, I would buy drinks for both of us, and we'd tip them over or pour them in the toilet. She got caught one night and was scolded by the manager. But with no alcohol, suddenly, I could see... I could see everything going on around me.

The other men who frequented the place, doing what I did the first night, putting their hands in places they didn't have permission to be, with girls who were muted by the vast power differential between us, imprisoned by their situation. One night, a watcher warned the bar that the police had arrived. They shut the lights out and locked the doors, failing to turn off the AC. For what seemed like hours, Jen and I huddled together, trying to keep each other warm while waiting. I was frightened. If I was caught and exposed to the US Navy, I'd lose everything. It was a federal crime to be cavorting with trafficking victims.

I felt trapped, too. I couldn't keep going there and allowing them to take my money. It was wrong. It was perpetuating horror and the destruction of these young lives and their patrons. If I took her home, we'd end up having sex. Because of the situation, I would never know if she wanted to or not. I tried for a bit to come in a bit tipsy to avoid noticing everything going on by visiting another bar nearby before arriving. I would wind up talking to another Filipina with kids and feeling the sudden pull and thrill of possibly bringing them home. I'd have to tear myself away from her to go to Jen's bar.

I felt alone. My world in Singapore seemed to rotate between church, the Filipina mafia, and work. Work was a drag, and I was scared to tell anyone at church. One day in quiet confession at church, I decided that I could no longer risk going to Jen's bar. I prayed that somehow she'd be let go. We hadn't seen each other for three weeks at that point. She had started a Bible study with the other girls she lived with, using several copies of *The Purpose Driven Life*, which I bought for all of them. She refused to go home with any other men, further sinking her into debt with her employer. They refused to give her passport back.

I eventually went on a business trip to Portsmouth in the UK with my division officer, Commander 'Dan'. We attended a technology conference for defense ministers, and I embarrassingly sat in the wrong seat during the gala dinner on a 200-year-old warship. Defense contractors had been given seats next to the dignitaries, but I sat down at the wrong table, in one of their seats, next to the ministers and armed forces heads. I listened to them have very bigoted conversations about racial disparities in their countries. Commander 'Dan' was very worried that I would say something to alienate myself and America. There was a pub crawl at the end, and we lost one member that night. Everyone argued over who would go into the strip club to look for him. The next day, we got on our flight and went home. In the taxi on the way home, I started to get a backlog of messages on my mobile phone.

The text messages rolled in... the latest first...

"I'm at the airport..."

"I'm at a hotel... we are waiting to be sent back to the Philippines."

"I was in a jail cell, tied to another woman."

In previous nights, Jen had told me that the police would come, and because of a spotter, the girls were drilled to bolt out the back door, sometimes throwing off their high heels and carrying them as they ran all the way back to their dorm rooms.

The Singapore F1 Night Race was coming to town. Its inaugural success the year before put pressure on officials and law enforcement to make sure the "squeaky clean city" maintained its image.[97] They stepped up sting operations for the illegal trafficking of persons. Prostitution was legal in Singapore but couldn't be anyone's primary means of income. What was typically nonchalantly overlooked and welcomed by many travelers (mainly men) to a world-class destination could become a black eye during one of the biggest sporting events all year.

The police didn't announce their arrival as usual, and in plain clothes, they pounced on Jen and Jeil's bar in Paramount. The manager and the girls were instantly arrested. While Jen stood there waiting to be questioned, she looked at her manager in cuffs being pressed against a wall and read his rights. Suddenly, she had pity on him, asking herself the question, "What kind of life did he have to end up in a place like this?"

I was sitting in the taxi next to Commander 'Dan,' trying to disconnect my pounding heart from my face, giving him short answers to his questions. I told the taxi driver to drop him off first before me. When my boss alighted at his residence, I said goodbye and then told the driver,

"Uncle, please take me back to the airport. You can restart the meter if you want. I forgot something."

Someone.

They had put Jen and the rest of the girls in jail for 48 hours and interviewed them individually. Jen was completely honest and told the whole story of how she ended up there. She and the other girls were put in a hotel for two days and then sent with an escort to the airport to be deported to Manila.

I arrived at Terminal 4, and there they were, with their pillows, teddy bears, and belongings. Jen, another young lady, and I ate at McDonald's before their flight. It was our first date, and we had ten chaperones. Jen's birthday was coming up, and I gave her a brand new phone I bought her on my layover in Dubai.

I gave her about 300 dollars worth of cash to get home to Cebu, back to her family, who hadn't seen her for five months. She hadn't been able to attend her husband's wake or say goodbye. The last night she had spoken with him, he had apologized for all he had done wrong to her, and they spoke of their hopes for the future when Jen could go to Singapore and 'find money'. A week later, he was lying in a ditch with nine bullets in his back. The 'agents' told her she'd lose her place, and that she couldn't bring her husband back to life, imploring her to think of her kids.

Her family had no idea what she was doing there or what she had gone through. What started as a desperate search for money became the beginning of a new chapter in both of our lives.

Part Four:
A Broken Road

*I think about the years I spent just passin'
through
I'd like to have the time I lost and give it back
to You
But You just smile and take my hand
You've been there, You understand
It's all part of a grander plan that is coming
true
Every long lost dream led me to where You are
Others who broke my heart, they were like
Northern stars
Pointing me on my way into Your loving arms
This much I know is true
That God blessed the broken road
That led me straight to You*

Rascal Flatts (performing "Bless the Broken Road")[98]

333
Chapter Twelve

A Rescue

She's just a girl and she's on fire
Hotter than a fantasy
Lonely like a highway
She's livin' in a world and it's on fire
Filled with catastrophe
But she knows she can fly away

Oh, oh-oh-oh-oh
She got both feet on the ground
And she's burnin' it down
Oh-oh-oh-oh-oh, oh-oh-oh-oh
She got her head in the clouds
And she's not backin' down

This girl is on fire

Alicia Keys (performing "Girl on Fire")[99]

In the Navy

When I landed in counseling in Singapore to deal with my anger issues the second time, I observed the enormous gap between me and the normal clientele at the Singapore American Club. The counseling center was in the corner offices of the behemoth premises with an Olympic-sized pool, other sports facilities, and conference halls. When I panicked over my heart palpitations, they sent me to one of the best heart doctors in the country. Commander 'Dan's kids went to Singapore American School where the tuition was Ivy League prices. As military members overseas, we were often graced with the lives of the rich and famous even though we were not.

It was here, with my counselor, behind the Olympic pool and the chatter of kids from the water polo club with doting mothers drinking 10-dollar lattes, that I discovered the triggers of my angry outbursts.

When I was five years old, long before Thailand, I had a Kindergarten teacher, Mrs. Dubois, at Clementon Elementary School, who would physically abuse me in the bathroom attached to our classroom. I remember it being spacious to accommodate a wheelchair and having a chrome pressure nozzle to flush like a lot of public bathroom facilities. But what happened in there is completely locked out of my memory. Darkness. I just know the intense guilt I felt leaving it each time. She would force me to sit alone, away from all the other kids, because I talked too much. I had some issues with having accidents in my pants as well and was made to feel ashamed. Some of the parents had let on to my mother that there might be something wrong, but it never came fully to light. I ran into Mrs. Dubois at a wedding randomly before she passed away. She had me as her student her last year before retiring.

My mother had been sexually assaulted by a family friend and grew up, as well, as a young lady, under some very difficult circumstances. Her underlying anger issues really impacted my sister and me growing up. Today, instead of being angry at the butter dishes being thrown at us or the slamming doors, I see my mom as a warrior who has battled and mostly won the fight against her past. She has been my biggest cheerleader my whole life, and as I've had to deal with my own anger issues, we've been able to openly discuss a path to healing and grace.

My mother, my Kindergarten teacher, and my 4th and 5th grade teachers created a trigger inside. When I felt a woman in authority stepping on me, I lost control. When these Chiefs crossed a certain threshold, something inside of me snapped.

Two of my favorite people in all the world were my supervisors, both ET2's—Nikki Foster on the USS *Bulkely*, and Jen Vaughn in the backdrop in London. They would both go on to become Mustangs. Not the cars or the horses, but a rare jump from enlisted, blue-collar navy, to officer, the white-collar version. I had a woman in charge of me my whole damn Navy career. The ratio of men and women in the navy at the time was about 6 to 1,[100] and of course, thinned out considerably like all glass ceilings, the higher in rank. Along with Nikki, my division chief, and both division officers on the USS *Bulkely*, all women. Jen and Jodie, the kind pregnant woman who knows all my dark secrets, both in London. The two chiefs (the ones I screamed at), and Rear Admiral Nora Tyson of my unit in Singapore who went on to become the first woman to command a carrier strike group, the most potent naval formation in the Milky Way.[101] The Master Chief who lost her chance to Lee to take my virginity. All women.

God was either toying with me or had something very valuable to bring into my life. It gave me the opportunity to resolve the long-running trauma I experienced as a child.

Mafia II

When the raid took place, two of the girls, Jeil and Megz, were stripped of their passports and released back into Singapore, told by the authorities that they couldn't work legally in the country. The authorities provided no shelter or resources for them. They were crucial witnesses to the establishment's owner, who was being charged with human trafficking. I invited them to stay with me in my 1900 sq. ft. apartment. Jeil cooked ungodly delicious food, like the first time we met, and the girls would hang around and watch the Kardashians on my cable network I barely turned on. I was a gaming addict, after all, and didn't have time to watch TV. I hate TV, right, Nikki? I found the Kardashians to be fascinating and was soon sucked into their daily lives as well.

Five other Filipinos, all with legitimate work and visa status, were already staying with me, so there were seven or eight of us living there at one point.

Most of them have moved on to bigger and brighter things. Joel became a flight attendant and migrated to Canada. Lanie, his sister, returned to the Philippines. Marisol moved on to work in jewelry sales, and I bought my engagement ring and wedding bands from her at her workplace in Singapore. She eventually made it back to Cebu and got married and had kids. Ghia was on three cruises in a year with her husband. She was working at the second venue opened up by the owners of the Pasir Ris beachside bar and restaurant—the one that led me through the doors into the world of the Filipina mafia forever. While she was living with me, I had to chase away her drunk and jealous boyfriend gone awry one night. Alvin had a love of Kobe Bryant strewn all over the walls of his room in my home. He reunited with his wife and children to make a life in Singapore together. Many of their family and friends passed through my doors as they came to visit Singapore.

Another friend of mine, Trezzi, one of the originals, was our waitress the night my buddy Todd and my niece showed up in Pasir Ris. She had heart issues, and we spent the evening at the public hospital. The nurse who attended her and the doctor were both Filipinos who had escaped the Philippines to work in the shining city of Singapore. Trezzi's husband would eventually move to Singapore and become a chef, and Trezzi would become part of the crew of a cruise liner out of Scandinavia. They would both send money home to help take care of their daughter.

One infamous night, while I was home in the US, my neighbor's wife complained that people were throwing a party at my 1900 sq. ft. apartment in Sembawang on Halloween. This wasn't the case.

My Filipino cohort wore Halloween costumes, and two of them were smoking outside early in the morning after work. The Navy officer who lived next door called my supervisor and complained. The supervisor was shocked that I had people living with me. It was forbidden without authorization, and they had 24 hours to pack up and leave. I was especially worried about Jeil and Megz, as they had no work or safe place to go. There was another generous soul willing to let them stay in his place. I wondered aloud how Jeil and Megz knew about him but never asked. I didn't have much choice. I went to see them and met the man. He was a Singaporean, estranged from his Mongolian wife. He was very into football gambling and had two other Russian prostitutes living with him. I sat and watched *Fight Club* with the girls and left. Jeil had found part-time gigs and a husband through cleaning houses eventually. Unfortunately, that husband turned out to be abusive and felt threatened by Jeil's entrepreneurial and take-charge spirit.

Jeil's story is fascinating. She was a 'juicy' girl in a bar off the US Army base in S. Korea. A 'juicy girl' is basically the name for the bar girls that would get short-term gigs to 'entertain' US troops in their off time around Camp Humphrey's in Pyeongtek. She rose from 'juicy girl' to manager of juicy girls and even had the owner pay for her kidney removal when she needed surgery. With her enterprising mindset, she went to Singapore to try her hand and ended up in the wrong place—Paramount Plaza with Jen and Megz. She's a sister to me at this point. Despite our beginnings and her pawning the love of my life off for sex to avoid it—there aren't too many more people in this world that I trust more than her. She was in our wedding as a bridesmaid. Now, she runs a successful catering business in her hometown in Mindanao. I've threatened to bring her on board when I build my award-winning hotel and resort chain. Watch, folks. It will happen.

Jen would later admit to me that she not only had a little baby girl but also boys, ages 8 and 6. She had anticipated I'd disappear after she told me over a virtual call. She wrote out the letter and read it to me. She ended it by saying that she completely understood if I walked away.

How could I? Jen and the rest of the supporting cast abruptly halted my narrow, selfish, and myopic existence. It was as if a puzzle piece, missing and obscuring the full beauty of the picture beneath, had been dropped into place and explained to me what my life was meant to be.

I called my parents. The years of disappointing confessions and cries for help suddenly became an unsaid and powerful new direction. We all felt it.

Years before, as a teenager, I had recurring dreams of walking with a woman at the Chiang Mai zoo in Thailand. In 2013, I was walking alongside Jen with my hand tightly wrapped around my daughter Khenyz's hand, and my son JM was running off ahead to look at the elephants.

Meeting my wife in that dingy hellhole rescued me. I should have been a million miles from there. Those memories will never be erased and haunt me often. Rather than tucking them away in shame, I use them to make the world more aware of the massive gap between 'them' and us. And when I say 'them,' I'm referring to myself as well, the John in this story—the morally compromised Navy sailor with thin boundaries and a credit card that night.

When people ask me how I met my wife, it's awkward—more awkward than the question, "Where are you from?"

Be the Voice of Girls

With long dark hair to her waistline, thick eyebrows, and hazel skin linked to a shy smile from a 15-year-old girl wearing an American college jersey underneath an unbuttoned brown and white checkered long-sleeve shirt—she slid out the door as the program ended, her face added to the Mount Rushmore of faces chipped into the sides of my skull. Her name was Mehrigül.

During the program, Mirey, the program's coordinator, leaned forward and said to me in a low voice,

"You see the girl there in the brown jacket?" I nodded. "She spent two days underneath the rubble of her apartment with her dead mother before they rescued her."

I was back in Hatay again for the first time since an earthquake leveled large swathes of the province, including Iskenderun, where I saw, for the first time, cleared rubble and deserts of flat land with dirt piled on top of what used to be apartments crumpled like a wad of paper by the enormous force of a 7.9-magnitude quake only 50 miles below the surface (most are far below that). Large, abandoned complexes crumbled were still in view, with dangling metal frames warped out of place, draped randomly on the sides. When my bus arrived, I saw the tent cities and hundreds of little temporary shelters for businesses to continue to operate.

Mirey had to take over the *Be the Voice of Girls* program for Fatma when Fatma's apartment crumbled like a Lego set, taking her and her daughter, Alara, sleeping on the 12th floor, from us. We met for coffee before I reunited with the program's alumni for the first time since then. Mirey's words chopped open the cuts of grief I had for months after Fatma's death—grief that sent me into a mental tailspin while secluded in my apartment 750 km away in Isparta, forced to teach online due to the public dormitories being used for victims and their families. Tears fell, and my teeth clenched to keep from sobbing... again.

"Mike, we are not okay. It's one year past, and we act as though nothing happened, but there are times when I just stand there and ask myself why I'm still here, and she and others are not."

She gave me a full account of the events that day and the aftermath. She told me how they had put the wrong body in Fatma's grave, and her sister kept dreaming of Fatma, saying, "It's not me. It's not me." Time passed, and suddenly, a local official came to the family and told them that they had made a mistake. They had found Fatma's remains and put her to rest in peace.

We walked to the building where the classroom was. It was not a mere block from where I had first met Fatma, Alara, Deniz, and Cemre, now waiting for us on a distant shore of the next life. When we got to Iskenderun's shoreline, I could see that the buildings eerily had sunk about three feet into the ground, forcing all the businesses to install steps down into the first floor of the buildings that didn't collapse. They had been condemned by the government, but the owners, having no place to go, were still there. Because the whole shoreline was three feet further down, flooding could be seen on the main boulevard after a recent downpour. There was no easy way to fix it.

I was suddenly relieved that Mirey was willing to be so open about the events that were obviously so painful to talk about. It allowed me to express my emotions before walking into the classroom and revisiting the other precious faces, a bit less cute and a bit more beautiful now, etched into my brain.

Fatma Dodurka started the organization *Be the Voice of Girls* three years before. The US Embassy in Türkiye initially rejected her request to fund the BVG startup, but instead of giving up, she requested that they take another look. Roger Cohen, the diplomat overseeing educational programs sponsored by Uncle Sam in Türkiye, gave her another shot. While on my 26-city adventure, Roger would ask me to stop in and co-facilitate on a Saturday with Fatma and the second cohort of girls in her program.

BVG was a grassroots effort to bring art and English together to build and strengthen girls' push toward leadership in a Turkish society that hadn't always been kind to the fairer gender. The Hatay region was the southern curl extending south along the Mediterranean, almost entirely surrounded by Syria on the other side of the coastline. It was proudly diverse and welcoming to a lot of refugee resettlements.

I arrived the first time on a Saturday, January 7th, a month before the earthquake. I was early, so I wandered a bit along the waterside park across the boulevard from where I would eventually meet everyone. I could hear *Erik Dalı* playing faintly down at the pier, which could easily be seen in the clear, sunny morning air. I eventually wandered back to our venue for the afternoon. I stood inside on the base floor near the entrance to wait. I was guarded by three stained-glass peacocks on the outer glass double doors. At about 11 a.m., I was cajoled by Fatma's warm Turkish hug and high-pitched giggle. Her endearing laugh came with bright red lipstick and a nose that would make Janine proud. Alara, her daughter, with short hair, wearing a bohemian sailor cosplay outfit and painter's cap, stood by and briefly greeted me in a spotless American accent one would hear somewhere in the Midwest or on the evening news.

Fatma asked me if I'd eaten yet. I lied and said I had. I had accidentally booked my hotel 20 miles away at an almost deserted resort that looked under construction. I was glad I was on time.

We went up to the third floor, where the stadium seating classroom was, with a spacious front stage area. It was an established public education facility provided by the local government. It had an oversized lectern, as if a panel of three judges might preside over the events, in front of a picture of Kemal Atatürk emblazoned on the wall next to the Turkish flag. A stray cat greeted us at the top of the stairs, which would later curl up on my lap as I watched the morning procession take place.

A girl who looked like she grew up down the street from my wife approached me and said in perfect English.

"Hi, I hear you lived in the Philippines."

Her name was Althea, but I nicknamed her "Cornell" for the rest of the day after a discussion with her and other girls about what American university they hoped to attend someday. Her mom and she were full-blooded Filipinas. Her mother married a Turkish man, and they moved to Iskenderun because of his work.

The girls came prepared to give a fashion show, where they would take comments from the crowd after each one explained details of their outfits. Some came casual. Some came looking like they had just arrived from their 22nd-floor office suite, hijab to boot, owning the company inside. They were navigating the topic with little difficulty using phrases such as 'pencil skirt,' 'overdressed,' and 'from time to time.' From where I was sitting, it looked like Atatürk was impressed as well, presiding behind the lectern for three—As the girls paraded in with giggles on an imaginary catwalk to music played from someone's cellphone.

The girls all floated in over the next hour or so. I had prepared myself for a lot of translation for the event but realized that none was needed. They were all selected from various public middle schools and high schools by Fatma. Her criteria involved them having fledgling art skills. It didn't have to be drawing. It could be music or writing as well. They had to demonstrate a propensity for art and English together to be selected. They were divided up into working groups named after US cities and states.

They set up and organized a Q&A session to ask me questions about different art disciplines. The first group, New York, Deniz's group, fired questions at me about handicrafts. I claim regularly that I can talk about anything, and I, for about 90 seconds, proved to myself it was true. But when they got to the traditional handcraft question, I really had no clue what to say. I wasn't Thai, so I felt guilty claiming theirs, and as an American mongrel, I only had my mom's German sauerkraut to boast about. That was culinary arts.

The next group, Los Angeles, really set me up for failure by asking me what my favorite Turkish cuisine was. Thankfully, I had just come from Gaziantep, the food capital of the world. However, Hatay was very proud of their dishes, and I knew none of them. Mispronouncing the Antep soup, *beyran,* as *bayram,* got some long stares and giggles as well. *Bayram* is a word used for Muslim religious holidays. They rescued me from a pickle by asking me if I liked salt or sweets more. I love a good Kosher dill. The final question was what was my favorite American food, and I didn't feel like explaining my mom's chicken and broccoli dish for the sake of time, so I said pizza... mumbling afterward that pizza is not originally American. It's Italian...

Utah asked me where I found inspiration to draw. Because I don't draw, I decided to change their question a bit from 'draw' to 'write'... and without pause, I said,

"I find inspiration through people like yourselves."

"Why do you write?"

"I write because I want people to see the world from a different perspective. I want people to learn something that may help us get along better and make the world a safer and better place."

Fist pump in the air. Giggles and laughs. I was in.

"When did you start writing?"

"I started writing when I was in third grade, but I never had the confidence to publish or open myself up to critique."

The final group, 'Ohio,' which included Althea, Alara, and Cemre, asked me about design. This was a nice segue into the activity I was supposed to lead in the latter part of the program. Fatma had asked me to help her students 'design' their own careers.

Deniz rattled on excitedly about how she didn't know if she wanted to be a poet or an astronaut. I felt like she and her group had already brought me to another world.

Afterward, Fatma and I sat and walked along the shores of Iskenderun, where I had been before things got rolling. She talked about how she wanted *Be the Voice of Girls* to go international. She also told me about losing her husband two years before, leaving Alara without a father.

After a huge seafood dinner, Fatma took me to see her brother at 11 p.m. so he could show me how to make the world-famous dessert of Hatay, *künefe*. I videoed the whole thing. He told me in Turkish while she translated. You could hear her high-pitched laugh throughout.

Eventually, we made it to her house in Kırıkhan. Sprawled out all over the living room was the artwork of the girls—various winter scenes with snow and landscape, an explosion of their expression and talent all over the place.

The next morning, Fatma and I had coffee and tea biscuits and talked seriously about her next step. The co-founder of BVG, Carl, an American who had lived in Türkiye for 18 years, had invited her and Alara to the US. He was an integral part of getting the girls' virtual team of educators together. They already had an appointment to get their visa paperwork approved at the US Embassy in Ankara. She asked me about the book I was writing. I told her it was a memoir of my life, having lived in eight countries and the amazing journey it has been. Most importantly, it was about the people who became friends from all corners of the planet.

She wanted the world to know how she was able to take a disparate group of teenage girls from different backgrounds and build unity, confidence, and everything and more that I witnessed until my very last day in Türkiye from those girls—forever monuments of memories in my mind. She fretted about English being her second language and being critiqued. I reassured her that when it comes to writing, there will always be someone who will disagree or criticize, and publishing is more than writing. It was about bringing people who resonate with your message together into the world spelled out in your pages.

That was the last time I saw her outside our midyear conference in Antalya. Fatma and her daughter Alara had recently moved from Kırıkhan, Hatay, to a 12-floor condominium called the Rönesans Rezidans in Antakya to be closer to Alara's art school. Infamously, the builder was caught in the aftermath of the earthquake trying to escape, making the building the center of the Turkish fury toward the rank corruption in the construction industry in a country where there is not one inch of territory outside a seismic zone prone to earthquakes.[102]

Deniz, our future astronaut, along with Fatma and the rest of the girls, piloted me to heaven. I hear Deniz still, reciting poetry in my dreams. I wake up sad.

Afghanistan

My head started to spin. My breathing felt heavy. I looked at my online students and immediately told them I needed to take a break.

I had just read the gruesome details of the botched pullout in Afghanistan by the US military on August 30th, 2021. The Biden administration was writing poetry with the symbolism of pulling out before the 20th anniversary of 9/11—instead of dealing with the gritty details of a safe and secure transition. It was infuriating.[103]

I had shortness of breath and tears streaming down my face. I had endured the humiliation of getting asked to leave the Navy. I had endured the thousands of us coming home with mental illnesses and missing limbs. I endured the gaping hole left in my heart after the war in Iraq that cost untold lives of Iraqis and billions of US dollars for naught.

I had endured my service and all its disappointment, serving in the US Navy from August 11th, 1999, to July 2011, holding on to the one nugget that because we had chased the Taliban out, girls could go to school and get jobs—rather than raped and kidnapped into forced marriages under the Taliban regime.

I watched the botched pullout in horror. The Taliban had reached Kabul before the US could get out. The writing was on the wall long before then, but I and the most extraordinary intelligence and military machinery in history were blindsided. They were so blindsided that when they attempted to retaliate for a suicide bombing at the airport in the final moments, they dropped a drone strike on an NGO's family, killing seven children.[104] The Biden administration said nothing. Generals were left to quietly admit fault.

I watched the live coverage of Joe Biden's speech. I shook my fist at him. He said that we weren't in the nation-building business and we had completed our mission to avenge 9/11 by stopping al-Qaeda and neutralizing the mastermind, Osama bin Laden.

He was right. The truth was that the last 20 years were largely a failed operation. It was the story of two completely different worlds—like my ride to work in Makati. Seventy percent of Afghans lived in rural areas. Most Afghans weren't reaping many benefits outside Kabul and other large cities to the north during the longest conflict in US military history.[105]

A long-form article in the *New Yorker* by Anand Gopal, called 'The Other Afghan Women,' helped me deal with my cognitive dissonance regarding my military service and the plight of Afghans in the bigger picture of history.[106] It was written from the perspective of a woman who saw all three invasions take place in the Sangin Valley in Helmand Province in southern Afghanistan. It spells out the ridiculous restraints put on women long before the Taliban had arrived. The Soviets, too, had brought education to women, largely rejected by the conservative society of the times. The Mujahideen, allied with the US to defeat the communists, had slit the throats of public officials in favor of women's education.

The investigative journalism from Gopal digs deeply into the mistakes of the international coalition forces led by the US in Helmand province and other similar places, where the wars were fought most fiercely, and how this convinced many to abandon them for the Taliban to bring peace. She lost 16 family members to coalition forces, and their house had been blown up by US special forces. Afghan forces would indiscriminately kill innocent people, while the US would turn a blind eye or be culpable themselves. The Afghans in power had no regard for those living in the disparate parts of the country. The allowing of women to find education or other human rights was largely ignored in most of the country. The difference now was that what little support they did have was gone, as Western aid and NGOs funding the education efforts didn't exist. But how different was the Taliban from the interlopers for most of the country?

While in Türkiye, I came across a young lady named Robina Azizi on social media. She's from Afghanistan. When Robina and I met online, she was 18. When I reached out to her, she immediately called me. We talked for over an hour, crying and laughing together. She leads an organization called *Girls in the Path of Change*. In their first year of existence, she had 600 or so girls secretly attending online education courses of some kind. She leads as a refugee. Her family had to illegally cross into Pakistan and live in asylum because her brother and sister are investigative journalists wanted by the Taliban. Germany answered her family's pleas for protection.

On my way to a conference in Lille, France, I was able to visit her and her famous sister in Bonn for a drink before they had to return to the camp before curfew. I worked with my growing network to find someone who could provide her with the means to finish high school. That was the first step of many to come.

On GPC's first anniversary, I had the BVG girls (*Be the Voice of Girls*) together with my colleague who taught in Ankara. We recorded their well wishes and congratulations.

I'm okay with the nugget that kept me sane during my time in the military. As inaccurate a reflection as it was, it was a glimpse into my aspirations for the future.

Chapter Thirteen

Can We Love & Relate in a Polarized World?

I want to leave a legacy,
How will they remember me?
Did I choose to love?
Did I point to You enough?
To make a mark on things

Nichole Nordeman (performing "Legacy")[107]

Claradise

I don't watch many films, but a film that always gets me thinking about unchecked technological innovation is the crime action thriller *Surrogates*, starring Bruce Willis.[108] In the movie, people lie in beds while rocking the world in robotic, human-like bodies. They get all the pleasures of being human but as robots. Spoiler Alert! It requires the protagonist (Bruce Willis) to give up being in his body for moments to solve the crime, as the antagonist has figured out how to kill people in their beds by electrocuting their "surrogate" bodies remotely.

This is to say that today, technology is creating 'superhuman' versions of ourselves as we lie in bed doing nothing. We appear to be entering worlds, battling enemies—whether political enemies on Twitter or just another team of online players in a plethora of popular titles. And no, it's not just teenage boys anymore—everyone has jumped in. These games started when I was a teenager, and we are still playing them. These worlds have only become richer and more exciting.

In 2022, there was outrage in the news when it was discovered that Susan Gibson, a politician running for election in the state of Virginia, was streaming live sex shows on a site called Chatterbate.[109] Her audience would watch and pay for private shows, tipping with tokens to initiate an ever-revealing or intense timeline of sexual activities, promising a climax at the end to keep lurkers and tippers glued to her portal. I wasn't outraged. I wasn't shaking my head, asking, "How could she?" I knew the world she had entered.

I don't remember how it started, but there was a young lady by the name of Clara (not her real name). She was Asian American, and she had an array of kawaii (かわいい) and provocative things we could tip for. But mostly, she was engaging. She loved to talk to those in her "room" and built personal relationships with us. After her show, she'd hang out, sometimes naked, sometimes not, to talk about life. She was funny and honest. She treated regular attendees kindly and even answered questions from those who hadn't spent money on her. Each visitor had a color designation based on the number of tokens in their account, which told Clara and other performers who to pay attention to. But she would entertain all of us, as long as we were polite.

One night, she'd give career advice; on another, relationship or financial advice. She was a cerebral young lady who would undress for a price, masturbate, or expose her most private parts as prescribed by her directory of services—20 tokens for saying "I love you, [insert name]"; 100 tokens to slap her butt. You tipped, you got it. She even had a guitar and would sing songs or allow playlist requests during the 6 to 8 hours she spent online each night.

She would talk about her life, her family, and how she first got started. In the beginning, she lied to her father, telling him she started a makeup artist channel, hiding her sex toys in her room. Eventually, she made so much money she could move out and get her own spacious condo in California.

Each night was a different adventure. Regular customers often became her moderators. Some moderators got paid, but some of hers just loved her. Moderators were directed to kick out rude or demanding viewers. She had no mercy on those without social graces. We were thrilled to hang on to our lives in her chat channel and watch her brashly dispose of thrill-seekers imposing their wants over hers. She was the queen of her world. We loved Clara.

I massaged my searing conscience by telling myself her content was somehow better than others on the platform, and by paying homage to her, I was endorsing "cleaner" fun. The focus for me was Clara, not so much sex—at least, that's what I convinced myself. I was hooked, but I refused to drop tokens for sexual acts. That was my red line. I eventually paid to be a regular so that when we entered, we were recognized as part of her fan club. I even subscribed to her Patreon page.

The more I learned about her, the more uncomfortable I became with the sexual aspects of the show. I got more and more uncomfortable seeing her perform sexual acts, so I would click off the browser tab when she performed and come back for the aftermath and social engagement. You would see an enormous drop-off of viewers, but I hung around, enamored by her conversations. Surely, that would stave off the nagging conscience screaming at me that this had to stop.

On weekdays, after work, I knew I had only an hour left to see her, and I'd find a remote place in the Gangnam bus station in Seoul, beside the Boots drugstore, to watch until she said goodnight. I'd get on the train and go home. Rinse and repeat all the way through my training for my new job.

She had a Discord channel dedicated to her called "Claradise." I started building relationships with people who subscribed to her channel. We'd have discussions, talk about life or games. She would join voice channels and play *League of Legends* with her fans. I would tell them about my life in Korea, and they would talk about their jobs too. There were memes, bits, and running jokes on certain members. She was an instigator and made it all the more fun. It was as if there was no sex at all at times, but everyone knew, in the back of their minds, why they were all there. No one goes on Chatterbate to make friends—only.

Many men vied to outdo each other by spending money on her. I mean *money*. I would see guys drop ten grand at one time regularly. There was a contest one night: one group of men tipped for her to keep her clothes on, and the other group tipped for her to take them off. A guy spent 25K USD for her to keep them off for the rest of the night. No sex. No toys. Unreal. There were milestone rewards for the biggest tippers decorating her bio. The men and women (yes, one of her biggest fans was a college-aged girl who eventually became a moderator) on the list had the pride and envy of others.

Clara was taking over my life. Ask me what was going on in my wife's life or my kids' lives at the time. At church? It dimmed in comparison to *Claradise*. I was in Korea with nagging loneliness. It was an escape from the perpetuating pain of not being home with my family in the Philippines. It was an escape from the nagging inadequacy I felt in my new job.

I can't remember if there was any significant moment when this ended. I remember realizing that it was a lie to say we "supported" Clara. No, it was all about us. Not her. I had been heavily involved in helping young people my whole life, and suddenly, I saw her in that light. She was a 20-something young lady who needed a real life. This was not one. Not a sustainable one. As much as it was a fantasy for us, it was for her as well. This had implications for her personal dating life, sexual health, and psychology. I couldn't ignore that any longer. I had to escape *Claradise*.

I wrote her a long message on Patreon explaining why I was dropping my subscription. I thanked her for the memories but told her I wanted more for her and couldn't continue supporting her in this way. I told her that someday I wished we could meet in the real world and have coffee and talk about real things... outside of *Claradise*. Know her real name, see her pursue real relationships. Have a boring or exciting career. A spouse and children if she wanted them... anything but this.

I've a thousand times decided against it, then found the courage to go for it. Back and forth, I've struggled, knowing my children may read this. My wife will know details I've never shared with her. "See a therapist, Mike. It's a private matter." Yes, but no. It's a silent matter for millions of people, and it has no end.

I'd love to say that was my last time on Chatterbate, but this is why I'm discussing it with you today. In a swift five minutes, I could be back at any time. The barriers to these worlds are thinner than ever. The country's government blocks the site? No problem, there are VPNs.

Fraudsters, cybersex rings, Tinder—all of these capitalize on our base desires, especially men. I talked to someone in the online dating industry, and it's all the same. It's a constant 24-hour ladies' night where the drinks are free for the ladies, and the men pay much more.[110] Ask an executive from Tinder, and they'll tell you exactly that. I get fraud messages on WhatsApp, Instagram, and my phone number at least once daily. I'm a 40-year-old white man and probably represent the culmination of sexual frustration and financial success in the Western world. We are constant targets. No one sees us as victims at all. We don't capture the imagination as such. We are often portrayed as the perpetrators and villains with our white man power all over the world. Surely it's okay if they take our money online, right? Add rich Asian men to that story, and we've pretty much covered all the villains. Yes?

Sports betting, in my opinion, might be worse. Exciting, unpredictable, but predictably producing euphoria and pulsing excitement that peaks to edge out the negative emotions caused by our daily lives. The only way to get back there is to do it again. And again. And again. Like a drug, it loses its vigor, thus asking for more intensity, brought on by greater stakes, more money, or more bizarre and dangerous activities.

Role-playing games, for example, are super popular, involving taking on a character in a world of fantasy. Based on the roll of the dice, certain skills are utilized to kill dragons, acquire special armor, and level up the character to go on and face more adventure. The massive multiplayer online (MMO)/RPG world brought whole communities of people onto a computer server to then act out their fantasies together. *World of Warcraft* put me in the wrong lane one day on my way to work because of my sleepless nights injecting endorphins, dopamine, and serotonin into my bloodstream in my mid-twenties. The creation of these worlds was a massive undertaking, but due to their popularity, it was worth the investment. The profits have made these fledgling software studios billion-dollar entertainment multinationals. What once couldn't possibly compete with cable TV or pay-per-view now has soccer moms ignoring their kids to play *Candy Crush* on the bleachers.

Take this world, then, and add flesh and blood. Replace dragons with women, replace swords and armor with real pleasure-producing devices in sensitive areas, and allow men to directly connect their credit cards to those devices to initiate a sexual response—thus providing stimuli for men and women to gratify themselves through masturbation.

Another world, like RPGs, a fiction romance novel, or a TV series. We enter other worlds for pleasure all the time. We are self-seeking, whether we are watching a highly-rated TV series on Apple TV or perusing Chatterbate for our niche sexual fantasy. Technology allows us to do that. Technology has more easily than ever created avenues of destruction. The destruction of our sexual lives, our marriages, and our commitment to our children—sucking all resources into cyberspace and lining the pockets of stakeholders of these fantasy enterprises.

That's the crux of the problem! This fascination pulls our focus away from the real world and the actual needs around us. I just finished over two hundred pages or so talking about it. I represent the 1st world, the top of Maslow's hierarchy of needs. We have education and resources at our disposal. What will our legacy be?

I have discussed the people I've met all over the world. I didn't meet them on Chatterbate—not to say that those people don't have needs and aren't important, but in venues like theirs and places like Paramount and Heaven with my wife and Susanna, respectively, we now have both arms tied behind our backs to do anything about them.

REFLECTION

Drugs seem to capture the imagination of Hollywood, politicians, and society alike, but I hardly think they are among the worst vices in 2024. Digitally laced cocaine comes in many forms. Slot machines are all digital now. Sex, of course, as described in intimate detail. The number of gamers and doom-scroll Tiktokers wrapped up in another world leaves few to care for immigrants, the poor, or policy-shaping in West Africa.

What has captured your imagination, preventing you from moving further to get involved with real people? What wormholes have potentially hijacked a large portion of your life and resources? It could be something fairly innocuous, like porcelain owls. It really depends on what impact it has on your ability to love and relate to others in the world you live in and beyond.

Barriers to Entry

Remember Lee from Angel Witch? The one throwing ping pong balls at us, and who took my virginity? One of our outings, not mentioned before, was to the beach. Reminiscent of my time growing up as a missionary kid, I told her I wanted to hang out on Jomtien Beach as I did as a child and write my economics paper due the following week in one of my online college classes. Jomtien Beach had changed a lot since the last time I saw it, circa 1995; it was 2008. There were condominiums and hotels lined up, replacing the quiet confines of the jungle beach resorts from over 20 years before.

While we were on the beach, suddenly, we were accosted by a sea of vendors selling—everything. There were men with full-on pieces of furniture, carrying a small teak coffee table on their shoulders and photo books full of pictures of their other wares down the road. We had massage therapists, pedicurists, and an endless array of food vendors, flowerists, you name it, it was presented to us. We settled on *moo ping* (หมูปิ้ง), with *khao niaow* (ข้าวเหนียว) and *som tam* (ส้มตำ), along with lots of seasonal fruit like rambutan or *ngaw* (เงาะ).

It was quite annoying to be pestered every other minute. On the beach, there were no walls, no barriers keeping vendors from plying cash-laden foreigners looking for a sunny adventure on the seasides, an hour bus ride away from the world's number one red-eye destination—Bangkok.

Cheap transportation, the economic gap between rich and poor, and technology brought the barriers down. It brought these girls from the poorest parts of Thailand to work in the bars and sell their bodies for money to feed their families back home. International destinations, such as Bangkok, Singapore, Hong Kong, and Kuala Lumpur, were hubs with redlight districts dotting their cityscape. The customers could fly relatively cheaply from their centers of prosperity to these beaches and not only get a tan and some souvenirs but indulge in their sexual desires to boot. Locals and crime networks alike saw the opportunity to make money, organizing travel and advertising on the World Wide Web, which was absorbing the world's investment dollars at a breathtaking rate. Just like the vendors on the beach, there was very little between us and them anymore. No walls could prevent the flow of information thanks to personal computers and, in the last 20 years, smart mobile devices and wireless infrastructure.

Work, of course, had brought me to Pattaya that week. I was working with the Royal Thai Navy and helping build military relationships in the region to counter the outward expansion of China's reach into Southeast Asia. When I flew home to Singapore, Lee messaged me a week later, asking me to help with her finances. With the help of Kaelira (from Joplin), who spoke Thai fluently, she translated a letter I sent after sending money once via Western Union. I wanted Lee to know that I was ashamed of using her for my pleasure. I wanted her to know that these unstoppable forces of economics and technology were no excuse for my actions. For her, this might have been routine. My letter may have been received with disappointment. I don't know. I have no idea how many men she was writing to—men who casually kept in touch, hoping to possibly return for more fun or, like me, just feeling guilty after leaving her 800 dollars poorer and no longer a virgin.

In the early 2000s, when I was stationed in the Navy in London, England, I was bored, perusing the web on duty (the place where I confessed to Jodie, etc.). I found these sites that connected Western men with Eastern European women, especially from the former Soviet bloc. These services were like any modern dating site or adult 'dating' site in that you would scroll through pages and pages of women supposedly looking for love and companionship, but most likely mainly looking for someone to care for them and get them out of their dire economic plight, especially if they had children. To connect with them, you had to, of course, pay money for tokens to send well wishes or express interest in them.

They would write back. I would immediately notice the tone and writing changes in the translation of the letter. The beginning of the letter would sound sincere, and then it was as if someone else was dropping obvious paragraphs in the middle advertising a desire for a romantic relationship. I found it a turn-off and suspected something awry, but I pressed on. I surfed the Internet for some information others might have on it and found a lawyer who knew about the industry in great detail. He had a free site and blog, and it talked about how these sites were overtaken by organized crime. The women, on one end, were probably innocent, but the bait letters were not and were designed to lead unsuspecting lonely hearts astray. They siphoned the pockets of unsuspecting, normally middle-aged divorced men and myself of our money. I remember my parents receiving a full-on brochure from Anastasia.com with sexily clad young ladies on the cover, inviting men on a meetup tour in Moscow and Odessa to 'date' and find a 'mate.'

Embarrassing, for sure, that my parents got wind of this, but what I discovered on the other end of this was the world of prostitution, human trafficking, and everything in between. My sister sent me a book called *The Natasha's* by an investigative journalist named Victor Malarek.[111] It spelled out some of the issues specifically in the Balkans, but certainly not isolated to it. Much of it involved UN troops, even Americans, either directly involved or turning a blind eye to it. A good movie to watch in this regard is *The Whistleblower* (2010), directed by Larysa Kondracki.[112]

While in London, you would walk up to their iconic red phone booths and see them covered in shiny call numbers brochures for escort/adult services. I'm not suggesting that all of these ladies were trafficked, but my eyes were opened forever to a world of women who, for economic reasons, were willing to compromise their safety and sexual health and trust total strangers to find them money.

Along with the Christian books Jen discovered, a growing volume of books on my bookshelf unearthed this universe. I started to learn more about people's migration, how this directly impacted the trade, and why it needed to be stopped.

Women aren't cigarettes. There is no price on our bodies. Ask my Black American friends about that. No amount of pragmatism should put our bodies on the market. What if we regulate prostitution like in Amsterdam, you might ask. Have you been there? Have you been to Canal Street? I have. The person I was with, a Dutchman, told me, "Mike, I won't say anything if you want an hour with someone."

Waves and waves of men from all over the world were coming to have their crack at their fleshly fantasies. It's rather horrifying that we need organized groups to "protect" the rights of sex workers to raise their wages and provide free medical care. This completely ignores the reality of a global market without borders that drives human slavery. As economics nerds, we call it the "race to the bottom" as the barriers to entry drop—the cheapest wages possible to get the product desired. If you commoditize a woman's body, then men will be racing to find the cheapest place to get it. Thai women were servicing scores of men a week in Singapore for 20 dollars a pop. Lee and Min in Pattaya and Phuket were "lucky" to get one customer per week. The US intelligence reports that siphoned through my communications spaces were available for me to read, and they said as such, and much, much more.

Taken captured the imagination of millions regarding the kidnapping of an ex-CIA agent's daughter and how he (played by Liam Neeson) kicks their ass.[113] From Suzanna to Clara, they are all along a very long spectrum with the extremes of under duress/kidnapping on drugs like in movies like *Taken* (2008) or completely doing it out of their own free will, as many sex worker rights advocates suggest is possible. Even to this day, I don't like the movie because it does not portray accurately the complexities involved.

Many choose to be there—Clara included, within the safe confines of anonymity and her large California life—but they shouldn't be. No one has a daughter in this life and hopes they will end up in Clara's or my wife's shoes.

Kidnapping and murder provide the proper 'shock' entertainment necessary to bring excitement back into our dull lives. They draw a very unimaginative straight line in the decision-making process for all involved, including the 'Johns' like myself. In a polarized world, that is convenient storytelling beset by an agenda. This hurts the chances of providing the proper help to all involved: Johns, sellers, and those whose bodies have become the product.

With the myriad of distractions, Lee, the best food on the planet, and a vendor every 45.6 seconds, I didn't write a line for my economics paper there on the beach. But by the time I turned it in, it was a start to telling my story, and these girls' stories, and what we should all be doing about it.

My eventual demise should be a warning. What started innocently—going to 'Heaven' intoxicated, rubbing a woman's feet surrounded by topless women on a catwalk—became much more. I would self-righteously and ignorantly be satisfied saying I didn't pay for sex while watching some of my married colleagues indulge and hearing exciting stories in Malta of shipmates visiting Russians in a secret brothel with removable stairs to prevent unpaying customers and girls from escaping.

On a different deployment, my ship pulled into Dubai, and we all ended up at a hotel basement club. There were Russian singers and Filipina wait staff, and apparently, I was going to get kicked out for repeatedly asking (I was super drunk) if they were trafficked and coerced into working there. My supervisor reined me in and promised the attendants that I would behave for the rest of the night. On a humorous note, I also told an Indian man and a Pakistani in that same basement club how wonderful it was that they were sitting at the same table, talking and sharing a drink.

On another occasion in the same city, we ended up at a club, and suddenly, a van load of women, mostly racially Black, swarmed in. I was very drunk and was dancing with one of them, and she whispered in my ear that I could take her around back for $100. In my drunken stupor, I asked my shipmate for $100, and of course, they refused, and we all went home.

My proud naivety was gone after that. The incident felt small, but the shame wasn't. The reality is that these women were most likely trafficked in from parts of the African continent, and I was $100 of cash away from using them for sex. Not rubbing their feet, not asking them to put their top back on, not talking to them about their lives. Not receiving letters from them, hijacked by the Russian mob, but straight-up—in the alleyway, disgustingly exposed, and using a woman for sex.

REFLECTION

Early on in my story, you found some of us, like my shipmate and me, in rehab with very thin boundaries. Boundaries are important. They help sound off an internal alarm, telling us we might be headed in the wrong direction. Of course, this book is about taking risks, but not risks that exploit others or leave us in a position to be exploited.

I don't expect all my readers to have quite the journey I've had, but many of you lack healthy boundaries that have led to serious regrets, financial mayhem, and being used or using others. I prefer the example of drinking buddies. Often, they are only your buddies when you drink. You are all mutually doing what my shipmate explained to me in the unsaid rules—drinking as much as possible while avoiding becoming a burden to others—which is a complete lie. Have you ever been the designated driver on nights with your friends? It's annoying. Just like me in Jen's bar with no alcohol. Suddenly, you can see everything. Having boundaries is the same. Suddenly, instead of being forced to take a sip when it's your turn, you can comfortably take back control of your decision-making process.

What are your activities amounting to these days? Are they purely self-seeking, or do they have a larger and more noble task? Do you find yourself doing things merely because others are doing them, and you feel silly taking a step back and going it alone?

Along with GPC in Afghanistan and BVG in Türkiye, I support a growing number of little girls around the world in the poorest countries: Lebanon, Haiti, El Salvador, Nepal, and Uganda. I support them because I want to increase their chances of succeeding in a world that has not valued women as they should. I know. I live with sadness and regret about my past each day. But as I kindly reminded a postmortem Tupac, it doesn't have to stay that way.

In what ways can you 'be the change we want to see in the world'? I love that cliché! Do we see the needs out there? Take a look. Don't allow your shame or guilt about your past to keep you from making the necessary changes in a world so divided. Don't wait around for perfection to arrive, and definitely don't wait around for the approval of others. That's what got me in this mess!

Africa

"What country, do you think, experienced the bloodiest conflict in 2022?"

"Ukraine."

It was a classroom full of Turks. The Palestinian conflict had just reopened its 70-year-old wound once again, and a bunch of protests in Türkiye had canceled some of my events out of fears of reprisal against Americans and their support for Israel.

"Nope. Ethiopia .. by about 2x the casualties."

Silence in the room.

The Tigrays, the Ethiopian government, and its allies were at it again, causing immense human suffering.[114]

"Why do you think I stand here in front of you today feeling safe?"

"Because we love you, Hocam."

"Exactly. We know each other. You know who I am."

I've had the pleasure of making wonderful friends from Nigeria, Ghana, Tunisia, Egypt, South Africa, and Uganda, but I've never actually set foot on the African continent. I did date a beautiful young lady who thought it was a country and couldn't point to it on a map.

Prior to the outbreak of war in Israel, I was meeting a South African friend of Irish and Greek descent in Istanbul, and we were enjoying a ferry ride on the Bosphorus. At our table were two young racially Black couples dressed up for an elegant night out. The two gentlemen were from Djibouti, and their dates were from Rwanda and Burundi, respectively. These folks were young entrepreneurs in the construction industry. They all spoke French and English fluently, and they were a mismatch to Gerts and me, dressed up to lounge around a house or look homeless. Gerts spoke a bit of French and decided to put himself out there.

One of the young ladies was explaining to me in great detail the culture of Türkiye and why it has such an advanced construction industry. This helped explain the public outcry and fury over the collapse of Fatma's high-rise and many others during the earthquake. The four of them were in the construction industry as engineers.

But I had an itching question to ask them: how were they treated in Türkiye? Were they treated based on the lifestyle they had earned as successful entrepreneurs, or were they viewed as poor immigrants because of the color of their skin?

The most outspoken gentleman answered. He talked about how stilted people are because they don't live outside the world they come from. He explained that this phenomenon was as true back in Djibouti as it was anywhere else in the world. It's typical for people to be extremely suspicious of others who are different. He said that is an experience they've had all over the world. He doesn't really blame them because, in many cases, the stigma or stereotype is true for many people back in his own country.

This was a very enlightening way of looking at life—not through the lens of how people treat you, but through the backstory that leads them to treat you that way. What contributes to the suspicion, bias, and, unfortunately, excuses for outright racism that people experience all over the world? It's the distance between our worlds. When we don't have any other information to go on, their reality is not ours. Media and like-minded communities reinforce those stereotypes, creating a simplistic reconciliation in our minds.

My new friend from Djibouti was very right. Not six months later, I'd be sitting along the shoreline of the Bosphorus with another African friend of mine from Egypt, asking me if Türkiye was an excellent country to emigrate to. I worried openly about people associating him with some of the Eastern neighbors like Syria and Iraq—not that there is anything wrong with them, but Turks often feel forced to accept them as refugees, and in terrible economic times, that has become a souring point for them.[115] Sound familiar? Yeah. If you're an American, this debate also rages on in our political sentiments. My friend spoke Arabic, and that night, I walked with him to the mosque so he could pray. He was well educated and talented, just like his Black African counterparts I spoke to on the ferry, but based on someone's lack of knowledge and distance culturally, combined with fear, he could be treated as unwelcome.

My young friend Bee had lived in Nigeria with a Muslim father and Christian mother until she was a young teenager and then moved to America. She was constantly berated for not being 'Black' enough as an American and insisted on calling herself a Nigerian American to safely explain why she was different. She experienced prejudice despite not looking any different than them. Ntšali, a racially Black friend from South Africa, experienced something similar. Her parents hailed from Lesotho, the little autonomous region in the middle, but she grew up going, soon after apartheid, to an almost all-white girls school. She went from that to moving across the country to go to college in the midst of a mostly racially Black community, but she didn't speak their language, and it was often assumed she did because of her skin color.

My Korean friends would often insist on showing me the latest viral video of Black-on-Asian crime. I don't really like watching violence in general, not even an Avengers movie anymore, but these viral videos and associated communities were confirmation bias that Black folks are going out of their way to hate Asians. My students working for Hyundai gave me some insight into why. I was teaching well-educated executives and engineers, and they all have very clear images of the LA riots in the 1990s—the beating of Rodney King by a bunch of white police officers. They don't focus on that. During the riots, angry Black protesters burned down the middle-class businesses of many Asians, including Koreans, for no reason whatsoever. The focus became multi-generational. It was a common fixation from then on that Black folks couldn't be trusted. I then went to look at hate crime statistics, and Black-on-Asian hate crimes barely registered compared to white-on-Asian crimes.[116] When I showed them these stats, they were quickly dismissed because those 'stats' created a disturbing counter-narrative to the ones they heard growing up.

The sobering reality is that news channels are quite adept. Social media companies are even more adept. Quite competent. They are curating news or providing algorithms that will get people to sit longer and click more, and it doesn't involve Ethiopia, Sudan, or Burkina Faso. For every George Floyd (may he rest in peace) in America that gets national or world coverage, there are thousands that have similar skin color, whose cries and pleas go unheard. It's a conundrum that keeps me up at night at times. Why is the Dark Continent still dark?

Unfortunately, the answer is easy. We don't have an imagination the further people are from our reach. We can accurately claim we aren't racist and believe in our hearts that all people deserve human dignity and respect, but if we don't know them, it becomes much harder to tangibly empathize.

Even the billions we drop in aid in Africa and globally have limitations in arousing care. Having grown up around NGO work and fundraising events, I am more than familiar with our financial systems that allow people who "care" to efficiently swipe a card and walk away with a shiny brochure and a monthly reminder and newsletter that may or may not be opened. If we aren't interacting on a social plane, however, then it becomes much more difficult for them to enter our minds at all—well, enter our minds in a way that doesn't excite our fears or enter into a means of exploitation that plagued my early years as a sailor.

Don't get me wrong. Having like-mindedness is not a sin. Feeling a sense of affinity with people similar to us is pretty natural. Ukrainians have a similar language and history to Russians, so it's not merely sharing culture or race that will bring about peace or community. It causes a great amount of distress as well, as we have seen in Ethiopia. Europeans know all too well, having fought wars denoted in decades, such as the Thirty Years War or the Hundred Years War. Progress has been made in Europe on all accounts. It's under strain, but certainly not the chaos it was in 1939.

Conquest looks different in 2024, and unfortunately, the same, as we see drone warfare, mines, and artillery battles in Ukraine maim and kill thousands. But now, economic conquests have become the norm in a shrinking planet, and they have now entered a digital sphere as giant behemoths of Silicon Valley and the Chinese disruptor TikTok seek to conquer the views and clicks of the world—bombarding us with targeted advertising. The battlefield entered our homes. We don't need to leave our homes to order to our hearts' content because of delivery apps and e-commerce. Legacy companies in finance, hunting for natural resources, and manufacturing are all still just as powerful, if not more. Just because our world has shrunk due to the digital transformation hasn't changed the essential components of human needs and wants. Sovereign wealth funds sitting on the world's most valuable resources have diversified their portfolios to include the growth of the digital space.

When I see these retirement cities being built in Florida, where people can wake up around other retirees and experience *Groundhog Day* to their hearts' content with golf, softball, and drinks by the pool, it makes me cringe. The wealth that gives us the ability to reach further than others is squandered, utilized to build fortresses from even our own families if we want to.

Martin Kimani, the UN representative of Kenya, during the emergency Security Council meeting on February 21, 2022, in response to Russia's invasion of Ukraine, said this:

"Kenya, and almost every African country, was birthed by the ending of empire. Our borders were not of our own drawing. They were drawn in the distant colonial metropoles of London, Paris, and Lisbon with no regard for the ancient nations that they cleaved apart. Today, across the border of every single African country live our countrymen with whom we share deep historical, cultural, and linguistic bonds. At independence, had we chosen to pursue states on the basis of ethnic, racial, or religious homogeneity, we would still be waging bloody wars these many decades later. Instead, we agreed that we would settle for the borders that we inherited. But we would still pursue continental political, economic, and legal integration.

Rather than form nations that looked ever backward into history with a dangerous nostalgia, we chose to look forward to a greatness none of our many nations and peoples had ever known."[117]

As the world falters and succumbs to tunnel vision each time Israel has a violent spat with its neighbors, we don't talk enough about the progress other countries have made—or model conflict resolution after them. Israel, take heed.

I echo Ambassador Kimani's words, but more so, I think we should reevaluate 'greatness.' In the same vein as Emma Lazarus and her hallowed words on Miss Liberty, greatness can look very different with an imagination further than conquest, whether political or material.

It's a shame we don't often see things the way my friend from Djibouti does—through their life experiences rather than through the narrow lenses of color, accent, or lifestyle. It's a shame we can't be more patient in understanding why people have the inclinations they do. In our daily lives, we have our 'borders' drawn up for us. We have to contend with the world we've been dealt.

Jumping into unfamiliar waters is scary and awkward but necessary to expand our world. It's no different than going to school to broaden our horizons. It takes work, discipline, and time to get a degree that helps us learn about the world we live in. We meet people—our teachers, classmates, roommates from different places. Relationships are very much a part of our formation as we move to establish our lives in a greater capacity, getting jobs, having families, etc. Often, though, we go to college and, like magnets, find the people exactly like us to feel more comfortable. It happens in urban locations as well. Cities are a huge mesh of diversity, but given the chance and lacking courage, we often seek out only people like us. Add screen time with Clara and other worlds; it gets all the more siloed.

One of my podcast guests, Chikka Oduah, is the Founder & Executive Creative Director of ZIKORA Media & Art's African Cultural Heritage Initiative. She is an award-winning journalist and filmmaker. She gave up a tremendous career in the US to move back closer to her roots. She, like Bee, is a Nigerian American, and she resides in Senegal. She's tired of the 'Dark Continent' bias that is perpetuated even by well-meaning people wanting to help. She focuses on the brilliant and rich cultural roots of the pan-African community. She is digging beneath those colonial norms to show the world what we can learn from them besides the primitive overtures of *National Geographic* or the barrage of ads showing starving children.

The same tools that bring us *Claradise* can be powerfully utilized to bring cultural richness from around the world to our doorstep. A multitude of brilliant content providers do this already. It just depends on how often you click and watch for more of them to enter your world. Cultures that used to eat dogs, for example, now decorate their households with lively little pooches. This arose partly because of the consciousness of worlds outside their own, coinciding with their upward mobility. It has wrongly been labeled 'Westernizing'—these cultures underneath the Starbucks signs and Levi's are all still fundamentally different.

REFLECTION

Intentionally grabbing lunch with a neighbor, especially in melting pots around the world, can transport us to the lives of those within their reach in the far corners of our planet because there is a chance they are only a few generations removed. Their food and their religious inclinations are now in our senses of touch, smell, and sight. Most importantly, as bonds form, they are now within our sphere of emotions. We can empathize. They have kids; they have divorced, they have grief—they have universal chunks of life that we can all relate to. What about economics? I learned some trade secrets in the car industry. A luxury sedan is 70 to 80% made up of the same parts as its mass-market edition.[118]

In the rich world, we often mindlessly add that credit card number in to give to the needy or support a cause that we believe in. I do, as well. And I will keep giving money to those in need. Having met people from Nepal and Uganda (an exciting story for another time) and my book cover artist from Lebanon is bringing me much closer to the lives of the little girls behind the monthly credit card billing statement.

What is 'greatness' to you? Is it the number of cars in your driveway, the number of sons you have? Can it be more? I challenge you to have a greater imagination of what greatness looks like past the machinations of the rich and powerful.

What people around you can help you build the necessary bridges to broaden your knowledge of the world around you? This can help you make more informed decisions in future elections, local policing strategies, or school PTA meetings. Take a trip on the wild side and search hashtags you wouldn't normally escape to while lying in bed or on the couch.

What barriers prevent you from reaching out? Is it language or feeling embarrassed? It's like going to the gym for the first time. But if you build a routine, habits can be life-changing, just like eating the right food and getting exercise.

Albuquerque

When my kids were scared of the dark, I would remark,

"It's the same exact place as the one with the light on. The only difference is you can't see."

When I was driving with a pastor friend of mine to a short-term project to help build a church on a Navajo reservation in Arizona, I had forgotten my glasses. It was a 20-hour drive from Joplin, Missouri, and I didn't want him to have to drive the whole way. When he got tired, he asked me to take over. Suddenly, the very flat and straight route we were taking became a winding path up and down a mountain range around Albuquerque, New Mexico. Because of my vision, it felt like, at each turn, we would drop suddenly into a dark abyss—like the one I saw from the top of my bunk bed as a child, or the one after meeting Jen. I was leaning in with my chin over the steering wheel, as if a few inches would make a huge difference.

What was behind the shades of darkness was just another chunk of asphalt first put there in the 1950s, partly in case of a nuclear war, when the Red Scare was more than a scare. The political motivation necessary for President Eisenhower's economic ambitions, inspired by the Autobahn in Germany, came from fear of being swallowed by the Communists.[119] In a sense, we see fears in the Cold War creating both the physical superhighway and the information superhighway. DARPA (Defense Advanced Research Projects Agency) first came up with the concept of the Internet and prototypes in 1960.[120] DARPA also played a significant role in developing the Covid-19 vaccines.[121] No doubt, fear is a driver of innovation and 'progress.' Not being able to see on the road presented opportunities to let my companion sleep and risks that couldn't be ignored.

I've met many respectable human beings who can't be persuaded away from the idea that September 11th was completely planned by the US government, or that we faked the moon landing using Hollywood tricks. So many people are skeptical of it that, before an international conference, I never assume that even the majority of people think it's true. Not everyone's brother-in-law is a rocket scientist. The most bizarre, of course, are the people who believe the earth is flat. But get this—it's not bizarre to them. They are convinced. They have websites, videos, and proven theories, and when you talk to them, they are much more prepared to prove the world is flat than you are, on average, to prove that it is not.

Lots of good literature comes from a jail cell. Oscar Wilde, the Apostle Paul, Nelson Mandela, Alexander Solzhenitsyn, and MLK all wrote from jail. But jail can also perpetuate lies as well. Adolf Hitler wrote *Mein Kampf* in jail. Lenin and Stalin developed their machinations in camps in Siberia. I got into a fight with one of my cellmates in Chesapeake about the CIA and their efforts against Black people. I was purely skeptical. I was also ignorant—ignorant of the plight of Black folks for generations. It didn't mean he was right, however. There is a line of truth in every pack of lies.

All other things being equal, three groups of people suffered the most casualties in the United States because of COVID-19—Native Americans, Black Americans, and rural White Americans from the South. There is evidence to suggest that this was not only due to socio-economic status but also due to hesitancy to trust institutions such as the NIH (National Institutes of Health).[122]

All three groups often refused to believe that any of the precautions or the efficacy of vaccines could save lives. As Makiba pointed out, with the meat-washing habits of many Black families, the unresolved issue of chattel slavery creates enormous fears of federal authorities even today among her demographic. We have rebuilt Germany, Japan, Iraq, and Afghanistan, and sent billions of dollars of aid around the world, but we missed the chance to rebuild the South for both Whites and Blacks.[123] We drove Native Americans out of their lands to the most remote and untenable places in our country and still fail to provide a scaffold of trust to their remaining members.

People who believe strongly in something are very willing to defend it at all costs. These emotional energies and convictions are infectious. When we espouse leaders who are openly willing to push fantastical narratives to get elected, our open and free societies are under threat. The Christian community I am in is often guilty of perpetuating these through the imagination of spiritual warfare. Everything is designed by 'Satan' to thwart their chosen leader, regardless of that leader's acumen, character, or track record. Their fears veil their own scriptures that testify that love overcomes fear. That our divine leader is Truth.

This book is full of embarrassing moral lapses. I will confess to you one more time. I haven't voted since President Bill Clinton's second run for office as the Democratic Party's nominee. That was 28 years ago as of the publication of this book. He (and his gargantuan noggin) was running against Senator Bob Dole in the Republican Party. I was 18 and exercising my right to vote for the first time. More precisely, I was exercising my desire to fit into the conservative bubble I belonged to at the time. Bill and Hillary represented a threat to the religious right. The Christian Coalition and other similar organizations, such as Focus on the Family from James Dobson, exhorted his downfall, and this backdrop kept my vote salient and on point with the lifestyle I was grounded in as an Evangelical Christian.[124]

At 18, in 1996, I was told that if I voted for Bill, homosexuals would take over our country. Babies weren't safe. His election would perpetuate the slippery slope that would destroy a country that God had blessed. Blessed with what? Free labor for 200 years erased the identities and cultures of African men and women.

The other side, politically, was not visible until reading *What's So Amazing About Grace*, where Philip Yancey describes his interview of Bill and Hillary Clinton. They were Christians and yearned for Christian fellowship in a political mire that painted Bill as the anti-Christ. Another story was of a gay friend of Philip's who was a talent for Billy Graham's organization. He came out as gay and lost his reputation. The reaction from the Christian community was—plainly not Christian.[125]

While many believe this mainly happens on one side of the aisle in American politics (and it is concerning), I've met professors from very prominent secular institutions who, without blinking, perpetuate fictitious narratives of nameless conspiratorial organizing to topple their firmly held convictions about women, the Palestinians, homosexuals—you name it. It's there.

With a vacuum of information comes the imagination of our fears, and it will build pillars, towers of a false sense of security we think we need to continue in life. The problem is that it leaves those who don't subscribe to the same fears or beliefs behind. Relationships can't be formed easily as long as the dualism exists.

I struggled with my anger. My uncertainty about my future drove me to media sources that placated a very simplistic idea of the United States of America that was dangerous. It was a wormhole that prevented me from building important bridges with those I had served with and the supporting cast of people who didn't have the same experiences I did. I started to realize that my difficulties and trauma pushed me to field a very narrow and hateful response to what 'America' is. Abuse and trauma do that when the system coughs you up.

I'm extremely grateful to my English students for giving me the opportunity to see my country from another lens. Instead of looking at the situation with bitterness, I now look at it as an opportunity. I have had the front-row experience that many have. I know what it is like as a foreign national, a suspicious-looking person, or just someone coming in from a certain country who gets harassed. I have a tiny, tiny inkling of what it must be to be a person of color suspected automatically of being more dangerous than others simply because of their appearance. I thank God now for giving me a rare insight into what it must be like to not look or sound like me.

One of my favorite COVID-19 stories has been about an Iranian scientist who the FBI detained because the spooks wanted him to spy on Iran for the US. He refused. He had previously enjoyed the benefits of living and working collaboratively with a private company in the US, but yet, because of his connections, he was coerced by the US government to spy. When he refused, he was then released, but he had never been granted access to the country via his visa. He was then arrested again and detained by my friends from DHS. While detained in a cell for illegals, far from the comfortable confines of Chesapeake City Jail, he got COVID-19 but survived.

He found a public defender willing to take his case and get him back to Iran. I come away reading this story appalled and nodding at the travesty and treatment by my government, but realizing that in his own country, he wouldn't have been so lucky to have a public defender be able to defeat the United States in a court battle to get him home. Quite the opposite. He would have simply disappeared. I walk away with faith that we have institutions that still protect people in America. They are far from perfect and need continual investment and reevaluation.[126]

My story and lack of success with law enforcement and border police have galvanized my desire to be a part of the solution. As America gets quite a bit less European, white, and Christian, we need changes. We need to take the best of what America has to offer and get rid of its worst legacies. What if we had protocols that thoughtfully created something besides fear when people approach the immigration counter at the airport? What if our immigration laws were transparent enough to prevent the enormous crisis mounting on our Southern border?

We love to watch the news or social media and shake our fist at someone, or sing hallelujah, or swear under our breath in disgust. Even if you feel that someone's perspective is a 'disease' (and it might very well be), is it that difficult to understand that the freedoms you have to espouse a particular view, lifestyle, or religion give another the same rights, and that's good for both of you? Could the dichotomy of plurality possibly have a net good for society?

Disappointment with leaders—political, religious, you name it—doesn't mean you need to disavow a whole community (say… cancel culture) to achieve your life goals. Most likely, those that you think are standing in your way are actually people you need to be holding out your hand to for help, or should be helping. You might find that ever-elusive satisfaction and joyful life there if you are willing to overcome your fears of doing so.

REFLECTION

Our fears are costly. Yes, they are designed to save your life, but in a media-intense context, they've been easily hijacked! What disappoints shapes your view of history and the landing place of your current existence. Abusive women and getting kicked out of the military had a profound impact on the colored glasses I saw the world through. Could the events you list down have pushed you to believe things that might not be true?

Think about your media consumption for a moment. What has constructed those preferences? What has led you to choose the political sentiments you have? Are those who oppose you completely wrong? Try taking an intellectually honest step by asking an all-important question:

"What if I'm wrong?"

It could be a religious belief, a long-held suspicion of a particular race, or a conspiracy you believe is gospel. No one is asking you to change your religion, but healthy skepticism can put you in a position to engage in more learning and, more importantly, give you more opportunities for friendships that could, indeed, like many of mine, last a lifetime.

Never Say Never

I said I'd never marry a Filipina—they are all gold diggers.

I said I'd never work for a Korean boss—they are all slave drivers.

I said I'd never be a pastor—they abuse their power.

I said I'd never join the military—yes, even that.

Life took me down these roads. I never thought I'd go to jail. I never thought I could enjoy teaching English as a second language.

'Dr. Zang.' His words sound ridiculous in the self-medicated, snake oil-selling world we live in. We are so used to being told that the solutions are simple and just around the corner. He helped set me on a course that allowed me to understand a deep fundamental truth about life: it's a struggle. I did end up in jail and rehab. I needed them. There are no pat answers. There are no 12, 5, or 7-step plans that will resolve all the conflict and disparity between us. Friction is when the rubber meets the road. It allowed me to drive 110 miles an hour in a construction zone. Friction is necessary, or we cannot go anywhere. The faster we become aware of this, the more places we will go if we aren't afraid to push the pedal to the floor. Growth comes when others reflect our identity, pitfalls, and gifts back at us.

My successes and discoveries, which I share with you here, are marked with scars and losses. When we don't see it this way, we find an unhealthy 'Claradise' to bury our pains and struggles in. After all, believing in a political savior, a football team, or betting everything on Bitcoin is easier than facing a boring job, an annoying spouse, or an empty bank account. Conspiracy theories are popular because they provide the zeal and energy to cover up the gaping reality that we don't know and may never know what really happened. We reach for extremes to get rid of the nagging loneliness of everyday life. "Dr. Zang" was preparing me to grasp the idea that joy is much deeper and comes from winning battles, not simply avoiding them—and these battles should never be fought alone.

The problem that creates polarity in this world is that, when presented with a choice, we shrink. We allow our fears to speak. I admit that having choice stripped from me may have created some of the thin boundaries I had, but conversely, it gave me tools to embrace. We really need to see life less from a consumer standpoint, where we stroll down the aisle picking what fancies us. Activism, beer commercials, and fitness apps—they present the best and worst to convince us to join their side. But in reality, we are all somewhere in between. We can embrace the East and the West with humility. We can respect the opposite gender without feeling threatened by their success (or authority). We can live within our means and gain empathy for those both lower and higher on the economic ladder. The awkwardness of being with people who don't look or sound like us is not a sign that something is wrong. It's a sign that something is right. You are living. Life has suddenly taken you further than you've been before.

I want my legacy to be more than a manicured lawn, a good golf swing, and a maxed-out life insurance plan. I want my legacy to be far more than that. I want my children to know that our kindness and neighborliness are what will outlast our sagging bodies or what we own.

Endnotes

1. Taylor Swift, *Anti-Hero*, track 3 on *Midnights*, Republic Records, 2022, Spotify, https://open.spotify.com.

2. Frankie Avalon, *Beauty School Dropout*, track 11 on *Grease: The Original Soundtrack from the Motion Picture*, Polydor Records, 1978, Spotify, https://open.spotify.com.

3. ABBA, *Mamma Mia*, track 1 on *ABBA*, Polar Music International, 1975, Spotify, https://open.spotify.com.

4. *Captain Phillips*, directed by Paul Greengrass (Culver City, CA: Columbia Pictures, 2013), film.

5. 1. Andrew Blankstein and Megan Garvey, "Paris Hilton Stunned by 45-Day Sentence," Los Angeles Times, May 5, 2007, https://www.latimes.com/la-me-paris5may05-story.html.

6. Jennifer Barnhill, "Why Divorce Is Particularly Hard on Military Families," Military.com, April 22, 2024, https://www.military.com/daily-news/opinions/2023/06/22/why-divorce-particularly-hard-military-families.html.

7. Kenny Rogers, *The Gambler*, track 5 on *The Gambler*, United Artists Records, 1978, Spotify, https://open.spotify.com.

8. Kelly Kasulis, "'patient 31' and South Korea's Sudden Spike in Coronavirus Cases," Al Jazeera, March 3, 2020, https://www.aljazeera.com/news/2020/3/3/patient-31-and-south-koreas-sudden-spike-in-coronavirus-cases.

9. *Heartland*, created by Murray Shostak, aired on CBC Television, 2007–2019, https://www.cbc.ca/heartland.

10. Eleanor Butler, "Turkish Delight as Inflation Rate Dips, Raising Hopes of Rate Cuts," euronews, September 3, 2024, https://www.euronews.com/business/2024/09/03/inflation-in-turkey-eases-further-when-are-rate-cuts-coming.

11. "2023 Turkey-Syria Earthquake," Center for Disaster Philanthropy, April 25, 2024, https://disasterphilanthropy.org/disasters/2023-turkey-syria-earthquake/.

12. The Black Eyed Peas, *Where Is the Love?*, track 8 on *Elephunk*, A&M Records, 2003, Spotify, https://open.spotify.com.

13. Garth Brooks, *Belleau Wood*, track 10 on *Sevens*, Capitol Nashville, 1997

14. "U.S. Military Spends More than the next 9 Countries in 2023," National Priorities Project, April 30, 2024, https://www.nationalpriorities.org/blog/2024/04/30/us-military-spends-more-next-10-countries-2023/.

15. James Palmer, "'fat Leonard' Was a Crook U.S. Admirals Called Bro," Foreign Policy, May 28, 2024, https://foreignpolicy.com/2024/05/11/fat-leonard-scandal-us-navy-malaysian-defense-contractor-scam-venezuela-pacific-security/.

16. Elijah Asdourian David Wessel et al., "Getting Reconstruction Right and Wrong: Lessons from Iraq," Brookings, March 9, 2022, https://www.brookings.edu/articles/getting-reconstruction-right-and-wrong-lessons-from-iraq/.

17. Glenn Greenwald, "Edward Snowden: The Whistleblower behind the NSA Surveillance Revelations," The Guardian, June 11, 2013, https://www.theguardian.com/world/2013/jun/09/edward-snowden-nsa-whistleblower-surveillance.

18. Austin Allen, "Emma Lazarus: 'The New Colossus,'" Poetry Foundation, November 22, 2017, https://www.poetryfoundation.org/articles/144956/emma-lazarus-the-new-colossus.

19. "Barack Obama's Keynote Address at the 2004 Democratic National Convention," PBS, July 27, 2004, https://www.pbs.org/newshour/show/barack-obamas-keynote-address-at-the-2004-democratic-national-convention.

20. "Obama Delivers Immigration Address in San Francisco," NBCNews.com, November 26, 2013, https://www.nbcnews.com/video/obama-delivers-immigration-address-in-san-francisco-73227331877.

21. Jonathan Masters and Will Merrow, "How Much U.S. Aid Is Going to Ukraine?," Council on Foreign Relations, September 27, 2024, https://www.cfr.org/article/how-much-us-aid-going-ukraine.

22. IU, 에잇 (*Eight*), featuring Suga, EDAM Entertainment, 2020, Spotify, https://open.spotify.com.

23. 1. "What Is a Starling Murmuration and Why Do They Form?," The Wildlife Trust for Lancashire Manchester and North Merseyside, November 15, 2018, https://www.lancswt.org.uk/blog/starling-murmuration-facts.

24. "Police Answer Mystery of Hundreds of Starlings Found Dead on Road," The Guardian, January 16, 2020, https://www.theguardian.com/uk-news/2020/jan/16/police-answer-mystery-of-hundreds-of-starlings-found-dead-on-road.

25. "Death Toll from Itaewon Crush Rises Again to 156," Korea JoongAng Daily, November 1, 2022, https://koreajoongangdaily.joins.com/2022/11/01/national/socialAffairs/korea-itaewon-itaewon-halloween/20221101114836184.html.

26. U.S.-South Korea Alliance: Issues for Congress - CRS Reports, September 12, 2023, https://crsreports.congress.gov/product/pdf/IF/IF11388.

27. Ock Hyun-ju, "Korean Media's Focus on 'gay' Club in Covid-19 Case Further Stigmatizes LGBT People," The Korea Herald, May 8, 2020, https://www.koreaherald.com/view.php?ud=20200508000751.

28. *Itaewon Class*, directed by Kim Sung-yoon, JTBC, 2020, Netflix, https://www.netflix.com.

29. "Fukushima Daiichi Accident," World Nuclear Association, April 29, 2024, https://world-nuclear.org/information-library/safety-and-security/safety-of-plants/fukushima-daiichi-accident.

30. Julia Jocobo and Cameron Harrison, "Doctor Dragged off United Airlines Flight after Watching Viral Video of Himself: 'I Just Cried,'" ABC News, April 9, 2019, https://abcnews.go.com/US/doctor-dragged-off-united-airlines-flight-watching-viral/story?id=62250271.

31. Yong Kwon, "South Korea's Reforestation Campaign," – The Diplomat, July 22, 2022, https://thediplomat.com/2022/07/south-koreas-reforestation-campaign/.

32. 나눔의 집, accessed October 15, 2024, http://www.nanum.org/eng/main/index.php.

33. Alexis Duden, "A Guide to Understanding the History of the 'comfort Women' Issue," United States Institute of Peace, September 16, 2022, https://www.usip.org/publications/2022/09/guide-understanding-history-comfort-women-issue.

34. Emma Baldi, "South Korea's Plan to Compensate Victims of Forced Labour Employed in Japanese Factories during Colonial Rule: A Step Forward for Peaceful Relations, but Not for Victims' Rights," EJIL, May 5, 2023, https://www.ejiltalk.org/south-koreas-plan-to-compensate-victims-of-forced-labour-employed-in-japanese-factories-during-colonial-rule-a-step-forward-for-peaceful-relations-but-not-for-victims-rights/.

35. Catherine Kim, "The Escalating Trade War between South Korea and Japan, Explained," Vox, August 9, 2019, https://www.vox.com/world/2019/8/9/20758025/trade-war-south-korea-japan.

36. "Invest Korea," 새창, September 8, 2021, https://www.investkorea.org/ik-en/bbs/i-308/detail.do?ntt_sn=490760.

37. Justin McCurry, "'comfort Women' Crisis: Campaign over Wartime Sexual Slavery Hit by Financial Scandal," The Guardian, June 14, 2020, https://www.theguardian.com/world/2020/jun/14/comfort-women-crisis-campaign-over-wartime-sexual-slavery-hit-by-financial-scandal.

38. "Gwangju Student Anti-Japanese Movement," October 6, 2024, https://en.namu.wiki/w/광주학생항일운동.

39. Casting Crowns, *Stained Glass Masquerade*, track 2 on *Lifesong*, Reunion Records, 2005, Spotify, https://open.spotify.com.

40. Sophie B. Hawkins, *Damn I Wish I Was Your Lover*, track 1 on *Tongues and Tails*, Columbia Records, 1992, Spotify, https://open.spotify.com.

41. Stephanie Petit, "Delilah: Inside the Radio Host's Highs and Heartbreaks," People.com, October 9, 2017, https://people.com/music/delilah-radio-child-suicide-history-divorce/.

42. "Life," John Stott, November 9, 2023, https://johnstott.org/life/.

43. Billy Graham, "Heros & Icons: John Stott," Time, April 18, 2005, http://content.time.com/time/specials/packages/article/0%2C28804%2C1972656_1972717_1974108%2C00.html.

44. Joshua Harris, *I Kissed Dating Goodbye* (Colorado Springs: Multnomah Books, 1997).

45. Michelle Boorstein, "Suit Accuses Sovereign Grace Ministries of Covering up Alleged Child Sexual Abuse - The Washington Post," washingtonpost.com, January 14, 2013, https://www.washingtonpost.com/local/lawsuit-accuses-neo-calvinist-church-movement-leaders-of-child-sexual-abuse/2013/01/14/6e671764-5e94-11e2-90a0-73c8343c6d61_story.html.

46. Jeremy Weber, "C. J. Mahaney Leaves Leadership of Sovereign Grace Ministries," Christianity Today, July 3, 2013, https://www.christianitytoday.com/2013/03/c-j-mahaney-leaves-leadership-of-sovereign-grace-ministries/.

47. "Joshua Harris Says He's Not a Christian Anymore, but His Journey Isn't over Yet," Premier Christianity, July 31, 2019, https://www.premierchristianity.com/home/joshua-harris-says-hes-not-a-christian-anymore-but-his-journey-isnt-over-yet/1822.article.

48. "Nixon Silent Majority Speech Text," Voices of Democracy, June 25, 2024, https://voicesofdemocracy.umd.edu/nixon-silent-majority-speech-text/.

49. David Cohen, Pat Robertson, evangelical and Christian political trailblazer, dies at 93, June 8, 2023, https://www.politico.com/news/2023/06/08/pat-robertson-televangelist-candidate-00006015.

50. Regent University - profile, rankings and Data | US News Best Colleges, 2024, https://www.usnews.com/best-colleges/regent-university-30913.

51. Hozier, *Take Me to Church*, track 1 on *Hozier*, Rubyworks Records, 2014, Spotify, https://open.spotify.com.

52. "Library Guides: Government Sources by Subject: Gays in the Military," Gays in the Military - Government Sources by Subject - Library Guides at University of Washington Libraries, October 3, 2024, https://guides.lib.uw.edu/c.php?g=341739&p=2304282.

53. 2Pac, *Changes*, track 5 on *Greatest Hits*, Interscope Records, 1998, Spotify, https://open.spotify.com.

54. Laats, Adam. *Fundamentalist U: Keeping the Faith in American Higher Education*. Oxford University Press, 2018, Chapter 5.

55. Text of obama's fatherhood speech - politico, June 15, 2008, https://www.politico.com/story/2008/06/text-of-obamas-fatherhood-speech-011094.

56. David Cloud, "Why Are You Opposed to Drums?," Why are you opposed to drums?, way of life literature, April 24, 2007, https://www.wayoflife.org/reports/why-are-you-opposed-to-drums.php.

57. *"A Shot in the Dark,"* directed by Brian Iles, written by Mike Desilets, *Family Guy*, Season 14, Episode 9, aired December 13, 2015, on Fox.

58. Sheila Flynn, "What Happened to JonBenet Ramsey? A Timeline of the Investigation," The Independent, December 14, 2023, https://www.independent.co.uk/news/world/americas/crime/jonbenet-ramsey-case-brother-house-b2464324.html.

59. David Stout, "Runaway Girl Is Found Dead after Torture, Police Say," The New York Times, August 16, 1996, https://www.nytimes.com/1996/08/16/nyregion/runaway-girl-is-found-dead-after-torture-police-say.html.

60. "Rev. Dr. Antipas Harris," Black Theology and Leadership Institute, accessed October 15, 2024, https://btli.ptsem.edu/rev-antipas-l-harris/.

61. Jane Ohlmeyer, "How Ireland Served as a Laboratory for the British Empire," Trinity College Dublin, the University of Dublin, December 31, 2023, https://www.tcd.ie/news_events/articles/2023/how-ireland-served-as-a-laboratory-for-the-british-empire/.

62. A. A. McConnell and D. T. Reid, "The Irish Famine: A Century and a Half On," Royal College of Physicians of Edinburgh, 1998, https://www.rcpe.ac.uk/sites/default/files/vol28_3.1_9.pdf.

63. Robert P. Jones, *The Hidden Roots of White Supremacy: And the Path to a Shared American Future* (New York: Simon & Schuster, 2023), Chapter 5

64. "580: The Hidden Roots of White Supremacy with Robert P. Jones," HolyPost, August 30, 2023, https://podcasts.apple.com/gb/podcast/580-the-hidden-roots-of-white-supremacy-with-robert-p-jones/id591157388?i=1000626195062.

65. A Religious Portrait of African-Americans," Pew Research Center, January 30, 2009, https://www.pewresearch.org/religion/2009/01/30/a-religious-portrait-of-african-americans/.

66. "Books about American Slavery (403 Books)," Goodreads, accessed October 15, 2024, https://www.goodreads.com/list/show/4913.Books_about_American_slavery.

67. Kate Shellnutt, "George Floyd Left a Gospel Legacy in Houston," Christianity Today, November 8, 2022, https://www.christianitytoday.com/2020/05/george-floyd-ministry-houston-third-ward-church/.

68. Oliver Laughland and Amudalat Ajasa, "'I Allowed Myself to Feel Guilty for a Very Long Time': The Teenage Cashier Who Took George Floyd's $20 Bill," The Guardian, May 23, 2021, https://www.theguardian.com/us-news/2021/may/23/christopher-martin-george-floyd-minneapolis-cup-foods.

69. Thomas P. Bonczar and Allen J. Beck, Lifetime likelihood of going to state or Federal Prison, 1997, https://bjs.ojp.gov/content/pub/pdf/Llgsfp.pdf.

70. "Squad Car Video of Philando Castile Shooting Released," CBSNews (YouTube), June 21, 2017, https://www.youtube.com/watch?v=V94Lphx6z6Y&t=1s.

71. Richard A. Oppel, Derrick Bryson Taylor, and Nicholas Bogel-burroughs, "What to Know about Breonna Taylor's Death," The New York Times, May 30, 2020, https://www.nytimes.com/article/breonna-taylor-police.html.

72. Phil Vischer, "Why Do White Christians Vote Republican, and Black Christians Vote Democrat?," HolyPost (YouTube), October 12, 2020, https://www.youtube.com/watch?v=W4eS2E-PoGo&t=1s.

73. Madeline F. Schultz, "VeggieTales Creator Phil Vischer Tells Stories Differently Now," Washington Examiner, March 7, 2020, https://www.washingtonexaminer.com/opinion/1928952/veggietales-creator-phil-vischer-tells-stories-differently-now/.

74. Meredith Deliso, "Tupac Shakur Timeline: Key Events in Rapper's Murder Investigation," ABC News, September 30, 2023, https://abcnews.go.com/Entertainment/tupac-shakur-timeline-key-events-rappers-murder-investigation/story?id=101497618.

75. U2, *One*, track 3 on *Achtung Baby*, Island Records, 1991, Spotify, https://open.spotify.com.

76. Rage Against the Machine, *How I Could Just Kill a Man*, track 11 on *Renegades*, Epic Records, 2000, Spotify, https://open.spotify.com.

77. Jared Gabriel L. Dela Rosa, Charlene Divine M. Catral, Nico Alexander Reyes, et al. Current status of hypertension care and management in the Philippines. *Diabetes Metab Syndr*. 2024;18(4):103008. doi:10.1016/j.dsx.2024.103008

78. Delta Dyrecka Letigio, "Talisay Tragedy: Three Deaths, a Burning House, an Hour-Long Shootout," Cebu Daily News, May 16, 2019, https://cebudailynews.inquirer.net/234446/talisay-tragedy-three-deaths-a-burning-house-an-hour-long-shootout.

79. "Village Chief's Senseless Murder Pains Wife," SunStar Publishing Inc., May 17, 2019, https://www.sunstar.com.ph/cebu/local-news/village-chiefrsquos-senseless-murder-pains-wife.

80. 1. Alexis Romero, "Duterte Says He Will 'wipe out' Parojinog Clan of Ozamiz City," Philstar.com, November 28, 2018, https://www.philstar.com/headlines/2018/11/28/1872538/duterte-says-he-will-wipe-out-parojinog-clan-ozamiz-city.

81. Segundo J. E. Romero, "Duterte's Rise to Power in the Philippines: Domestic and Regional Implications: Heinrich Böll Foundation: Southeast Asia Regional Office," Heinrich Böll Foundation | Southeast Asia Regional Office, September 26, 2016, https://th.boell.org/en/2016/09/26/dutertes-rise-power-philippines-domestic-and-regional-implications.

82. Stephanie Hancock, "The Killing Squads: Inside the Philippines' 'War on Drugs,'" Human Rights Watch, October 27, 2022, https://www.hrw.org/news/2017/03/02/killing-squads-inside-philippines-war-drugs.

83. Mobile phone theft - the Guardian, December 2001, http://image.guardian.co.uk/sys-files/Guardian/documents/2002/01/08/mobilephone.pdf.

84. "Land Grabbing in Philippines : Via Campesina," La Via Campesina - EN, March 11, 2014, https://viacampesina.org/en/land-grabbing-in-philippine/.

85. Philip Yancey, *What's So Amazing About Grace?* (Grand Rapids: Zondervan, 1997), 101–102.

86. Bruce Springsteen, *The Ghost of Tom Joad*, track 1 on *The Ghost of Tom Joad*, Columbia Records, 1995, Spotify, https://open.spotify.com.

87. Rojonell Culvera, "The Steady Growth of the Philippine BPO Sector," Philippines, May 12, 2023, https://www.jll.com.ph/en/trends-and-insights/research/the-steady-growth-of-the-philippine-bpo-sector.

88. Anna Kireeva, "Middle Class in the Philippines: Understanding and Income Ranges |," Digido, September 19, 2024, https://digido.ph/articles/middle-class-philippines.

89. Philippines Foreign Direct Investment, accessed October 15, 2024, https://tradingeconomics.com/philippines/foreign-direct-investment.

90. Anna Leah Gonzales, OFW remittances hit all-time high in 2023 | Philippine News Agency, February 15, 2023, https://www.pna.gov.ph/articles/1218913.

91. "Why Does Bamboo Grow so Fast?," BBC Science Focus Magazine, September 2, 2021, https://www.sciencefocus.com/nature/speed-bamboo-plant-grow.

92. Hong Chen, Haitao Cheng, Ge Wang *et al.* Tensile properties of bamboo in different sizes. *J Wood Sci* **61**, 552–561 (2015). https://doi.org/10.1007/s10086-015-1511-x

93. Sina Youssefian, Nima Rahbar, Molecular Origin of Strength and Stiffness in Bamboo Fibrils. *Sci Rep* **5**, 11116 (2015). https://doi.org/10.1038/srep11116

94. Katharina, "How Much Ownership Should Angel Investors Get When Investing in a Startup?," Angel Investing School, February 20, 2024, https://angelinvestingschool.com/how-much-ownership-should-angel-investors-get-when-investing-in-a-startup/.

95. The Corrs, *Somebody for Someone*, track 3 on *In Blue*, Atlantic Records, 2000, Spotify, https://open.spotify.com.

96. Rick Warren, *The Purpose Driven Life* (Grand Rapids: Zondervan, 2002).

97. Alex Kalinauckas, "Six F1 Grands Prix Are Now Held at Night. Singapore Was the First.," The New York Times, September 20, 2024, https://www.nytimes.com/2024/09/20/sports/autoracing/f1-singapore-grand-prix-night.html.

98. Rascal Flatts, *Bless the Broken Road*, track 3 on *Feels Like Today*, Lyric Street Records, 2004, Spotify, https://open.spotify.com.

99. Alicia Keys, *Girl on Fire*, track 1 on *Girl on Fire*, RCA Records, 2012, Spotify, https://open.spotify.com.

100. 2020 demographics profile of the Military Community, 2020, https://download.militaryonesource.mil/12038/MOS/Reports/2020-demographics-report.pdf.

101. Regina T. Akers, "The Navy's Aircraft Carrier Force Centenary: Women Carrier Aviator Trailblazers," The Sextant, March 22, 2022, https://usnhistory.navylive.dodlive.mil/Recent/Article-View/Article/2974189/the-navys-aircraft-carrier-force-centenary-women-carrier-aviator-trailblazers/.

102. "Trial Concerning 269 Luxury Residence Deaths in Turkey Earthquake Begins," Turkish Minute, April 21, 2024, https://turkishminute.com/2024/04/18/trial-concerning-269-luxury-residence-death-turkey-earthquake-begin/.

103. Jim Inhofe, "Afghanistan Was a Predictable, Preventable Disaster," Foreign Policy, August 19, 2022, https://foreignpolicy.com/2022/08/15/afghanistan-withdrawal-pullout-military-taliban-chaos-evacuation-biden-inhofe/.

104. Eleanor Watson, "A U.S. Drone Strike Killed an Aid Worker in Afghanistan. Many of His Family and Colleagues Are Still Stranded There," CBS News, August 16, 2022, https://www.cbsnews.com/news/afghanistan-drone-strike-zemari-ahmadi-family-colleagues-resettlement/.

105. Shannon Bettypiece, Peter Alexander, and Mike Memoli, "Biden Defends Afghanistan Withdrawal: 'Not Extending a Forever Exit,'" NBCNews.com, August 31, 2021, https://www.nbcnews.com/politics/white-house/biden-address-end-afghan-war-amid-criticism-over-chaotic-u-n1278142.

106. Anand Gopal, "The Other Afghan Women," The New Yorker, September 6, 2021, https://www.newyorker.com/magazine/2021/09/13/the-other-afghan-women.

107. Nichole Nordeman, *Legacy*, track 5 on *Woven & Spun*, Sparrow Records, 2002, Spotify, https://open.spotify.com.

108. *Surrogates*, directed by Jonathan Mostow (Touchstone Pictures, 2009), featuring Bruce Willis.

109. Jack Shafer, "So What If a Candidate Livestreamed Sex Acts with Her Husband?," https://www.politico.com/news/magazine/2023/09/12/candidate-livestreamed-sex-acts-00115395, September 12, 2023.

110. Gavin Butler, "Straight, Middle-Aged Men Are Being Charged More to Use Tinder Plus," VICE, August 9, 2024, https://www.vice.com/en/article/straight-middle-aged-men-are-being-charged-more-to-use-tinder-plus/.

111. Victor Malarek, *The Natashas: Inside the New Global Sex Trade* (New York: Arcade Publishing, 2003)

112. *The Whistleblower*, directed by Larysa Kondracki (Samuel Goldwyn Films, 2010), film.

113. *Taken*, directed by Pierre Morel (20th Century Fox, 2008), film.

114. "New Figures Show Conflict-Related Deaths at 28-Year High, Largely Due to Ethiopia and Ukraine Wars," Peace Research Institute Oslo (PRIO), June 7, 2023, https://www.prio.org/news/3058.

115. Ramon Mahia et al., "The Long-Term Impact of Syrian Refugees on Turkish Economy (FEM43-05 Report)," https://www.femise.org/, September 2019, https://www.femise.org/en/slideshow-en/the-long-term-impact-of-syrian-refugees-on-turkish-economy-fem43-05-report/.

116. "Facts and Statistics," Hate Crimes, September 25, 2024, https://www.justice.gov/hatecrimes/hate-crime-statistics.

117. "Thank You, Mr. President, I Thank under-Secretary General ...," United Nations, February 21, 2022, https://www.un.int/kenya/sites/www.un.int/files/Kenya/kenya_statement_during_urgent_meeting_on_on_ukraine_21_february_2022_at_2100.pdf.

118. Mingyu Guan et al., "Five Trends Shaping Tomorrow's Luxury-Car Market," McKinsey & Company, July 8, 2022, https://www.mckinsey.com/industries/automotive-and-assembly/our-insights/five-trends-shaping-tomorrows-luxury-car-market.

119. Richard F. Weingroff, "Original Intent: Purpose of the Interstate System 1954-1956," Original Intent: Purpose of the Interstate System 1954-1956 | FHWA, June 30, 2023, https://highways.dot.gov/highway-history/interstate-system/original-intent-purpose-interstate-system-1954-1956.

120. Mitch Waldrop, "DARPA," https://www.darpa.mil/, 2015, https://www.darpa.mil/attachments/(2O15) Global Nav - About Us - History - Resources - 50th - Internet (Approved).pdf.Global Nav - About Us - History - Resources - 50th - Internet (Approved).pdf.

121. Lalani, Hussain S et al. "US Taxpayers Heavily Funded the Discovery of COVID-19 Vaccines." *Clinical pharmacology and therapeutics* vol. 111,3 (2022): 542-544. doi:10.1002/cpt.2344

122. Vázquez, E., Juturu, P., Burroughs, M. *et al.* Continuum of Trauma: Fear and Mistrust of Institutions in Communities of Color During the COVID-19 Pandemic. *Cult Med Psychiatry* **48**, 290–309 (2024). https://doi.org/10.1007/s11013-023-09835-3

123. Allison Keyes, "America Is Still Reckoning with the Failures of Reconstruction," Smithsonian.com, October 27, 2021, https://www.smithsonianmag.com/smithsonian-institution/a-profound-demand-to-make-good-on-the-promises-of-freedom-180978924/.

124. Philip Yancey, "The Riddle of Bill Clinton's Faith," Christianity Today, April 25, 1994, https://www.christianitytoday.com/1994/04/riddle-of-bill-clintons-faith/.

125. Philip Yancey, *What's So Amazing About Grace?* (Grand Rapids: Zondervan, 1997), pages 226-228

126. Laura Secor, "The Man Who Refused to Spy," The New Yorker, September 14, 2020, https://www.newyorker.com/magazine/2020/09/21/the-man-who-refused-to-spy.

KICKSTARTER backers ..
Thank You!

신동혁 Clark Josiah Shem C. Dabuet
Margit Takacs
William L. Buot
Greg Birdsall
Ntšali Anita Tjan Lorenz
최욱
Rebekah Rickards Joshua Craft Hüseyin BAYKUŞAK
Leia B 김영유
Julia Haynie Lance Eaton David Chien Rosemary 'RO' Fajardo
Faith Yuri Belén
Kristen 정성문
PullaWagon.com Caleb VanSumeren
Eryck Stamper
Rachel Anneese Marshall
Aycan Yaman

So Much!

Junhyuk Kim Jen Vaughn
Josh, Elicia, Mason, Savannah, Austin & Byron Loring
Russell Creed Pam Davis
Cisco Bready John McGraw Chulmin Ahn
Saskia Mark Donald 김병우
Dan Vickers
Marie Suazo
Aaron Stubbs Scott and Laura Gutwein
Jesse Khopang
Basirat 'B' Sarah Styf Megan
Jenny O'Fee Corianne Kunz
Kellea Geraldine Bethany Kunz
Corrine Dan Askins
Ghia Yoshito Darmon-Shimamori
Michael Noll-Hussong
Arnel Omilio Fabonan